ADVANCE PRAISE FOR

Reinventing Martial Arts in the 21st Century: Eastern Stimulus, Western Response

"The author presents the situation of selected martial arts traditions of China and Europe in today's social contexts. At the same time, he shows both social sensitivity and broad erudition. His research on Mexican traditions brings a fresh perspective to the analysis of cultural influences and theoretical reflection on the heritage of martial arts. Also, the qualitative methodology used here is most appropriate for an in-depth description of the attitudes of martial artists. It includes, but is not limited to, autoethnography. I highly recommend this book to researchers and enthusiasts of martial arts/fighting arts."
—Professor Dr Wojciech J. Cynarski, 10th dan of Idokan

"Dr. Jennings' *Reinventing Martial Arts in the 21st Century* is a fresh, extremely current piece. Written in a clear, precise and simple language, it addresses many of the topics inspiring contemporary social research on martial arts—their hybridization with other movements systems, their consideration as self-help or therapy practices, or their protection, revival or reinvention as intangible cultural heritage, to name a few. It is solidly structured and developed, presenting findings on all these fields, based on the author's original research and knowledge as a veteran martial artist. No doubt this book is a brilliant contribution to the field of study of martial arts and combat sports."
—Carlos Gutiérrez García, Associate Professor, Department of Physical and Sport Education, Universidad de León, Spain; Editor-in-Chief of *Revista de Artes Marciales Asiáticas*

"Most martial arts celebrate their long historical traditions, ancient roots and aim to inculcate their learners with respect for expert practitioners and their values. Those that originated in East and South East Asia spread across the rest of the world in the twentieth century, and now flourish in societies very different from those where they originated. Alongside the globalised martial arts an academic field of research—martial arts studies—has grown up. Its focus is not only on those Eastern and South-east Asian martial arts and combat sports, but also on those from Africa and the Americas (such as Capoeira and Xilam), and those claiming European origins such as Savate, HEMA (Historical European Martial Arts) or Breton wrestling. Some of these are self-conscious recreations; others are evolved varieties of earlier activities. One important theme in martial arts studies is studying how different forms of combat change and develop; a second research area is focused on how practitioners can benefit physically and mentally from participation.

"George Jennings has, in this book, drawn together several of the key themes in martial arts studies which became highly visible during the COVID-19 pandemic. Drawing on ethnographic work done before, during, and since the height of the pandemic in Europe, key themes in martial arts studies are explored. Jennings has worked intensively on three martial arts (Taijiquan, HEMA and Wing Chun), and also draws on the research about other activities such as Venezuelan Stick fighting, Savate and Xilam. The text addresses core themes in martial arts studies while blending the standpoints of the practitioner, the teacher, and the researcher."
—Sara Delamont, Reader Emeritus, Cardiff University, United Kingdom

"George Jennings tackles the western reinvention of traditional martial arts in terms of McDonaldization, heritage studies, and sport science to discuss emerging forms of virtual community, therapy and self-help. Through evocative auto-ethnography Jennings demonstrates the advantage of training in swords while taking notes. The result is a highly readable academic account of colorful vignettes and vivid insights shared from a lifetime in martial arts and scholarship."
—DS Farrer, University of Exeter, United Kingdom

"This book offers a fascinating exploration of multiple overlooked aspects of the living and breathing richness and diversity of martial arts as lived practices, often intertwined with different livelihoods, issues and aspects of health and wellbeing, and ways of growing. Jennings speaks fluently in a range of voices, allowing different levels and kinds of focus and attention, from large perspectives to attention to less obvious areas of life and practice. This work will be of particular value to ethnography, anthropology and social science students and researchers of martial arts, culture and society."
—Professor Paul Bowman, Cardiff University, United Kingdom;
Author of *The Invention of Martial Arts* (2021)

Reinventing Martial Arts in the 21st Century

Sport in East and Southeast Asian Societies

Geopolitical, Political, Cultural and Social Perspectives

J.A. Mangan
Series Editor

Vol. 3

The Sport in East and Southeast Asian Societies series
is part of the Peter Lang Regional Studies list.
Every volume is peer reviewed and meets
the highest quality standards for content and production.

PETER LANG
New York • Berlin • Brussels • Lausanne • Oxford

George Jennings

Reinventing Martial Arts in the 21st Century

Eastern Stimulus, Western Response

PETER LANG
New York • Berlin • Brussels • Lausanne • Oxford

Library of Congress Cataloging-in-Publication Data

Names: Jennings, George, author.
Title: Reinventing martial arts in the 21st century: Eastern stimulus, Western response / George Jennings.
Description: New York: Peter Lang, 2023.
Series: Sport in East and Southeast Asian societies: geopolitical, political, cultural and social perspectives; vol. 3
ISSN 2689-3460 (print) | ISSN 2689-3479 (online)
Includes bibliographical references and index.
Identifiers: LCCN 2022042268 (print) | LCCN 2022042269 (ebook) |
ISBN 978-1-4331-8293-8 (hardback)
ISBN 978-1-4331-8294-5 (ebook pdf) | ISBN 978-1-4331-8295-2 (epub)
Subjects: LCSH: Martial arts. | Martial arts—Social aspects.
Classification: LCC GV1101. J46 2023 (print) | LCC GV1101 (ebook) |
DDC 796.8—dc23/eng/20220930
LC record available at https://lccn.loc.gov/2022042268
LC ebook record available at https://lccn.loc.gov/2022042269
DOI 10.3726/b17408

Bibliographic information published by **Die Deutsche Nationalbibliothek**.
Die Deutsche Nationalbibliothek lists this publication in the "Deutsche Nationalbibliografie"; detailed bibliographic data are available on the Internet at http://dnb.d-nb.de/.

© 2023 Peter Lang Publishing, Inc., New York
80 Broad Street, 5th floor, New York, NY 10004
www.peterlang.com

All rights reserved.
Reprint or reproduction, even partially, in all forms such as microfilm, xerography, microfiche, microcard, and offset strictly prohibited.

I dedicate this book to all those people who have punched, chopped, kicked, stabbed and beheaded me (in the context of martial arts classes and training!), as they are all my teachers.

Contents

Preface		ix
Acknowledgments		xxix
List of Abbreviations		xxxiii
1	Introduction: Conceptualising the Martial Arts in Contemporary Society	1
Part I	Reimagining the Martial Arts	19
2	Chinese Martial Arts as Art Forms	21
3	Martial Arts as the Basis for Mixed Movement Systems	39
4	Martial Arts as the Social Structure for Self-Help	59
5	The Restructuring of Martial Arts as Therapy	79
Part II	Reconstructing the Martial Arts	99
6	Regulating the Martial Arts Industry: The McDojo Critique	101

| 7 | The Revival and Protection of Martial Arts as Heritage | 123 |

PART III Living and Breathing the Martial Arts — 143

8	Teachers, Networks and Relationships in the Martial Arts	145
9	Investing into the Martial Arts and Related Practices	163
10	My Martial Arts Journey: An Autoethnography	183
11	Conclusions and Future Directions	207
	Index	217

Preface

Martial Arts before, during and after COVID-19: Three Arts, Three Stories, One Pandemic

I began planning this book in 2019 to meet the expansion of the Sport in East and Southeast Asian Societies series, thinking that it would be ready for 2020, but it has taken three years to finish the writing of my first monograph. Something unexpected swept from East Asia to change contemporary martial arts and society. This major global event in the 21st century has been the Coronavirus (COVID-19) pandemic that is believed to have begun in Wuhan, China in late 2019 and is still affecting many people at the time of writing, with new strains emerging across the world.

Research and early commentaries on the pandemic and martial arts has helped us know more about how martial artists might return to training in a safe manner (Anderucci, 2020), how we might train specific supplementary routines alone, or even utilise distance learning previously overlooked for civilian self-defence (Koerner & Staller, 2022) and the ways in which specific schools have adapted to the governmental restrictions such as staying at home – by continuing social and learning activities online (Jennings, 2020). The following short set of stories tells the tales of three martial arts that I have practised and researched as an ethnographer: Wing Chun Kung Fu, Historical European Martial Arts (HEMA) and Taijiquan (Tai Chi Chuan).

The first set of vignettes are from 2017 to 2019, when travel and physical exchanges permitted travel of practitioners and teachers from different countries to work in singular spaces. The second trio of vignettes returns to these three martial arts schools to show how their pedagogies were flipped online in the spring to summer period of 2020, making use of the technological advances of the 21st century. The third set of tales returns to these training sites to show how the pedagogies had adapted to social distancing and awkwardness when returning to human touch.

These are impressionist tales that follow the convention set out by Van Maanen (2011), which is designed to invite the reader into the social and sensuous world of a fieldwork setting while minimising the authoritarian and theoretical voice of the author. This genre is a way of representing ethnographic research, making the most of long-term immersion in fieldwork sites, as I have done over several years. As such, this chapter makes a contribution to knowledge by showing how three different martial arts schools operated before, during and after the main wave of the pandemic and subsequent lockdowns. The reader will notice the contrasts between the special events (a Wing Chun seminar, a guest workshop and a Taijiquan course) to the regular online training from the main instructors and their supportive network of students, followed by gradual adjustments to partner training and the use of physical equipment. We begin with the story from Bridge's Wing Chun Academy in which two guest instructors from the United States gave a two-day seminar over one weekend, only for the school to close its doors once the "stay at home" mandate was enacted. One theme that unites the three groups in dealing with the issue of the virus and the related problems of isolation, loneliness and lack of touch is humour among tightly-knit martial arts communities, which features in the second set of tales.

Bridge's Wing Chun Academy

Weekend seminar from a martial arts couple. Bridge's Academy is a former chapel converted to a full-time Chinese martial arts centre. Led by the charismatic Sifu John Bridge (seen in Jennings, Brown, & Sparkes, 2010), now in his fifties, it is hidden within a tough working-class community of long terraces in a sadly run-down seaside town, accessible through a narrow alley descending to the temple-like entrance, with its pagoda-like surroundings. Bridge had learned from three main teachers in the UK until he sought out his current Sifu, Master Li, who is from the former Portuguese colony of Macao but is has been based in the United States since the 1970s. A year before Li would return to British soil after a 20-year absence from his first European seminar, two of his senior students, Sifus Karl and Jemima, visited England for a weekend seminar. This pair are a real-life husband and wife team who run their *Kwoon* (School) in the South-West United States. Their seminar was followed by a holiday in the English Westcountry and Wales, the latter venue being the home of a Wing Chun student they have befriended while she had visited Master Li in the U.S. There was even a Wing Chun instructor who had travelled all the way from Greece, where some of the senior members of the lineage had visited recently. The couple, Karl and Jemima, have an excellent reputation for professionalism and exactitude when it comes to the biomechanics of Wing Chun; with my friend and regular training partner George (real name requested) recalling that Sifu had told me, "they like things really precise over there [in the USA]." He added to my surprise, "but they're not as interested in learning Wing Chun for self-defence as we are. Over in their state, people carry guns with them in the supermarket. If someone tried to attack them, they would just get their gun out and shoot them. If someone hits them in *chi sau* [sticking hands], they just reset." This was apparent in the level of precision expected from the participants, who included Wing Chun practitioners from as far and wide as the West of Scotland, the English East Midlands, three different schools in South Wales and people in the Academy. They all came in their groups, with their own uniforms bearing the mark of their associations – since Master Li had disbanded his European federation. I bought two of the t-shirts from Karl and Jemima's school in the U.S. lying on Sifu's counter, which have an attractive design involving Chinese symbols such as the plum blossom that is distinctive to Wing Chun and other Southern Chinese martial arts.

The first day of the weekend seminar involved honing the basic movements of Wing Chun Kung Fu, from the basic stance to turning and punching in the air, followed by techniques in the air. These gradually became more complex, with kicks in the air developed using combinations at mid and lower gates of the body (as in the midsection and knees). Students formed a large circle around the edge of the large hall, while Sifus Jemima and Karl gave demonstrations from the centre. This position differed from the convention series of rows in a class, and it enabled the guest teachers to walk around the room to check on each student in equal measure. Jemima stood in front of me, noticing that I was exaggerating the pulling mechanism in an excessively circular fashion. This was something I was working on it at home in order to explore the circles within the Wing Chun system, as in when dragging the opponent's arm back with one first while firing out the other. However, this exaggeration was exposed by someone with a very discerning eye for the finer aspects of the system.

Once our basic movements were checked on the first day, we moved onto partner training on the Sunday. Karl and Jemima wanted to get out "rolling" mechanism correct, and each of them would check on how it felt. Karl moved with me in a slow and thoughtful fashion, and I could feel his solid structures coming up from his strong stance. My own teacher crossed the room to take a look at me. "He's crap!" He joked, laughing as I smiled to meet the joke. He meant this in a sarcastic manner, as he had normally regarded me as a skilful student who had been trained to a high level. Karl did not seem to register this humour, and he defended me with a serious reply in a steady, monotone voice: "He's doing very well." It was interesting to note how the very professional couple wouldn't mock the students or make jokes about any other Wing Chun school, while Sifu Bridge felt comfortable to joke about many things with both his students and peers. During a demonstration of a partner exercise, Jemima corrected Karl, and suggested a different way to explain the technique, leaving John to quip: "We know who's in charge at home, don't we, Karl!" Everyone laughed at this joke, including the guest instructors, who obviously had a strong bond with John, understanding his cockney working-class and direct sense of humour. Karl often deferred to Jemima, and he noted, "there is no doubt in my mind that she could hurt me." The two also became very passionate about their teacher Sifu Li, noting that "there's always something that he can spot with your technique to make you better." Jemima later added, "you keep on getting better and better each day… and then you die" smiling with the realisation that our goal of perfection will never be reached.

Not only did the Wing Chun practitioners travel down for the seminar, but also their partners. My girlfriend Barbara stayed with me in a hotel near the harbour, while one of the Scottish instructors' girlfriends came along with him. "I'm not very good…It wouldn't be worth your bother." She said in a strong Scots accent when I offered to work on a drill together. The Greek Wing Chun instructor was greatly impressed by the style of Wing Chun that Master Li had developed off the basis of his own Sifu's style, noting its superiority. However, his long-suffering wife was waiting patiently with Barbara on the Sunday afternoon, whispering to her, "when is this going to end?!" To the outsider, Wing Chun can look rather monotonous and static, as it is more about inside sensations felt through proprioception. Barbara was surprised that I was interested in Wing Chun, as it appeared to be rather violent for her: "I was wondering to myself, why does George like this?! But then again, I can see you deeply concentrating in the drills, as in a form of meditation" she added, taking her perspective from a mindfulness facilitator and researcher.

Reuniting the Kung Fu family online.
Two and a half years on from the seminar and later weekend seminar from Master Li and his son (also travelling for the corresponding family holiday enabled by the student fees from the weekend), the COVID-19 pandemic led the UK Government, like many governments around the world, to initiate measures including the stay and work from home policies. Letter from the Prime Minister's office were posted to each household, while martial arts schools had to close with no idea when they would return, and Sifu Bridge used the Facebook platform to set up a private member's group that George and I could join, along with another former student who lived far away.

Normally, it would be very difficult to learn from our formative teacher on a regular basis, as the special events of the quarterly seminars and the occasional guest seminar would enable us to learn more about Wing Chun from our teacher who lives two and a half hours away (as far distance by British standards) in another country (England), which had slightly different restrictions due to the Welsh Government's localised control over the pandemic. However, now that no one could learn in person – even the locals – Sifu developed twice-weekly online classes to teach Wing Chun on the same evenings as he normally taught in the gym, making sure the times suited his senior student and confidant, Jim, who has a young family. Using the Messenger application connecting to the Facebook group (renamed from "Dragon Gym is Closed" used to announce the closure of the doors to the more vulgar "Dragon Gym Fucked Off" with the exchange of jokes, memes and action plans), he started a group call with current and former students united by his lineage. People answered the call from their homes, sometimes with a beer or snack in hand after a hard day's work online, with many taking a brief break at 8 p.m. for the "clap for carers" in honour of the National Health Service (NHS) workers who were struggling to maintain the health system afloat during the pandemic. Clangs of saucepans erupted for a moment as we took a break midway through the class.

The classes varied from demonstrations involving students copying Sifu's movements to more theoretical sessions in which we took copious notes. At the time, Sifu was working as his own elderly mother's carer, and was living in her home near his *Kwoon*, which had a spacious kitchen with a new floor that made sound effects when he moved. Using his mobile phone, Sifu was able to show us students his footwork and stances, even placing the phone onto the floor…until his dog appeared wanting attention! With these domestic responsibilities, Sifu did need to open the kitchen door for the dog to go to toilet while other students had interruptions from their young children, whose bedtime was pending. We waved at the kids, as their unexpected entrance and antics made people smile and laugh. Another source of unexpected laughter came from the "pizza face" function that Sifu had imposed over his real face. This turned out to be accidental, as Sifu had learned about this function from a friend in a previous chat, but did not know how to turn it off. This was funny for a few minutes, but after a while, it became frustrating for me, as I was very motivated to continue my lessons with Sifu in his usual format, having my notebook and pen at the ready. After hanging up and starting a new call, we could then concentrate on our learning, with our teacher's normal face resurfacing. Besides the visual interruptions, we sometimes noted the sound effects each other made in the air, with my former senior Ben noting, "I like the swoosh noises that George makes." I was proud of this effect, which seemed to be aided by the relaxation that I was developing from my Taijiquan training.

Sifu wanted students to study the videos he posted on our members-only Facebook group, which included a palm and chopping sequence in the air, which consisted of eight techniques (as with the eight stances, eight punches and eight elbows corresponding to the eight directions characteristic of our lineage). He appeared to have filmed this while visiting another *Kwoon* either in the warmer climes of the South West United States or Macao (with him wearing shorts and a vest), and he would then test our understanding by asking us to demonstrate. This was a new sequence that I wrote down in my technical notebook, which I would then take photographs of and send to my training partner George (who could not attend due to him working evening shifts) via WhatsApp, as he told me he was able to read my rather illegible handwriting often taken very quickly as I watched, interpreted and tried to emulate the movements while standing up. Sometimes Sifu laughed at my extensive notetaking, making the others chuckle at my different mannerisms and habits. My manner of speaking and profession often made me feel different from the other, more local, working-class students. It seems rarer for students to take notes by hand these days as they spent more time on YouTube scrutinising videos and training off handouts and posters – as did Kyle, a beginner who had plastered his walls with posters of the fundamental sequences and maxims of our style of Wing Chun.

The case of Bridge's Academy shows a martial arts school led by a charismatic teacher who is connected to many international figures in Wing Chun. His decades of martial arts experience make students old and new take notes and reunite for special events. However, in this sleepy seaside town in a country where "there's no career" (in the dismissive words of Steve, my old senior brother who stayed for the sole reason of his Kung Fu family) and a great deal of transition for university and graduate jobs, Sifu now finds it hard to sustain his eclectic school, which had to streamline into Wing Chun and private lessons in the day. He admitted that, "like with many of the traditional martial arts around the bay, we've taken a hit due to the popularity of MMA." Unlike the large cohorts of people in the 1999 seminar photograph on whom Steve once remarked, "were all young then," his current students are mainly men in their thirties and forties, with a few of university age who away for much of the calendar year. However, one thing remains constant in this academy: The use of humour, especially from the teacher to his students. The Blade Academy is also led by a charismatic, fun-loving man whose students rallied behind him for a special event before the pandemic and for community-led, weekly meetings for wellbeing, connection and martial skill development.

A return to the seminars.
George and I reconnected after the lockdown, revising old copies of the red and blue sash syllabus that he had at home. As he had maintained a firm friendship with our Sifu, he sometimes messaged John Bridge to check on the meaning behind the rather vague lists of techniques and sequences on the syllabus. On one occasion in my kitchen, we were able to position George's phone against my computer to have a video call while we showed our interpretation of the techniques due to be revised in the seminar. Sifu became confused with the two George's, ordering "George" to do a technique against "George", which made us all laugh. I then suggested we use our middle names, with mine being Bradley and George's being Alan. This allowed for a smooth communication of instructions and an effective response to feedback as we tried to keep within the camera frame so that our teacher could give us feedback.

The first seminar post-lockdown involved many students, and it finished with an extensive Chinese buffet in an all you can eat restaurant close to the gym. One intermediate (blue sash) student was wearing a Grinch jumper over his uniform, with his blue sash dangling out of the bottom of the comical Christmas top. The other students were wearing their uniforms and belts ready for the formal post-seminar photograph, students lined up in two rows around their teacher in the centre. George and I enjoyed the comradery with our teacher and senior students, and got to know some of Sifu's more recent pupils. George and I, lacking the conditioning of the regular students in Dragon Gym, damaged our knuckles against the heavy bags. As usual, the punches would be counted from one to ten, starting one side of the hall, moving to the next side and then the second row of students who had moved their water-based bags to the rear of the hall. We compared our hands, lining them up against each other while grimacing. "Yours are worse!" Said George, who has managed to borrow one of the gym's old pairs of bag gloves. I recall Steve, my old senior, joking that these were "the gloves of death" due to the foul stench they left on one's hands after wearing them. Our knuckles took many weeks to heal in the dark winter months, and I was adamant that I would be prepared for the next gathering, ordering specialist wraps and gloves on Amazon. Taking these in my bag along with some Cornish pasties that George and his partner had prepared for us the day before, we arrived at the gym considerably early. It was a bright and sunny day, so we moved away from the dark alley to get some Vitamin D before the indoor event took up all of the daylight.

One student arrived, waiting on the steps in his motorcycle gear as some other students arrived. The turnout was reduced this time, and with Sifu in pain after some surgery on his nose and shoulder (due to a growth and chronic pain respectively), we had a far easier physical workout led by Jim, who now took responsibility for the warm up, first empty hand form sequence (Siu Lim Tao). This was a common routine in Bridge's Academy, which made use of the Kung Fu family system in which senior students (*sihing*) would work with beginners and oversee the routine aspects of the class. The Sifu would then come in and check on the beginners as they moved around the air or hit bags. In the first seminar, Sifu leaned into me and whispered, "get closer," only to return a few minutes later to whisper once again, "you still need to get closer." I did this despite the pain I felt in my hands, and the fear of torn skin around my knuckles. It had been years since I had struck a heavy bag, as I had moved away to my own internal training of stances and forms, along with partner training.

The second seminar involved more partner training, but after some minutes, my right shoulder started to flare up while working with a young, well-built student. Fortunately, Sifu decided to modify the drill, which was in part due to the pain he was experiencing. Doctors had told him that he had occupational injuries from training Wing Chun and rolling into the upper *bong sau* position, which reminded me of my own postural issues caused by the art (which I shall describe in Chapter 11). When Sifu asked to demonstrate a technique with me, he hissed, "be really light", as I deliberately held back from using the normal force for my techniques. He did not correct me while we worked on the drill, but I still knew that he could dominate me with his high level of skill and speed, which were remarkable for a man in his fifties.

George and I returned to Wales in his car, reminiscing about old times and different training methods such as the resting squat and hanging from a bar, which one influencer that George follows "swears that it takes away all his aches and pains." We also struggled to remember all the other students' names, and George chuckled: "I do like it when I go into the kitchen and make a cup of tea behind the counter, and no one knows who I am." We were the mysterious former students living in Wales who would come down to the gym, which felt like a second home to us. However, I was becoming concerned about the health of our teacher, who was now working as a deliveryman for the National Health Service (NHS) procurement department while living with chronic pain and the resulting fatigue. During a break in the seminar, Jim had told us that the evening class was only two hours, rather than the two and a half hour session I had benefited from as a university student. How could Sifu sustain teaching Wing Chun while doing this job? He has been his mother's carer, but she was now living in a nursing home on the other side of the country, near his sister. With those benefits as a carer removed, he was forced to seek out work that took him far and wide across the county and neighbouring region. I only hoped that the doors of Bridge's Academy, what students affectionately call Dragon Gym, would stay open for many years to come. It was badly in need of a deep clean and refurbishment, with ivy growing into the corner of the gym from a neighbouring building. Perhaps this was the case for many martial arts centres trying to recover from the pandemic in an era when MMA attracts many of the young people of towns and cities in Western society. Another martial art movement that appeals to the youth is Historical European Martial Arts (HEMA), accounted for in the next section.

The Blade Academy

"He's forgotten more about fencing than I have ever learned": Guest workshop from HEMA maestro Angelo.

Billy Marshall is an athletic instructor loved and respected by his students. On his Academy Facebook page, one student noted on his motivations to continue training: "Not only are you an amazing fencer and instructor, you're bloody hilarious!" Billy tries to make his Blade Academy a safe, inclusive and fun atmosphere to learn Historical European Martial Arts (HEMA) as a serious martial art (as opposed to a sporting model). He had undergone a strict apprenticeship under Angelo, a renowned Italian fencer and medieval historian in Southern Italy. From stories Billy and his wife Issie (who also learned HEMA in the same fencing academy "chapter" in Italy) had shared with us, Angelo was depicted as a brutal, unforgiving instructor who once gave Billy a physical punishment exercise for leaning against a wall while listening to him explaining a theoretical principle. He also cautioned his students not to talk back to Angelo, who was very strict on discipline. Billy was still in awe of the man, often exclaiming to his students that "the man has forgotten more about fencing than I have ever learned." He actually said this in front of Angelo when he visited for a guest workshop, and Angelo then whispered sharply, "don't say that! What if I mess up?!" In an interview, Billy revealed that he has never seen Angelo "mess up", and even if Angelo was having a bad day, "he could still kick my arse just to prove a point."

Within the first year of him founding the school in 2018, Angelo was invited to give a guest workshop on a topic of his choice, which happened to be "bloody German longsword…of all things!", noting the irony of an Italian living in Italy teaching Italian longsword to Italians now teaching a guest session on a German manuscript on the weapon. Billy's jokes about "filthy Germans" are not in regard to Germans in general, but a reflection of the rivalry and banter between different schools of thought in fencing. Billy prefers Fiore de Liberi's school of fencing, as it is "pretty brutal in places," although Billy admits that Fiore himself was "probably not a nice guy…he was elitist and sexist to begin with." Indeed, the fencing of Fiore's 14th century society was one of the male aristocratic, right-handed elites and not for women or the peasantry. This HEMA Academy is open to people of all ethnicities, religions, social backgrounds, and genders (including non-binary identities welcomed in a special Warrior Women event led by Issie). Yet, it does tend to attract people of a white ethnic background largely following Christianity or no faith, despite the main branch being located in a predominantly Muslim, Middle Eastern district of a cosmopolitan city that is full of Turkish kebab houses, Lebanese grill restaurants and shisha lounges. Billy is careful not to joke about religion, spirituality and other sensitive topics such as gender (eventually ceasing any innuendo jokes during the warm-ups such as "try not to make eye contact with anyone when doing this exercise"), instead preferring to joke about the antics of his eager, energetic students. With my high-energy character and evasive style of fencing that often leads me to bump into people fighting behind me, Billy often refers me to as a "maniac," once noting on the group Facebook group: "George…your maniacal laugh will haunt me tonight" after I cackled continually when faced with multiple opponents in unit combat event. Students start to coin nicknames for each other, with Templar John (so-called for him being a Knights Templar reenactor) telling me to my surprise, that mine was "Ninja."

After the seminar, we followed our tradition of visiting Bentley's, a dessert restaurant open to 11 p.m. in an area devoid of pubs and bars. The staff there had become accustomed to us turning up sweaty, all dressed in black, carrying our heavy bags full of equipment. Alun, one of the students, once remarked that "there's no surprise to hear that you all went to Bentley's the other week…they're all a bunch of sugar heads here." Indeed, while few of the Academy seem to drink alcohol, they almost exclusively enjoy munching on waffles, crepes and pancakes after a draining evening workout finishing at 10 p.m. It turned out that Angelo and his girlfriend Monica were also very much into sweet things as well as coffee, with Billy returning from a trip to Italy with a renewed addiction to caffeine, "because they're fiends out there." Billy and Issie supported the seminar by taking Angelo and Monica on a tour of Welsh castles, returning bronzed from the sunny weather and exposure in the many ruined fortresses. As always, we hugged each other goodbye, as if saying goodbye at an airport, even though we would be reunited in two days' time for the Friday night class.

A calendar of online events.
Although Billy is yet to become a fully professional instructor, he trains and teaches as if his life depends on it. Whenever he has a free morning, he goes to the gym and meets up to spar with some of his close students or any other HEMA instructors visiting the area. In fact, Billy plans his work shifts for the afternoons to enable his to follow his chosen lifestyle, although this is in part as he is not a morning person and has some sleeping issues. When the pandemic hit the country, Billy used an emotional video to immediately announce a formal alliance with a neighbouring HEMA academy that followed a similar philosophy towards HEMA as a martial art (rather than a sport). He also included a group photograph of the students who attended his final class before the first lockdown, which lasted from the spring to the summertime of 2020.

As I have shown in Jennings (2020), the Academy was quick to adapt to online teaching. Looking back at this, Billy reflected on how many martial arts instructors he knew were resistant to the idea of teaching online, only to later be offering online distance learning courses. These were already set up in some commercially successful schools, such as Samuel Kwok's online Wing Chun course mentioned later in this book. Billy and his team of close students and friends worked hard to keep the Academy members and their loved ones occupied with free classes, workouts and movie nights. Some partners joined us for High Intensity Interval Training (HIIT) workouts, and they even sat next to their partners to watch some of the deliberately selected bad movies that made us laugh. People used Zoom to be able to make comments about the poor acting, ludicrous plot and terrible fighting skills of the key characters. Counting down "three, two, one!," these films were simultaneously played through our personal Netflix accounts, and the Zoom chats followed, often lasting up to 30 min after the movie, as we were then able to talk about training tips and different kinds of specialist swords.

Each week, students' sword collections seemed to be growing, as the cottage industry of HEMA equipment seemed to be bolstered by the pandemic, with people collecting more weapons now that they had the time to train at home and explore other aspects of HEMA. Some students had to adapt physical exercises depending on their home environments, with one student renting a first-floor apartment being conscious of any jumping exercises that might irritate his neighbours below. With bad weather meaning we were training indoors, I was concerned about hitting my kitchen ceiling with my synthetic longsword, which did eventually happen, leaving a mark that is noticeable to this day. As my own home armoury was limited, I often resorted to other makeshift weapons in my home, such as an umbrella for the shorter side sword, leading Callum, a senior in the group to comment: "I'm loving the umbrella, George." I felt like a Victorian gentleman fending off ruffians in the streets of London with my Bartitsu skills!

Wednesday night became firmly fixed for movie nights while Friday evenings was for HEMA training at home, focusing on longsword and then side sword and dagger when the weather turned for the worse. This class was extended to include a HIIT workout led by Adam, a budding stuntman now working in various Netflix series. He was also a practitioner of Japanese Ninjitsu, and with his knowledge of physical conditioning, he led us through gruelling workouts in a highly professional manner, making use of the timer app on his phone while demonstrating the exercises from his partner's parent's patio. I made the use of my sofa to tuck my feet in for sit ups and the bottom of my stairs for calf raises, while using my portable iPad to change the angle so that Adam could check on our technique. Sometimes Billy would take these sessions, and through his friendship with Samantha, he organised a yoga evening training session for the students on Tuesday evenings. This was accompanied by a Dungeons and Dragons night on Sunday led by Len, a keen gamer and the Academy's webmaster. Looking back at this festival of activities every week, I was reminded of a song by the band The Darkness, which boasted of different extra-curricular activities each evening.

Post-lockdown hygiene and the New Normal.
Billy and Issie had read into the Government's strict guidance for gyms and fitness facilities, also consulting with the managers of the large leisure centre where they rented a multi-sports hall. The fire doors were left open in order to ventilate the hall, and although we could converse outside without the COVID-19 protective masks, we had to put them on once we entered the rear fire door next to the car park. The Academy had been busy planning for this reunion, designing their very own COVID-19 facemasks proudly bearing the logo of the Academy over a black design – just like their all-black uniform with the white logo on the breast. Billy came over to us students, giving us an elbow greeting instead of his usual handshake and a hug. He had us line up to listen to the new regulations about mask wearing, distancing and using shared equipment such as the cones deployed for footwork drills and fitness exercises. "Once we line up at a distance, you can take your masks off if you like, but make sure to put the masks on again once you leave the closing formation." Billy explained. We then saluted with our right first to our hearts (where the Academy badge was), to then begin a modified warm up involving running on the stop, strafing left and right and either jumping in the air or collapsing to the ground in a plank position (or as a burpee exercise if we so wished). I placed my mask in my hoody pocket for safekeeping, while being cautious about moving in the wrong direction (left or right) should I accidentally bump into someone. Some of the students had caught the virus over the lockdown, and over the course of several weeks, some had succumbed to the illness, requiring them to self-isolate for two weeks.

After the warm up, Billy introduced a dynamic footwork drill making use of the forward steps, backwards steps and sideways motions. We would move forwards in a rapid fashion to squat down to pick up a plastic orange cone, to then shuffle backwards and then to the right, leaving the cone on the floor. The cone would then be picked up, as we moved to the left and then forwards, leaving the cone in its former place. After using the cones, we would wipe them down with antibacterial sheets so as to contain the spread of the virus. Over the course of several weeks, Billy came up with some ingenious adapted training methods and ways to drill techniques without breaching the 1.5–2 metre distance regulations. Having spoken to my old friend Carlos in a catch-up over Zoom, it was not as regulated as his Kendo association in the Netherlands, which had strict rules about training in groups and using partner drills. However, the grappling aspects of the system were not covered in the class, and nor were close-range techniques such as the pommel strike, involving the use of the bottom of the sword while trapping the opponent's arm. There is no unifying governing body for HEMA, which meant that Billy and Issie had to adapt the training sessions as COVID-19 measures were gradually lifted. This is also true for Wing Chun and its fellow Chinese martial art Taijiquan examined in the next section.

The School of Internal Arts

A day course across the border.
It was time for the one-day course. Aidan was kind enough to offer Andrew and I a lift to the short course led by Barry, a senior instructor in our Taijiquan organisation who happened to by the main teacher Malcolm's father and first teacher who was now learning from his enigmatic son. For some reason, during the night I had a feeling of foreboding before we set off for the journey. Once we reached the Prince of Wales Bridge heading to England, all of a sudden, Aidan clutched his chest and bent forwards, straining for breath at the wheel. Was he having a heart attack?! "Oh my goodness, I suddenly feel unwell in this country that feels superior" he joked, as we got to the border. Andrew, being a relative newcomer from South Africa, did not quite understand the difference between English, Welsh and British identities, and Aidan was making a joke about the stereotypical English sense of superiority – something I relayed to my family, which made them laugh.

The discussion was rich and energetic, with Andrew and Aidan discussing different martial arts and body-mind practices, including yoga. Andrew had noted that many of the large organisations had cult-like qualities, with the notorious Bikram Yoga being noted for the sexual harassment of young female students (as seen in a Netflix documentary, *Bikram: Yogi, Guru, Predator,* 2019). However, he was happy that Malcolm seemed humble and approachable, and not seemingly interested in such unseemly behaviour. Aidan, a black belt in Aikido, noted that Aikido teachers were often very insular in their views, preferring for their students to avoid cross training with other teachers. "But David's not like that at all. He's happy for us to travel to the course" reflected Aidan on our own instructor, who was humble about his role as a gateway to the larger organisation he was a part of. Andrew, meanwhile, had already got to train with Malcolm when he gave a special session in Manchester. "Explode the joints!" Andrew had told me, using Malcolm's instructions. "He's very different from his father. Very different," he added, upon reflection from this session.

I had found Barry to be very soothing in his tone, as well as polite, often asking us to do things with a "please" at the end of the message. He was also honest about the time for each exercise, with "two more minutes, please." This differed from our own teacher David, who Aidan joked about: "We all know that David lies…one minute is never one minute!" Andrew had also noted the extent of David's lesson plans one week, and he told us how very little of it actually got covered in the two-hour session.

Barry was a tall and powerfully built man who moved with great poise and relaxation. During the break, he sank and sat into a low stance from the "snake creeps down" posture, and Aidan whispered in my ear, "now, he doesn't move like a 61-year-old man, does he?" I had heard from a more senior Taijiquan student that "Barry says he likes training Taiji because he can move like he's 21 again." Later in the class, Barry explained some of the theory behind the slow movement training in Taijiquan, which was supposed to strengthen the fascia, which is "three or four times stronger than muscle." He added, "you don't become weaker doing Taiji, you become strong – super strong." This was later reinforced by David, who begged the question, "why would you practise a martial art that makes you weak? We want a soft yet strong, powerful body." We finished the seminar with a group photograph, bunching tightly together under the banner of the international association.

Starting the weekend with an online workout.
My Saturday mornings help me begin the weekend in the best possible way: with a Taijiquan class that I can take from my home – even in pyjamas on lazy mornings. This was not an original part of David's weekly classes, which were either evening sessions or the occasional day course at the weekends. Now, from 10:00 to 11:30 a.m., we have a Saturday morning class from the comforts of our living rooms, bedrooms and kitchens. In fine weather, I was able to train outside on my patio, although my knees did feel the pain when we went through the usual dynamic stretching routine on the floor. As with the Wing Chun class, I utilised my iPad, which had a far better connection on Zoom. This device was also portable, enabling me to move across the house for more suitable spaces for certain exercises, as in my long, thin kitchen and the soft rug in my lounge. David once joked: "My next-door neighbour is having an open house day today, and lots of people are going to come round. I've promised him I wouldn't go out in the garden with my sword" to which one normally quiet student, Kevin, responded with a short laugh, "is that dressed in ice hockey gear?!"

This use of home space has extended to furniture, as I occasionally sit on the sofa for some theoretical classes from David, while using two meditation cushions (a thick round cushion and a square, thin one). After COVID-19, David has provided us with a free meditation class on Thursday mornings from 7:00 to 8:30

a.m., which he stresses it "sitting practice, not meditation…is the foundation of meditation." He also distinguished levels of deep meditation with the phrase "there's meditation and then there's meditation proper…" joking that "I'm doing this slowly so that George can take his notes." Although not Taijiquan, it is part of David's personal practice that he is willing to share with his regular students. The School of Internal Arts "is not pure Taiji," as my Chinese friend Ma Xiujie noted, spotting several exercises from Chinese medicine, as in the lion pose on the ground. There is also some discursive borrowing of terms, such as mindfulness, which is now more frequently mentioned since the development of the meditation class (e.g., "keep your mindfulness in the kua"). However, the school does approach specific traditions (such as meditation) and techniques (such as leg stretches) in a Taijiquan way, with David often reminding us not to stretch to far or "make it a willpower thing" due to the Daoist belief that this would cause mental tension, further reinforcing the cycle of thought, emotional reaction and eventual build-up of physical tension in the body. At the end of these sessions, David asks for students' feedback on the sensations that they had felt. "Thanks for taking us on this journey!" Said the energetic and smartly dressed Ben, who David once joked was "the pinnacle of fashion" with his designer glasses, hats and original sports gear.

The joy of post-lockdown touch.
We eventually returned to the usual hall on a Tuesday evening, although the booking in the school hall on a Thursday night had been lost due to COVID-19 affected the diary of events in that smaller venue. We continued with some of the regular solo exercises while returning to more complex ones, with this being the second class of the evening for intermediate students. David had used the lockdown period to reorganise his syllabus and training protocols in order to have a clearer divide between the beginners (who are up to "cross hands" in the Short Form) and the intermediates beyond this stage. This made the organisation of space far easier, as beginners didn't need to stick to the right side of the hall while the more advanced were on the left. Despite us having the same instructions again, David reinforced them with soothing calls to "move from the scapula, not from the hands. Try to keep the hands light" as we rotated our hands in large circles around our heads, behind our torsos and out to the side. However, at this stage, David started to stress *attention* over *intention* – with the latter concept being very important for beginners. Walking away from his silver thermos, he remarked, "look at the flask, look at its lovely grooves. Then stepping back…" he moved away from the flask, showing how one could be attentive to an object,

just like we could be attentive to the sensations in our bodies without having to stress the intention too heavily. David often contrasted this approach to the popular way of practising Taiji without such principles, which he had once called "Taiji for dummies," noting that his teacher Malcolm sometimes referred to those large commercial approaches to institutionalised Taiji with very fixed postures as "McTaiji." This dualistic thinking is necessary in the beginning, with phrases such as "to stretch the back, you must relax the front" common in class. David is clear in his distinctions, adding that "people are either in a state of tension or collapse. Otherwise, they are sinking." And it is this sinking that he wants to develop in his students for their partner training, which offers a degree of pressure testing for the practitioner.

To our surprise, David called a stop to the individual training exercises, and asked us to turn to face a partner. We were going to learn to feel the lines across the body by touching the opponent's forearms with our fingers, as they brought their arms out to near extension. I rolled up my sleeves to enable my partner to feel into my fascia – something understood as the *huang* in the Chinese worldview we were being taught. We would try to sink our mass to the floor through our feet, later manipulating this by moving from the *kua*, an area inside the groin (according to Chinese medical theory), which David explains in Western terms as the inguinal crease, two ligaments that originate from the hips. This training then extended to a push and tug game to feel the difference when using physical strength. David asked to work with me, as we used our physical force against each other. As I was over twenty years younger than David, I was able to push him back by marching forwards and grunting. We both smiled with glee, as neither of us had had such an interaction before. Then David showed us the difference, by sinking and releasing, making my trip over, only to roll over my shoulder, avoiding getting my hip smashed on the hard floor. "Nice roll!" Commented the ever-joyful Sandra, a bio scientist in her late fifties. Turning to face my new partner Ted, a psychotherapist specialised in the LGBTQ+ population, he commented, "you have done lots of martial arts training, haven't you?" At the end of the class, former firefighter Aidan came to congratulate me on my development – something he had not manage to feel during the lockdown. "David wouldn't use you to demonstrate if he didn't see that you were good." Aidan said, motivating me with his words of encouragement, which were reinforced with a "well done mate" message the next morning.

Aidan, a former student of Aikido and Chen Hsin, was overjoyed with the return to working with other people in partner training, noting in the WhatsApp group, "it's great to work with another body again." I was able to work with

Dominic, one of the most advanced students in the class, who moved away from my issuing of force, to stagger away after I had taken his root away from him. We continued with this training the following week, and I face off to Dominic. However, this exercise was to be more complicated, as it was once of the more advanced pushing hands sequences involving grasping the opponent's upper arm, pulling them (or "plucking" in Taijiquan terms), for them to later return the movement by first swinging the rear arm out and upwards, for it to scoop underneath the partner's forearm. The level of complexity to be developed by intermediate students required close training with partners, a pedagogical element our teacher worked further only when face-to-face interactions were safe post-lockdown. While the impact of the COVID-19 pandemic has been experienced differently across and within nations and populations (an analysis that is beyond the aim of the present manuscript), my original approach to examine three different martial arts using a temporal outlook, i.e., *before*, *during* and *after* the pandemic, provides the adequate preamble to the focus of my book as summarised next.

Summary

From these sets of stories from events only a year or two apart, we can see how the community formed within the regular physical training have been supported by infrequent, special events through the guide of seminars (Wing Chun), workshops (HEMA) and courses (Taijiquan). These are not the only kinds of events in these martial arts, as competitions are common in HEMA, as are retreats for Taijiquan. The events required careful planning of logistics such as travel and accommodation around the stay. However, the COVID-19 pandemic meant that long-term planning had to be shelved as teachers and students became accustomed to a "new normal." All of the three schools had to adapt to the crisis of the global pandemic by seeking out creative ways to continue learning and teaching while maintaining a healthy sense of humour with jokes from the teachers, quick responses from the students and some gentle teasing to recognise the unique characteristics of the members of the group. This ties to a recent article on HEMA in which I examined the use of humour within the pedagogy in terms of how left-handed people are now welcome in fencing and wider Western society (Jennings, 2022), despite there being historical stigma associated with left handedness, and stigma in some contemporary societies outside the Western context.

In this book, I will examine how martial arts have been reimagined, reconstructed and reinvented for different purposes that are deemed to be important in contemporary society while considering the experiences of the practitioners themselves who have spent many years moving along their martial arts journeys, often meandering between different styles and systems from different cultures, both East and West. My research traces and articulates a story of reinvention of practitioners and their arts over longer periods of time, with a focus on Western practitioners of the martial arts that are either from the Eastern side of the globe, or have some influence from them in their philosophy, pedagogy, structure or practitioner biographies.

References

Anderucci, C. (2020). Gyms and martial arts school after COVID-19: When to come back to train? *Advances in Physical Education, 10*, 114–120.

Jennings, G. (2022). "Filthy lefties!": The humorous stigmatisation of left-handed fencers in historical European martial arts (HEMA), 136(2), 17-36.

Jennings, G. (2020). Martial arts under the COVID-19 lockdown: The pragmatics of creative pedagogy. *Sociología del Deporte, 1*(2), 13–24. https://doi.org/10.46661/socioldeporte.5242

Jennings, G., Brown, D., & Sparkes, A. C. (2010). It can be a religion if you want': Wing Chun Kung Fu as a secular religion. *Ethnography, 11*(4), 533–557.

Koerner, A., & Staller, M. (2022). Coaching self-defense under COVID-19: Challenges and solutions in the police and civilian domain. *Security Journal, 35*, 118–132.

Netflix. (2019). *Bikram: Yogi, guru, predator.* Dir. Eva Orner.

Van Maanen, J. (2011). *Tales from the field: On writing ethnography.* Chicago: Chicago University Press.

Acknowledgments

This is my first full-length academic book, and I have many people to thank for sharing their ideas and stories about the martial arts for the past two and a half decades. Since starting martial arts training in 1998, I have benefited from excellent teachers and mentors in Taekwondo, Kendo, Judo, Kickboxing, Wing Chun, Xilam, Taijiquan and HEMA. Many of them featured in the preface under pseudonyms to protect their identities, but hopefully, if they read this, they know who they are. My martial arts seniors and fellow students have also been inspirational for my development, and I am grateful for their punches and kicks! Special thanks to Tim Chow for getting me into the martial arts in the first place, and the Chow family for opening my eyes to Chinese culture.

No research project would be possible without its core set of voluntary participants, and my varied participants include some of the rich characters presented in this book (such as "Billy" and "David") as well as some of my influential seniors such as "Aidan" and George. They took a great deal of time looking through their interview data and how I represented them in the later chapters of the book. Although I wasn't able to include all of the participants and interview data due to space limitations and the focus of the book, I do hope to include their voices in future articles.

I am blessed to have some close colleagues at Cardiff Met who showed interest in my book and the eventual reading of it. David Brown has been an outstanding supervisor, colleague and friend over the past 18 years (since I approached him as a 19-year-old dissertation prospect), and I know we will eventually write our own book together. The members of the Qualitative Research Methods and Social Theory (QRMST) group have been very receptive to my ideas as well as my growing number of guest speakers. David Aldous and I still have to collaborate on some writing, but he has given me space in his research group to voice my ideas. Robyn Jones, my line manager Liz Lewis and other members of the Cardiff Met management have always helped me in terms of my research and innovation hours, giving me the headspace to read, write, think and rethink about the martial arts. Lisa Edwards has been a caring friend since I arrived at the university, and I appreciate the moral support from my Portuguese friends Manuel Santos and Mara Mata, including our virtual dinner during COVID-19.

Outside Cardiff Met, I am indebted to the guidance from veteran ethnographer Sara Delamont, who has become another firm friend in the Welsh capital. She welcomed me with open arms to the Ethnography Seminar Group at Cardiff University, which enabled me to share many research ideas and data to bright and upcoming social scientists. Like David Brown, I see Sara an excellent model for how to be a great professional and person in the coming decades. Lyn Jehu of the University of South Wales and his family have been very firm friends over these past five and a half years, and I have learned a lot about Japanese culture and martial arts from them. Professor Paul Bowman also deserves my thanks for setting up the ever-expanding Martial Arts Research Network in which I have presented several papers eventually written up for his journal. I really hope that our project on humour in martial arts communities can continue soon. Paul's comrade in arms Ben Judkins has also been very enthusiastic about my work, and I hope I am able to write another article for his popular Kung Fu Tea blog. Colleagues at the Documents Research Network (DRN) Aimee Grant and Maria Pournara (now at Swansea University) have supported by other blogs in our website in terms of how documents on the martial arts can be used as forms of data. Some of those documents also feature in this book, as in self-help books.

The renowned historian of sport Professor J. A. Mangan has been the ideal series editor for me, as his positive and crystal-clear feedback, rapid email responses and helpful advice has enabled me to get the book into this exciting series on Sport in East and South East Asian Societies. He and the professional staff at Peter Lang such as Ni La and Suma George provided me with plenty of time to write this 94,000-word monograph, which sometimes felt like constructing a second thesis during my full-time job. However, in the end, thanks to their encouragement and the smooth production processes aided by Jacqueline Pavlovic and Naviya Palani I feel far more confident about writing another monograph, and hope I can count on their support for such an endeavour. Like Sara Delamont, the name of J. A. Mangan conjured up images of an elite academic figure, but I found working with them both to be relaxed, flexible and upbeat.

Although peer reviewers can sometimes evoke reactions of annoyance and disbelief, I can look back at their comments as important stepping stones for my professional growth. Editors of books and collections that I have been part of have also helped me expand the topics that I have explored, and I am particularly grateful to Alex Channon, my old housemate Lorenzo Pedrini, Xiujie Ma and Joaquín Piedra for their sustained support of my work. Like my Italian friend Lorenzo, Matteo di Placido has also been a great appreciator of my work and ideas, and I was pleased to see his critical adoption of my Theory of Martial Creation in a recent article. Other Spanish friends who have been great sources of motivation and wisdom include Vicente Beltrán and Alex Jiménez. In a post-pandemic world, I hope to reunite with these friends soon, and return the hospitality I have received in their country. Eduardo González de la Fuente and Angélica Cabrera Torrecilla will soon come to Cardiff after five years on meeting in Prague – testament to the friendship and strong academic bonds that we have forged. Carlos Gutierrez has been a brilliant person to work with in *Revista de Artes Asiáticas* (RAMA) and later ICM UNESCO with the seasoned martial arts scholar DS Farrer. Special thanks to Miso Lee and Aisling Clardy for their platforms to share my ideas and research findings to a wider audience.

In the early days, my mother and grandparents were invaluable for my ability to step through the doors of martial arts classes, sometimes giving me lifts to the classes and courses beyond my reach. Their thoughtful presents for Christmas and birthdays got me into the Bruce Lee and fitness crazes of my youth. My brothers Matthew and Laurence have also shown interest in my authored work and I am proud of their achievements, too. I have definitely got my work cut out as the eldest brother!

My long-term partner Bárbara Ibinarriaga Soltero has been there for me since the initial book proposal ideas, always being there to listen to my ideas and put up with my frustrations with academic life. She gave a lot of her own time and energy checking through the document so that it was formatted and presented correctly according to the publisher's guidelines. Barbara also cast her eagle eye and PhD research skills over the manuscript to offer some comments that enabled me to elaborate on some confusing points that needed more contextualisation. We spent a lot of time in some of our favourite cafés in Cardiff while I was writing sections of the book, so I will look back at those moments with great fondness. No doubt we will have many of our own research collaborations in the coming years and decades. Thanks for your help, *cariad*!

List of Abbreviations

Anterior Cruciate Ligament	ACL
Brazilian Jiujitsu	BJJ
British Academy of Film and Television Arts	BAFTA
British Combat Association	BCA
British Council for Chinese Martial Arts	BCCMA
Chartered Institute of the Management of Physical Activity	CIMSPA
Combat Sports and Martial Arts	CSMA
Continued Professional Development	CPD
Coronavirus	COVID-19
Daoist Internal Arts	DIA
Digital Versatile Disc	DVD
Documents Research Network	DRN
Eastern Movement Forms	EMFs
Health Advancement Research Team	HART
High Intensity Interval Training	HIIT
Highly Sensitive Person	HSP
Historical European Martial Arts	HEMA
Intangible Cultural Heritage	ICH
International Centre of Martial Arts for Youth Development and Engagement	ICM
International Feldenkrais Federation	IFF
Israeli Defence Force	IDF

Lesbian, Gay, Bisexual, Transgender, And Queer Community	LGBTQ+
Live Action Role-Playing Game	LARP
Martial Arts and Combat Sports	MACS
Martial Movement Method	MMM
Mixed Martial Arts	MMA
Multiple-Choice Quiz	MCQ
National Health Service	NHS
People's Republic of China	RPC
Physical Health Education and Lifelong Learning	PHELL
Qualitative Research Methods and Social Theory	QRMST
Revista de Artes Asiáticas	RAMA
Royal Air Force	RAF
Special Operation Forces	SOF
Tai Chi and Qigong Union for Great Britain	TCUGB
Tai Chi Union for Great Britain	TCUGB
Traditional Chinese Medicine	TCM
Traditional Sports and Games	TSG
Ultimate Fighting Championship	UFC
United Nations Educational, Scientific and Cultural Organization	UNESCO
United Kingdom	UK
Unique Selling Points	USPs
Video Home System	VHS
Virtual Reality	VR
Young Men's Christian Association	YMCA

1

Introduction: Conceptualising the Martial Arts in Contemporary Society

The Reinvention of the Martial Arts

Reinvention, reconstruction, revival, renaissance, resurgence, research, return… the list could go on. Many re- prefixed, process-based words are used in this book and by the practitioners, innovators and influencers within it, as this is a text concerned with the reshaping and redesigning of martial arts for different people, purposes and contexts. They are process words that are nouns but also verbs concerned with long-term visions, actions and projects around how martial arts are being used beyond their original purpose of self-defence, protection and military training. As the main title of the book suggests, it asks the question: how are the martial arts being reconstructed in the 21st century? Or more specifically for this book series on Sport and East Asia, what are the ways in which East Asian martial arts practices and techniques are being reconstructed in the Western context?

This is not to deny that there are new martial arts being developed today for the need of human survival in difficult circumstances. People will always be interested in learning how to defend themselves and their loved ones and nation, so the dominant model of martial arts as codified, socially acceptable fighting systems will of course continue. Special Operation Forces (SOF, as they are known in the military lexicon), will be at the forefront of this kind of experimentation and advocation of specific martial arts systems. Our love for entertainment means that martial arts will continue to feature in movies, television series and now online streaming, as well as video games specialised in armed and unarmed combat. Bowman (2019) has shown the influence of the different forms of media (including advertising, television and comedy sketches) in the discursive construction of the martial arts – most notably the Asian martial arts such as Kung Fu, Karate and Judo.

Martial arts are of course invented or constructed at some point in history, and many are not as old or "traditional" as non-specialists might think. Yet they are also reinvented and reconstructed for different purposes, as the society they exist in changes in terms of new rules, practices, norms and values. This might involve clubs and federations becoming more inclusive in terms of gender and the roles of women in organisations as in Savate in the UK (Jennings & Delamont, 2020), or other cases where martial arts are recreated for nationalist purposes and military training. Some martial arts become sports, other forms of moving meditation, while some die out only to be rediscovered and popularised by networks of innovators. The globally popular arts of Aikido, Judo, Taekwondo and Kendo were all formed during the late modern, end-of empire (and postcolonial) periods. Other popular versions of arts like the Ip Man style of Wing Chun (as taught by Ip Man in Hong Kong from the 1950s to 1970s) were also modified and codified during this period of modernity. Wartime martial arts used for maiming, killing and capturing an opponent were transformed into systems of human development and self-cultivation, as well as methods of civilian self-defence. Other fighting systems were made more socially acceptable as demonstration arts for folk events such as festivals and carnivals that are unique to specific towns and communities. Many of these arts were further modified in various formats to become combat sports such as those seen in the recent Tokyo 2020 Olympic Games, as in Karate, Judo and Taekwondo. Martial arts can therefore be sports, although there is already a large body of literature on the modernisation and civilising of systems such as Judo (Villamón, Brown, Espartero, & Gutiérrez, 2004), Venezuelan stick and machete fighting (Juego de Garrote) (Ryan, 2017) and Mixed Martial Arts (MMA) and its main competition, the Ultimate Fighting Championship (UFC) (Sánchez García & Malcolm, 2010).

Many martial arts have specific qualities, philosophies and practices that make them suitable for particular sectors of society. In fact, most martial arts were created with specific people in mind: a warrior class such as the Samurai / bushi, a slightly built ethnic group such as the Aeta (Ayta) people in the Philippines or the Jewish people of Europe experiencing violent antisemitism. Some of these arts have been used for different purposes. Krav Maga is a notable example of this. Founded in Europe by a Jewish boxer and wrestler, Krav Maga was initially used for Jewish people to defend themselves from Nazis and their sympathisers during the build up to the Holocaust. With the founding of the nation-state of Israel several years later, Krav Maga is now used by the Israeli Defence Force (IDF) but also other armed forces around the world. I could join a class in Cardiff, Bristol or other cities in the UK without having to be of Jewish origin extraction. As the founders of arts pass away, others take on the mantle of leadership and development, and the art can move beyond their control as other people interpret its potential in novel and refreshing ways. Other approaches to reconstructing the martial arts are as forms of liberal education, as in the generally peaceful Japanese Aikido used to develop leadership skills in the United States (Levine, 1991). For several decades now, calls have been made for the Asian martial arts sequences to be used to teach children for relaxation purposes and to learn discipline (Sparkes, 1985), with some new empirical studies on more recent, popular martial arts showing promise for youth development (e.g., Blomqvist Mickelsson, 2020).

A motivation for writing this book is my interest in the connections between the past, the present and the future. We know a lot about the development of martial arts over the centuries, particularly in terms of the founding of the modern, popularised styles in the 19th century and their continued formulation, diffusion and sportification into the 20th century.

Reinventing Martial Arts in the 21st Century would appeal to martial arts scholars as well as specialists in anthropology, history, social psychology and sociology. Sport scholars might find the work useful in showing martial arts can be used beyond competitive and demonstration sport in events such as the Olympic Games. The book is written in an accessible academic style for diverse audiences with the aim of it being useful for martial arts instructors, practitioners and leaders and for those whose first language might not be English. The conclusions point to future directions and applications of the ideas raised in the book, and the reader might be in the perfect position to do just that.

Positionality and the Scope of this Book

I am a British researcher who has lived in England, Scotland, Mexico and now Wales. The context I have lived, worked and trained in will determine my position on the martial arts, while the languages I can speak (English and Spanish) influence the sources I read, the data collect and how I analyse this date through specific theories and concepts. I am hesitant to use terms such as "West" and "East" in this text, as they can cause the impression of a false dichotomy. The Global North and South are also influential terms in the social sciences today, so this text tries to consider a very global, "big picture" perspective on the martial arts beyond the introspective, ethnographic accounts I am accustomed to writing. Elements of what are often referred to as the "Eastern," "Oriental" or "Asian" martial arts might be a certain kind of punch launched from the hip, of the practice of bowing and kneeling while wearing a coloured belt or a uniform. These rituals and "traditions" are specific practices taken out of their culture of origin.

The most obvious application of martial arts is for fighting: on the street, in the ring or cage and on the battlefield. However, they can also be used to enhance athletes' performance in terms of mobility and injury prevention, while their philosophies might be harnessed in terms of personal development and self-help. Asian martial arts, with their global recognition, might also inspire the development of more localised martial arts practices searching for long-lost warrior traditions and even world heritage. Reconstructing the martial arts covers these topics, which to date have received little coverage when compared with sportification, modernisation, globalisation and even martial arts tourism in their homelands such as Okinawa for Karate.

This book does reflect my biography and professional trajectory to date, as I write this in 2021-22, having studied various martial arts since 1998. On a personal level, I have utilised some of the techniques and basic movements of the martial arts in exercise rehabilitation. While a member of the registered charity Action After Stroke, a student-led voluntary association in the University of Exeter, I experimented with kicking techniques against resistance from myself when working with stroke survivors. Some of the basic qigong techniques and body loosening exercises I had learned from Taijiquan were adapted to expand these people's mobilities. Years later, while living in Mexico I started to imagine how I could create my own martial arts movement system based on the techniques, postures and exercises I had learned as a student and ethnographer of various fighting and human development systems. This included eye exercises for peripheral vision, which would be beneficial for people in all walks of life. During my time in Mexico, I was fortunate to be able to learn the basics of the martial art of Xilam, which takes a decolonial and nationalist perspective on Mexico in which the art is used to develop model citizens aware of their history and ancestry.

However, I must admit my limited knowledge in other fields. For instance, I know little about computer games and Virtual Reality (VR) compared with

Introduction: Conceptualising the Martial Arts | 5

many of my contemporaries, and these are industries where martial arts have featured for many decades. As the gaming world develops from the two-dimensional Nintendo *Streetfighter* games I grew up with, it is likely to see the West adapting East Asian martial arts for educational purposes but also for edutainment. Netflix and YouTube Originals Series such as *Cobra Kai* can be funny and nostalgic return to the *Karate Kid* films, with their mockery of identity politics and generational differences, but they also teach us about contemporary society, boyhood and family. *The Matrix*, with its virtual fights using techniques of Kung Fu and Jujitsu might have seemed fanciful at the time of release, but they might be part of the future of martial art around the world. Futurology might play a role in martial arts studies and sport studies as we imagine new visions of society.

Nonetheless, as I am a cultural sociologist, this book is more about longer-term trends that have come to prominence in the first two decades of the twenty-first century. There were signs of these trends, movements and initiatives in the late 20th century and perhaps even earlier in some cases (as in the French Judo for health and the Feldenkrais movement in terms of therapeutic martial arts stemming from the 1960s, see https://feldenkrais.com/), but there is now sufficient media attention and deployment of ideas around martial arts as therapy, self-help, movement systems, cultural heritage and revivalist movements for me to write entire chapters on them. I hope that when taken together, these chapters add to the knowledge on the martial arts, combat sports, movement systems, mind-body traditions, therapies and self-help techniques to show how they can work side-by-side. Martial arts can of course transform into sports, but they can be much more than that.

Where possible, the main empirical chapters typically follow a common structure: beginning with a short "hook" to contextualise the situation in contemporary society, followed by a brief review of literature on the research and arguments around the topic. I then select two to three international case studies of notable organisations, movements, arts and individuals that reflect the approach to martial reconstruction. This is followed by a discussion and analysis to help build and test a working definition of the martial arts – the framework I am attempting to develop and test in this monograph. This is in the aim of contributing in a balanced way to theory, data and method: new theory informed by established theoretical ideas, different forms of data often found from open-access sources, ethnographic studies and autobiographical reflections and the methods that have been used to gather and analyse these sources. Where possible, I have tried to support the chapters with a range of studies across the decades, from different countries and regions and from a spectrum of authors across the academic disciplines. My apologies in advance for missing any studies or researchers in this particular edition and text. As our field is forever expanding, there are so many studies and individuals I have am yet to cross paths with. Hopefully I will become more aware of new groups, institutions and pioneers in future studies and books.

Defining and Redefining the Martial Arts: A Work in Progress

All the above empirical investigations and scholars might have varied notions of what a martial art really is, and it is apparent that most of them do not attempt to define or categorise the martial arts. I believe all definitions have something to offer in terms of this discussion, and each of them holds valid perspectives. Strangely, dictionary definitions of martial arts – even those in reputed sources such as the Oxford and Cambridge dictionaries – remain biased towards the Asian styles, which leaves out the forms of combat in the Americas, Africa, Europe and Australasia. Public-facing, accessible Encylopaedias such as that of Crudelli's *The Way of the Warrior: Martial arts and fighting systems from around the world* (2008) have become increasingly international in scope, and this is seen in the very recent (and soon to be expanded) online collection by the ICM UNESCO *World Martial Arts: A Preliminary Report*, which also divides the martial arts according to geographic regions (see ICM, 2021). These kinds of reference books also note the founder and history of the arts, and offer some insight into their popularity today. In this book, I am not studying all the possible systems and their variations such as hybrid styles, but certain trends that have emerged in the last few decades. As the 21st century enters its third decade, stable trends as becoming more prominent, and I set out to examine these in turn.

There are now many different definitions of the martial arts around the world, within specific academic circles and in many languages, but all of them are inspired in some way by theory and previous definitions. As Meyer (2021) has recently remarked in conjunction with his own social scientific survey research, there are common acronyms in different languages such as the English "Martial Arts and Combat Sports" (MACS, now pronounced as a word in itself), and the French academic tendency for their translated "Combat Sports and Martial Arts" (CSMA), as seen in the recent JORRESCAM conference and an upcoming special issue of the Francophone journal *STAPS*. Definitions and preferred terms will of course change over time through the influence of certain readings and influential theories, and my use of MACS (Channon & Jennings, 2014) for the triadic relationship between combat sports, self-defence systems and traditionalist martial arts was in fact informed by the relational, triangular body cultures model of Henning Eichberg (1998) – a tripartite approach between achievement sport, fitness exercise and native / folk games. For instance, an art such as Taijiquan can become a sport (as in its place in Chinese Wushu), a form of rehabilitative exercise or an esoteric family art. From later reading and connections with Martinková and Parry (2016, 2021), I became open to the notion of "martial activities" such as martial sports, martial games and martial arts, with martial therapies being regarded as a "minor category" – perhaps deemed minor in the sense of their relatively rare practice and global dissemination.

My own discovery of definitions and models of the martial arts is still emerging and therefore open-ended, and I hope this book offers the opportunity for future conversations about the similar flexibility of what we study in the field now recognised as martial arts studies. Although Bowman (2017) has called for theory over definitions and data, we could argue that definitions stem from theory, reading and research involving the collection and analysis of data, and like theory, are open to adaption and refinement. In this text, I wish to build on my working definition of the martial arts that allows for the place of reimagination, reinvention and reconstruction of these martial activities for different populations and problems, as in martial arts therapies and therapeutic martial arts. In 2020, my initial definition of the martial arts was intentionally inclusive of all styles and systems around the world, with a direct influence of pragmatism (Shilling, 2008) and the sociological imagination (Mills, 1959), with its focus on solutions to problems:

A martial art is an imaginative, adaptable system of fighting techniques designed to deal with problems in combat / or society.

This followed my development of the Theory of Martial Creation (Jennings, 2019) in which I strived to explain how and why a martial art might be founded by an experienced martial artist living in certain cultural, economic, social and political conditions (as in the case of Bruce Lee). For me, a martial art is created by a martial artist in response to a particular problem in both interpersonal combat and wider society. The martial denotes an element of combat while the influence of society will dictate the needs of a given person in specific cultural, economic, environmental, political and social circumstances.

Phenomenology is key theoretical tradition in martial arts research, as seen in the work of Brazilian mixed martial arts scholars such as Cristiano Barreira (2017) and other work drawing on autoethnographic and autophenomenographic approaches interested in first-person perspectives on direct embodied experiences (Allen Collinson & Owton, 2014; Allen Collinson, Vaittinen, Jennings, & Owton, 2016). At the JORRESCAM conference in 2020, I received feedback from Barreira on the need for a phenomenological consideration of what a martial art is not. I have thus expanded the definition to include the following italicised terms:

> A martial art is an imaginative, adaptable system of *physical* human fighting techniques designed in order to deal with *perceived* problems in combat and society.

The perception is key, as with experienced, influential martial arts founders creating new systems and styles, they can use their vision (and wider senses) of combat and concerns about society in order to develop a system that an ordinary layperson would not be able to do. This is because of the perception of the world in terms of risk of assault, flaws in current martial arts systems and new strategies required for dealing with new forms of weapons. Martial arts founders might also perceive an existential threat to their fellow human beings as in rising levels of physical inactivity, isolation and loneliness, which might be combated through online martial arts courses to promote a holistic sense of health and wellbeing from physical, mental and social aspects of the person. The expertise of martial artists collaborating with specialists in psychotherapy and counselling (as in the fightingandspirit project) enables a shared vision based on a common perception of issues in society (such as anxiety and negative self-concept) and an agreed strategy of how to utilise aspects of the martial arts to deal with them.

In addition, there is the inevitable element of anthropology and the aspect of humanity in creating, maintaining and transmitting the martial arts. Dogs and other animals such as roosters can fight each other, and are unfortunately still trained to hurt each other in illegal pit fights and so-called "blood sports", but they do not have martial arts per se. Bull fighting is also not a martial art, as there is no consent between two or more human beings in order to fight under agreed rules – with the consent being something vital in MACS (Channon & Matthews, 2021). Only human can create, teach and pass on a martial arts system, hence the addition of "human" to my finalised definition:

A martial art is an imaginative, adaptable system of physical *human* fighting techniques designed in order to deal with perceived problems in combat and society.

In this way, despite eloquent and original arguments to the contrary (Goto-Jones, 2016), martial arts video games might not be regarded as a martial art because of the lack of direct physical human interaction between players, even in online gaming between multiple living people. With no direct physical contact between bodies or via objects such as swords and sticks, there is no interpersonal physical interaction that makes these martial arts deal with a direct threat in combat. This is not to decry the value of video games, which can fuel the imagination of the martial artists (imagination being the first key word of my definition) and perhaps even work on reflexes and skills as technology continued to develop through VR.

Martial arts can of course involve group activities and multiple opponents, but the direct physicality is key to making the martial art as it is, just as a sport need the physical presence and action of the body rather than the twiggle of thumbs on a control pad or keyboard (although the localised use of muscles in the hands and sitting for long periods can of course be exhausting). This connects with debates around e-sports being sports. This is something that has led the martial arts project to be halted for the time being, as the COVID-19 pandemic prevents many people – especially vulnerable and anxious newcomers – from gaining the benefits of these new forms of intimate, non-sexual interactions in close proximity.

Indeed, social scientific research (as in Channon & Jennings, 2013) has already noted the prolonged and painful aspects of touch that students learn to overcome through their journey in the martial arts. Martial arts will inevitably involve some degree of pain or discomfort, which could range from the fatigue of holding a posture in Taijiquan to the shock of receiving a blow to the stomach in Systema (and dealing with this distress through special breathing techniques). We learn to overcome the stress and anxiety of being pinned to the floor or cornered by a group of people in order to utilise the range of options available to us. Many advocates of martial arts therapies would suggest this translates to everyday life – the real fight we face through the internal conflict between our thoughts, feelings and actions. Warrior-inspired philosophies (as in the Mexican martial art of Xilam) often stress the need to unite these thoughts, feelings and actions as one in order to live a good life as a modern warrior. The martial arts therapy project Fightingandspirit also claims to help unlock the inner warrior in each of us, which can be unravelled through specialist courses to work on aspects of the human being and their psyche using the specific techniques and practices of the martial arts to battle the recognised ills of today exacerbated by a hyper-individualised, competitive society: loneliness, social anxiety and low self-worth.

As I have shown, there are now many contrasting and overlapping conceptualisations of what are now known as the martial arts. Such definitions may help us begin thinking about martial arts therapies and therapeutic martial arts activities. My own definition is inspired by anthropological, historical, phenomenological and sociological approaches common in martial arts studies in an effort to follow the interdisciplinary approach taken in the field (Bowman, 2015) as it becomes transdisciplinary – moving from academia to applied projects that hopefully make a positive difference in people's lives around the world. Readers are most welcome to test this definition out while considering the elements that make martial arts unique among physical cultures, therapies and mind-body practices. This might help address common questions raised by the likes of the Fight Back Project led by Georgia Verry in Australia: What is it in martial arts that makes people say "it saved my life"? (www.fightbackproject.com).

Outlining the Structure of the Book

The academic (and pracademic) field now recognised as "martial arts studies" has emerged in the last decade, and with this, has come debates around theory. One of the leaders of martial arts media studies in the English-speaking world, Paul Bowman (2019), calls for a deconstruction of martial arts in terms of the myths around tradition, origins while being critical of aspects of power, racism, etc. Based on extended fieldwork informed by my cultural sociology perspective, this text focuses on many grass-roots organisations and fledgling industries in order to study the reconstruction of the martial arts in a largely positive sense. In order to analyse this complex and varied process. The working definition of the martial arts outlined in the previous section guides my analysis in the later empirical chapters.

The reinvention process often takes many years and decades, but under pressure from a crisis, it can happen very quickly to the urgent requirement to continue martial arts practice. The Preface set the stage for the showcasing of the reinvention of martial arts pedagogies in a short space of time. The COVID-19 pandemic swept through many countries in the world, and affected them differently in terms of policy, law making and medical logistics. My ethnographic studies of Wing Chun Kung Fu, HEMA and Taijiquan were shared through three tales per art: before the pandemic, in which there was scope for international seminars, travel and physical touch; during the pandemic, when the martial arts classes had to be flipped online using streaming technology and creative use of home space and materials; and after the lockdowns, when the pandemic subsided enough for the three martial arts schools to return to training in an adapted fashion considering rules on hygiene, new possibilities for remote learning and concerns about the cost of living and the sustainability of a business. This adds to my previous publication on the adaptations that HEMA and Taijiquan undertook in relatively short space of time of the lockdowns and restrictions (Jennings, 2020).

This backdrop sets the scene for some of the challenges of the early 21st century that will drive the continued process of martial reinvention. Part One of this book is called "Re-imagining the Martial Arts", and it is composed of four chapters that reflect the eclectic possibilities of this reinvention beyond the conversion of martial arts into sports. The first empirical chapter (Chapter 2) continues along the theme of conceptualising martial arts. It does this by focusing on the main noun (*art*) of this compound word to consider how the martial arts are expressions of human creativity and innovation. I use one extensive case study of the Chinese martial arts to explore this concept, with frequent reference to many organisations in the United Kingdom. These schools and organisations reflect the creativity of teachers and those around them in developing new ways of teaching, transmitting and training the martial arts to new generations of students.

Moving on from this focus on one cultural origin (China), I show how martial arts can also be culturally hybrid and eclectic. Chapter 3 examines how elements of martial arts – their specific techniques of the body and practices – have been utilised by influential movement coaches to develop their mixed movement systems. This chapter uses two key case studies for the analysis of this process: Ido Portal's movement culture and Cameron Shayne's Budokwon Yoga. Both of these men have extensive backgrounds in the martial arts and related physical cultures, and they have developed their reputation through working with celebrities and competitive fighters, media interviews and their own extensive set of videos. I analyse the discourse shared in these interviews and demonstrations while considering the rich potential for the martial arts to be used for human performance. Beyond helping those suffering with physical, mental and emotional issues, the many techniques and training methods of the martial arts can assist elite athletes and performers looking for that extra edge in competition. Combined with other physical cultures, martial arts can offer a powerful tool as movement systems as part of the broader "movement movement."

Chapter 4 continues with this interest in performance and human betterment through the emphasis on martial arts as the structure for self-help. Over the last few decades, martial artists have begun to embrace the genre of self-help books, and several martial arts instructors from different disciplinary backgrounds have started to pen such texts for both martial artists and the general public. I use three case studies of such authors in this chapter: Shannon Lee (Bruce Lee's daughter and current holder of his estate), Geoff Thompson (a former bouncer turned author and playwright) and Steve Jones (a Wing Chun instructor and personal trainer) to show the varied approach to considering self-help from the perspectives of Bruce Lee, a more Western model and the Chinese perspective. The interest in healing individuals by expert counselling, therapy and training also accompanies the rising use of self-help. Although self-help books have been around for decades (and, according to Polly [2018], even stimulated Bruce Lee's ambitions to become the most famous Asian movie star), there is now a sub-genre of martial arts self-help books. Written by martial arts experts and instructors for open-minded readers who have an affinity for these systems, the martial arts self-help books reflect our increasingly individualistic societies in the Western context. Becoming more assertive, disciplined and living in a clean manner are attitudes and values emphasised through specific warrior philosophies.

One long-term interest in the martial arts has been in its therapeutic potential, which is examined in Chapter 5. Martial arts might be conceived as forms of therapy (as psychotherapy or physical therapy), or at the very least therapeutic and cathartic – something different to Western medicine, psychiatry and physical surgery interventions that might be useful for less severe ailments. Punches and kicks can expel stress and even challenge our inner demons, while talking therapy might add to the narration of trauma built into the body. Chapter 5 delves into the concept of martial arts therapy by examining key movements and ideas such as trauma-informed martial arts therapy and another project I am involved in, Fightingandspirit, which aims to combine martial arts and therapy by training both the therapists and members of the public. This chapter also closes Part One by suggesting an open theoretical framework around the reinvention of the martial arts, which are applicable to the concepts of arts, movement systems, self-help and therapy.

After the consideration of how martial arts might be reimagined in different ways, Part Two titled "Re-constructing the Martial Arts" outlines some of the key aspects of the reconstruction process of the martial arts industry and plethora of the martial arts as a whole. As martial arts become more prominent in society, there have been calls for a professionalisation of the industry and an international governance of the martial arts. These are covered in Chapters 6 and 7.

Chapter 6 introduces a grass roots critique around the extensive range of low-quality martial arts schools that often charge exuberant fees while teaching dangerous practices. Some are even led by criminally dangerous individuals with abusive intentions towards children and other vulnerable people. This McDojo critique is led by pioneering influencers in the martial arts who use their large social media following to highlight bad practice among instructors who are often deluded and abusive to their students. I use another three set of case studies to highlight the varied nature of the critique and definition of what a McDojo might be while examining the extent of the analysis, which ranges from comical videos to more serious, investigative documentaries.

Moving away from the darker side of abusive, mistrustful and charlatan instructors, the martial arts are also about the transmission knowledge and the preservation of (in)tangible cultural heritage. Chapter 7 focuses on martial arts as revivalist movements, which can be seen in Historical European Martial Arts (HEMA), re-enactment and the recently created Mexican martial arts such as Xilam and SUCEM. Perceiving this to be a moment of martial arts renaissance, I examine the broader revivalist industry as a whole, paying attention to the wholesalers and craft manufacturers of swords, armour and protective gear used in HEMA and the related martial activities such as reenactment. In addition to examining these expanding cottage industries, I share insights from my ethnographic and netnographic research into the recently invented Mexican martial arts, and how they have been received by the online martial arts community in that region in terms of trolling and praise from different factions of this community. With many of those Mexican martial arts being concerned with ancestral culture and knowledge from Mesoamerica, I then consider the topic of cultural heritage. There is now a global recognition of the martial arts as rich expressions of cultures, ethnic groups and regions. Some martial arts are already starting to be recognised as part of UNESCO's list of intangible cultural heritage. Chapter 7 continues the concern for preservation and conservation with its analysis of martial arts as heritage. Looking at the work of the International Center of Martial Arts for Youth Engagement and Development (ICM, based in South Korea) and related organisations, the third section of this chapter examines the role of heritage research, caretaking and cataloguing as some rare and highly localised martial arts become close to extinction. I also consider the potential influence of HEMA on the coding and recording of Asian martial arts as enthusiasts work to revive the fighting systems of other eras.

After considering these national and international cases of how martial arts can be reimagined and then regulated, I turn to a more micro-level analysis of the stories of committed instructors and practitioners of the martial arts in Part Three, "Living and Breathing the Martial Arts." These relate to some of the themes from the previous chapters, but are more concerned with the process of reinvention of the practitioner through the transformation and self-cultivation (and, I would argue, shared cultivation). Chapter 8 provides two case studies of my own instructors and ethnographic informants and gatekeepers, Billy Marshall (of the Blade Academy) and David James (of the School of Internal Arts), both featured in the preface. Taking heed of calls for a relational sociology, these stories introduce themes set around their relationships developed through the martial arts, such as their marriages to their wives (who they met through training), close friendships akin to brotherhood and loyalty to their teachers. This sets the scene for Chapter 9, also focusing on two long-term martial arts practitioners, George and Aidan, who, like Billy and David, have crossed between martial arts traditions and supplementary body-mind practices. These two stories shed light on the investment that martial artists make in terms of decades of their lives, physical energy, investment of leisure time and personal finances, which are understood in terms of Bourdieu's multiple forms of capital reinvested into a martial habitus that benefits these men in their daily lives. The final chapter is my own story, told using the genre of an evocative autoethnography. As I began the book with a set of short stories and episodes, I close the text in the same manner, tracing my martial arts story from my early exposure to the mediated martial arts as a small child to my future research directions are a scholar-practitioner of various systems of combat. This leads me to address the topic of reinvention of the martial arts and martial artists, returning to my working definition of the martial arts and an emergent theoretical perspective of martial reinvention.

A disclaimer should be made at this point, however. This book pays attention to the often overlooked aspects of the reconstruction of martial arts: as therapies, movement methods, approaches to self-help, cultural revival and cultural heritage. This is because of my background in the exercise and sport sciences, my experience with exercise rehabilitation with stroke survivors and my academic specialism in cultural sociology. As each martial artist and martial arts founders leaves their unique approach to their chosen style, I have offered my own perspective on a global phenomenon, and this includes details from my research since 2004, my practice since 1998 and the work of my colleagues, contacts and acquaintances. This book is, of course, part of a series on sport and East Asia, so I have paid particular attention to the martial arts from that region. However, the martial arts are now recognised as more than a sport or fighting system from the "Orient", as styles such as Afro-Brazilian Capoeira as recognised in the UNESCO's list of intangible cultural heritage. I have therefore considered the Global North and South, as well as the original idea of examining the stimulus from the East and the Western response as agreed with my ever-supportive editor, J. A. Mangan, who coined the original subtitle of "Eastern stimulus, Western response." Depending on one's definition of these complex systems, wrestling and boxing might also be classified as martial arts. Indeed, wrestling is one of the most widespread forms of physical cultures in the world, with styles ranging from Africa to Western Europe.

I write this book as an interdisciplinary social scientist and martial arts scholar. This is my first monograph after over 15 years of researching Wing Chun Kung Fu, the traditionalist Chinese martial arts, Xilam and other recently created Mexican martial arts and now Taijiquan and HEMA. It is also the manifestation of ideas generated from 23 years learning different martial arts. I have studied the Chinese martial arts in relative depth, along with some Taekwondo, Kendo and Judo, but I cannot claim to know all the Asian martial arts or even those from one particular culture. Although I have lived in England, Scotland, Mexico and now Wales, I cannot speak for all the Western world and for all martial artists. The book does reflect my ethnographic, life history and autoethnographic approaches with various anecdotes, examples and case studies drawn from my ongoing empirical investigations as a cultural sociologist (that are reflected in the Preface and in my autoethnography). However, the book does try to paint the big picture of the various ongoing martial arts reconstruction projects around the world that began in the late 20th century and continue in the first few decades of the 21st century.

I hope you find this book stimulating in terms of questions about transformation, cultivation, reinvention and reconstruction – questions that continue to fascinate me after over 20 years' involvement in the martial arts.

George Jennings
Cardiff, Wales, United Kingdom, May 2022

References

Allen Collinson, A., & Owton, H. (2014). Intense embodiment: Senses of heat in women's running and boxing. *Body & Society, 21*(2), 245–268.

Allen Collinson, J., Vaittinen, A., Jennings, G., & Owton, H. (2016). Exploring lived heat, "temperature work" and embodiment: Novel auto/ethnographic insights from physical culture. *Journal of Contemporary Ethnography, 47*(3), 283–305.

Barreira, C. (2017). The essences of martial arts and corporeal fighting: A classical phenomenological analysis. *Archives of Budo, 13*, 351–376.

Blomqvist Mickelsson, T. (2020). Modern unexplored martial arts – What can mixed martial arts and Brazilian Jiu-Jitsu do for youth development? *European Journal of Sport Science, 20*(3), 386–393.

Bowman, P. (2019). *Deconstructing martial arts*. Cardiff: Cardiff University Press.

Bowman, P. (2017). The definition of martial arts studies. *Martial Arts Studies, 3*, 6–23.

Bowman, P. (2015). *Martial arts studies: Disrupting disciplinary boundaries*. London: Rowman & Littlefield.

Channon, A., & Jennings, G. (2014). Exploring embodiment through martial arts and combat sports: A review of empirical research. *Sport in Society, 17*(6), 773–789.

Channon, A., & Jennings, G. (2013). The rules of engagement: Negotiating painful and intimate touch in mixed-sex martial arts. *Sociology of Sport Journal, 30*, 487–503.

Channon, A., & Matthews, C. (2021). Communicating consent in sport: A typological model of athletes' consent practices within combat sports. *International Review for the Sociology of Sport* (online early).

Crudelli, C. (2008). *The way of the warrior: Martial arts and fighting systems from around the world*. London: Dorling Kindersley.

Eichberg, H. (1998). *Body cultures: Essays on sport, space and identity*. London: Routledge.

Feldenkrais Method official website. Available at: https://feldenkrais.com/. Last accessed 28 May 2022.

Goto-Jones, C. (2016). *The virtual ninja manifesto*. London: Rowman & Littlefield.

ICM UNESCO. (2021). World Martial Arts. Available at: http://unescoicm.org/eng/library/global_martialarts.php. Last accessed 29 May 2022.

Jennings, G. (2020). Martial arts under the COVID-19 lockdown: The pragmatics of creative pedagogy. *Sociología del Deporte, 1*(2), 13–24. https://doi.org/10.46661/sociodeporte.5242

Jennings, G. (2019). Bruce Lee and the invention of Jeet Kune Do: The Theory of Martial Creation. *Martial Arts Studies, 8*, 60–72.

Jennings, G., & Delamont, S. (2020). Style, stamina and mobile masculinities: The reinvention of Savate in the Anglosphere. *Sport in History, 40*(3), 370–394.

Levine, D. (1991). Martial arts as a resource for liberal education: The case of Aikido. In M. Featherstone, M. Hepworth, & B. S. Turner (Eds.), *The body: Social process and cultural theory*. London: SAGE.

Martinková, I., & Parry, J. (2021). Mixed martial arts is not a martial art. In J. Holt & M. Ramsay (Eds.), *The Philosophy of Mixed Martial Arts: Squaring the octagon* (pp. 4–15). London: Routledge.

Martinková, I., & Parry, J. (2016). Martial categories: Clarification and classification. *Journal of the Philosophy of Sport, 43*(1), 143–162.

Meyer, M. (2021). *What is martial arts? The six-attribute model as an empirical approach to field terminology*. Kanazawa: Heiko Bittmann.

Mills, C.-W. (1959). *The sociological imagination*. Oxford: Oxford University Press.

Sánchez García, R., & Malcolm, D. (2010). Decivilizing, civilizing or informalizing? The international development of Mixed Martial Arts. *International Review for the Sociology of Sport, 45*(1), 39–58.

Polly, M. (2018). *Bruce Lee: A life*. London: Simon & Schuster.

Ryan, M. J. (2017). *Venezuelan stick fighting: The civilizing process in martial arts*. London: Lexington Books.

Shilling, C. (2008). *Changing bodies*. London: Sage.

Sparkes, A. C. (1985). Martial movement sequences. *Bulletin of Physical Education, 21*(1), 40–43.

The Fight Back Project official website. Available at: https://www.fightbackproject.com/. Last accessed 30 May 2022.

Villamón, M., Brown, B., Espartero, J., & Gutiérrez, C. (2004). Reflexive modernization and the disembedding of Judo from 1946 to the 2000 Sydney Olympics. *International Review for the Sociology of Sport, 39*(2), 139–156.

Part I
Reimagining the Martial Arts

2

Chinese Martial Arts as Art Forms

Considering Martial Arts as Arts

The Introduction chapter raised the notion of martial arts being arts as in painting a portrait, sculpting a stone statue or playing a musical instrument. These activities involve skilful use of precise techniques that can be honed for many years and decades into old age, where someone might be considered an accomplished artist. However, the idea of martial arts being arts per se might be strange to many outsiders, with some celebrated artists such as the multi-Academy Award winning actress Meryl Streep questioning the inclusion of Mixed Martial Arts (MMA) in this category (Kornhaber, 2017). This led to some interesting defences from advocates of martial activities, including comments on the aesthetics of martial arts movements as well as cultural expression. As we have seen, academic debates have been made about how to define and categorise a martial art, and we might also ask if the abstract noun "art" is appropriate for activities centred around fighting and the potential harming of another human being in or out of the formal training, learning and competitive environment. Although there are some martial arts that actively avoid harming the assailant with punches and kicks by way of controlled locks and throws (think of the pacifist art of Aikido, the Way of Harmony), many systems involve striking, joint breaking, eye gouging and painful manipulation techniques, not to mention stabbing, thrusting and cutting actions in the weapons-based systems.

As the martial arts themselves are becoming inclusive in terms of who can learn and complete, I offer an open and inclusive definition of the martial arts. Arts themselves can be inclusive of people with disabilities, and they can teach people about cultures other than their own. The martial arts can also offer this inclusive sense of belonging. Moreover, arts can (and should) be accessible for people of all ages, and hence they are potentially lifelong pursuits. The martial arts can be adapted to suit the needs of people are they get older, and it quite common for a person to have a varied career in various styles, from the explosive, sporting approaches to more meditative, spiritual schools as they enter old age.

Perceiving the martial arts as forms of art like painting, music and sculpture which also have their genres, flexibility and longevity, I define a martial art as the following: An imaginative, adaptable system of human fighting techniques designed to deal with perceived problems in combat and / or society. The martial arts, like all arts, stem from the human imagination, which in this case, is normally the imagination of the founder(s). Stories of dreams and epiphanies abound in martial arts folklore, as do tales of inspiration from animals and nature (as in many of the traditionalist Chinese martial arts). These myths of the martial arts might be modern inventions, but they do point to an imaginative potential. In more concrete terms, today's practitioners can imagine what to do with specific techniques and training methods. Experienced martial artists can therefore imagine how to use martial arts in new ways, as in adapting Karate for wheelchair users, which is now being done by groups around the world.

This returns to an earlier argument about how and why a martial art is formed. In Jennings (2019), I outlined the Theory of Martial Creation to explain this via the case studies of Victorian-Edwardian Bartitsu in Britain, Jeet Kune Do in 1960s California and Mexican Xilam over the last few decades. Taking elements of pragmatism through a historical perspective, I highlighted key aspects of the crisis in the life of the founder and the society that they form part of. With the crisis (or problems) being the centre of a martial art, the founder or innovator develops a strategy to deal with it. This is only possible if this person (or group of founders) has experience in one of more martial arts, as many systems build on the existence of their contemporary fighting systems.

Combat-based problems still form the basis of the majority of martial arts. This is understandable, given the "martial" marker in the compound term. The problem might be how to deal with fighting on the floor (as in Brazilian Jiu Jitsu), a way to fight a one-on-one duel (as in fencing) or a manner to box an opponent without knocking them down (as in Italian *boxe populare*). As research into Historical European Martial Arts (HEMA) has shown, fencing styles have evolved over the centuries to move from fighting an opponent in armour on the battlefield to fencing against one opponent in a salon. The variations in these problems might be in terms of rules to match the needs of society in terms of perceived violence, the need for greater safety or the banning of swords (e.g., in 19th century France, which helped stimulate the Le Canne cane fighting aspect of Savate).

As such, many martial arts are also concerned with society at large. In the 21st century, commonly agreed problems include climate change, unsustainable methods of food production, new international conflicts, a resulting refugee crisis and rising levels of physical inactivity. Not everyone perceives these as problems, of course. There are vaccine and climate change deniers and people on extreme end of political spectrums, and this variation allows for different perceptions. Many contemporary martial arts have been inspired by a concern for the environment, for an indigenous culture and by the worrying levels of preventable disease caused by lack of human movement. These problems are perceived, spoken (and written) about and then acted upon by knowledgeable visionaries who also perceive a way to solve the issue. Their dreams might be fanciful at times, but they offer an utopian vision to how society might and should be, rather than how it currently stands. Some founders are ardent patriots and nationalists wishing to transform their nation, while others wish to help other human beings through accessible ways of sharing their knowledge.

How can we perceive these styles as arts? One approach is to consider the perception and interpretation of influential martial artists who have taken techniques, movements, sequences, mantra and manuscripts and made them their own – leaving their mark on the art in question. In this chapter, I explore the notion of martial arts as arts by identifying the great diversity in interpretation of martial artists and instructors who have developed their own approach to practising, teaching and transmitting their system of choice. To do so, I have selected the example of the world-famous Chinese martial arts Wing Chun Kung Fu and Taijiquan, which I have practised and researched for the longest. Their global popularity and regional diversity are also important reasons for this selection. Wing Chun and Taijiquan also represent respectively a Southern Chinese martial art chiefly known as a self-defence or traditionalist style and what might be classified as a Northern Chinese martial art ordinarily practised for health and meditation. Finally, these arts are also notorious for their internal politics of lineage, with many people claiming to be more authentic, progressive or realistic. The political aspect of the martial arts is now becoming recognised in scholarship, with a recent Martial Arts Studies conference dedicated to the topic (www.mast udiesrn.org), and it deeply intertwined with the realities of perception, interpretation and judgement in the martial arts.

Perception, interpretation and judgement occurs in distinct circles within the arts. After all, the arts have their own genres and sub-genres with their unique characteristics and audience. Visual arts, fine art, music and many other forms are common across many cultures and societies. In terms of sub-genres, cinematic art has its Westerns, romantic comedies, action movies and of course, the specific martial traditions of Japanese Samurai films, 1970s Kung Fu films, accompanied by the Wuxia swordplay films reimagined in *Crouching Tiger, Hidden Dragon*. And so do the martial arts, with their socially recognised and self-identifying genres seen in sports martial arts (normally referred to as combat sports), internal martial arts, weapons martial arts, performance martial arts and so on. Of course, many martial arts will straddle two or more categories, as self-defence or traditionalist martial arts quite often involve the training of weapons. Genres in art can sometimes be merged to create new forms of human and cultural expression. For Bruce Lee, through his vision of the *Jeet Kune Do* philosophy, martial arts were one of the highest forms of self-expression (Lee, 1975).

There are people who love romantic comedies for their safe narratives and loveable characters but cannot stand horror movies for the sadism and shock of unexpected events, and there are those viewers who only select action movies when finding a film for the weekend. The same can be said of the martial arts, with aficionados of mixed martial arts and boxing who have little time for the performance martial arts of Wushu, which they regard as a mere dance, "a con" or a "wishy-washy," inferior form of martial arts (as several tough martial artists with backgrounds in boxing and door work have told me). I have met practitioners of boxing and HEMA who do not regard Wing Chun a martial art because it has no sparring, while certain Wing Chun exponents might feel that to be a martial art, a system requires meditation, philosophy and qigong (as one of my old participants once questioned an instructor). There will probably never be a universally agreed definition or taxonomy of the martial arts, but nearly all martial artists will agree that the martial arts in general are genuine arts. The passion, energy and time put into their skill development is akin to the arts, and their sensitivity and deep knowledge is also like an art connoisseur.

The present chapter begins with an exploration of the history and development of each art before focusing on the British context, which is followed by local case studies of regional and institutional change following the trajectories of notable martial artists. I have kept the majority of the examples as open case studies, as the readers will be able to check the information cited in the websites and practitioner-facing literature such as textbooks. Again, this chapter follows the blend of macro, meso and micro levels of social scientific analysis advocated by Brown and Leledaki (2010) in their discussion on researching Eastern Movement Forms (EMFs). The macro can be seen in the global transmission (globalisation, internationalisation and glocalisation) of the Asian martial arts, with institutional levels of transformation reflected as the meso level of society. Finally, the micro level is what can be seen, heard and felt by the human senses as in my own observations in fieldwork, informal conversations, interviews and autobiographic reflections. These three levels of society are of course intertwined, and this is commonly reflected in this and other empirical chapters in the book.

Wing Chun Kung Fu

The art of Wing Chun Kung Fu provides a notable example of constant evolution and adaption over the last few centuries. It has spread around the world from its homeland in the Guangdong (Canton) Province of South-East China. From former colonial bases such as British Hong Kong and Portuguese Macau, Wing Chun spread to the United States, Australia and Europe through migration of a first wave of influential master-teachers such as Wong Shun Leung, Chu Shong Tin and William Cheung in Australia. Many British practitioners first learned the art from first-generation Chinese / Hong Kongese teachers who settled in the UK, such as Simon Lau. However, after some years of seeking the right teacher and lineage for them, many well-known teachers and authors later travelled to train with those Sifus in Australia and the U.S. and their senior students, with some, such as Alan Gibson, switching lineages from the Ip Chun (Hong Kong) branch to that of Wong Shun Leung under David Peterson, a notable senior student. This notable movement is seen in the two editions of his well-known text *Why Wing Chun Works* (Gibson, 2001, 2012), in which the stance, position and drills are completely different. Others sought out the older teachers in Hong Kong to become a member of their last disciples before they passed away.

Depending on the lineage, Wing Chun might be spelt Ving Tsun (with the initials VT avoiding the acronym of WC, a.k.a. "toilet fist"), Wing Tsun (WT) or Weng Chun – all of which are influenced by a key innovator such as Leung Ting of Wing Tsun, which spread around Europe through its base in Germany. Some of these differences are for branding and marketing purposes: to enable their own brand of Wing Chun to stand out in relation to what it is not. Advocates of specific systems might argue the case for their own original approach to the art – perhaps citing an older or distinct lineage making them a more authentic form of Wing Chun, as in Shaolin Weng Chun (the Hung Fa Yi lineage) led by Garrett Gee (Gee, Meng & Loewenhagen, 2004). This particular lineage cites other forms of Wing Chun as "popular Wing Chun" that express the art aspect of martial arts. Conversely, these authors claim that Shaolin Weng Chun – a style more closely associated with the Shaolin Temple – is reflective of what constitutes science in the martial arts. The number 108 (the official number of techniques in many Wing Chun solo form sequences), for example, is not seen as a lucky Chinese number, but one that has a deeper meaning of dimensions and levels of technique.

I have also met some interesting Wing Chun instructors who are forming their own unique, mixed lineages. The coaching researcher and Wing Chun Sifu Dave Bright of Worthing Wing Chun, for instance, combines his old Wing Tsun lineage (which he has trained for the longest) with a rare lineage that has been learning from a teacher in Hong Kong. The latter style is apparently an older branch than the well-known Ip Man lineage, and it does not have the Siu Lim Tao form of the characteristic *bong sau* (wing arm) technique used while "rolling" in *chi sau*. It is a representative of Foshan Wing Chun more akin to what Leung Jan might have practised and taught. These pedagogical and technical differences please Bright, as he was having doubts about the place of the foundational first form, along with the aching feeling cause by moving the elbow high into a *bong sau*. Along with my colleague Alex Channon, I was fortunate to learn a fundamental double blocking system that involved using two hands for attach (from one partner) that was matched with double blocking techniques from the second partner. This was completely new to me, and it incorporated several hand techniques unknown to me at the time.

Martial arts books written for practitioners are often a combination of history (with added mythology), philosophy and how-to instructional material using photographs. Wing Chun offers plenty of such texts written in numerous languages that stress a different orientation to the art. For example, Manchester-based Michael Tse and his teacher Ip Chun tend to emphasise the health and longevity aspects of the art. This is likely down to Tse's further training in Qigong and Taijiquan, as he is a renowned practitioner of these two arts as well as Wing Chun. In the book *Wing Chun: Traditional Chinese Kung Fu for Self-Defence & Health*, Tse (Tse & Ip, 1998) even argues that he would not teach a person who came to him learning how to fight. Instead, they focus on the Daoist aspects of

Wing Chun along with the Qigong training offered by the first solo form of the Ip Man lineage, Siu Lim Tao (sometimes rendered "Siu Nim Tao" by other lineages). Here we can see the influence of other martial arts on the interpretation of Wing Chun and how the practitioner-instructor judges prospective students and people's character.

In a different end of the spectrum, the noted German Sifu Keith Kernspecht has stressed the combative aspect of Wing Tsun. In his *On Single Combat*, Kernspecht (1997) downplays the important of cultivating Qi energy – while not renouncing it – by focusing on physical strength and power (as seen through pictures of him lifting heavy weights and revealing his bulky, muscular torso). He is an example of a martial artist who has turned to teaching the police and armed forces, and numerous respected fighters come from this lineage such as the renowned Turkish-German fighter Emin Botzepe, who went on to found his own organisation. Keen to test Wing Chun in live combat and follow challenge matches, these men's schools also involve sparring and contact training, which differs to the majority of Wing Chun schools that stop the force of their strikes upon impact against a training partner's body – sometimes stopping short of contact. His network of friends includes Geoff Thompson, who also focuses on the realistic aspect of martial arts for survival and self-defence. We will return to Geoff in the chapter on martial arts as self-help (Chapter 4), which shows how people's perspectives on the martial arts can change with time and age as combat typically – and hopefully – becomes less important and frequent in their lives.

My own instructor John Bridge (pseudonym) came from a working class borough of the East End of London, and he initially learned Wing Chun there in one of the first schools established in the capital. There were several schools in the capital city in the early 1980s, but few were open to people of non-Chinese descent like him, a white Englishman. After relocating to the South West of England, he joined an international Wing Tsun organisation in which he grew to become a senior instructor in the United Kingdom. After a brief stint as a senior instructor for another Chinese-British teacher, he founded an independent Wing Chun organisation before seeking out his current Sifu, who is based in the United States (see also the Preface). Each time he learned from his new teacher, he had to adjust his stance, footwork and drills, and so did his students, with some of them resenting these radical changes. Only when he became independent (after a falling out with his current Sifu) did Bridge start to openly mix the drills from his four principal teachers, making a unique blend of Wing Chun lineages. For example, a recent seminar involved iron palm training using the standard Wing Chun wall bag full of rice, alongside ground fighting techniques.

Bowman (2021) has noted that in a given martial arts class, there might be a variety of external conditioning exercises that are not specific to the martial arts. Press ups (push ups) are very common, as is jogging on the spot and even dodgeball and basketball to warm up in large leisure centre venues. Martial arts instructors might tailor the exercises to condition specific body parts, as in press-ups on the knuckles, and even this might be targeting in a different way, depending on the knuckles used on impact in the given style (with the final three being prevalent in Wing Chun). Today, with the societal importance of health, fitness and weight management, many Wing Chun schools undertake a vigorous warm-up of 10-20 minutes, or something longer akin to a workout. The London Wing Chun Association is one such example of a modern, well-equipped school that makes use of Western scientific training principles and the latest technology. It does not forget about the wooden dummy, wall bag and weapons, but it supplements the student training with abdominal conditioning and even running regimes. This approach can attract a different kind of student looking for fitness, body image and Western ideals of health as well as self-defence and personal development.

Some of these innovations are possible with distance from one's main teacher. James Sinclair, the founder of the UK Wing Association, was one of the early non-Chinese students of Ip Chun. After some political disagreements, he decided to retain his own independent organisation while focusing on physical conditioning and external training.

Many Wing Chun instructors combine this martial art with another world-famous Chinese system, Taijiquan. Other lineages, due to historical connections between organisations such as Leung Ting's Wing Tsun schools, continue to teach Wing Chun alongside the Filipino stick fighting methods of Escrima, Arnis or Kali – even if those teachers are no longer affiliated with their former schools. The simultaneous attack and defense, close quarters combat and aggressive style all cross over between these arts. In more recent decades, online discussions of the internal aspects of Wing Chun have included claims that Wing Chun is the Taijiquan of the South of China (with Taijiquan originating in a more northern region of China). Again, many proponents of internal Wing Chun will claim that the art is an internal system focusing on relaxation and internal mechanics, rather than an external one relying on muscular force. Meanwhile, other teachers such as my own teacher's teacher (*Sigung* in Cantonese) suggest Wing Chun is a balance between internal aspects such as timing, structure and energy with external elements of speed and power. For him, we must start from the inside of the mind and body, developing the correct position, structure, timing, etc. before working on speed and other aspects of combat. There is therefore a great variety in interpretation of theory and practice in Wing Chun as well as how it is judged or regarded by the aficionados of the art.

The dualistic notion of internal and external martial arts has been debated by scholars. Some claim the distinction is political, with the Daoist influence on the martial arts infiltrating the Chinese arts during the 19th century, a time of nationalist Chinese activities attempting to counter the expansionist, imperialist ambitions of Western powers. Such nationalist revival movements culminated in the Boxer Rebellion of the early 20th century in which many Kung Fu styles may have died out with their final practitioners gunned down by colonial forces. However, the dualism between internal and external continues to this day, as seen in my recent fieldwork on Taijiquan and Neigong (inner skill or training) in the UK.

Taijiquan (Tai Chi Chuan)

We have already seen how Wing Chun operates along a vast spectrum, from one concerned with health to one stressing fighting application and body conditioning. Similarly, one of my main PhD informants, a well-respected Taijiquan instructor, once described Taijiquan as a broad church, from the very spiritual and New Age approaches to the martial and athletic varieties involving competition and combat. The art, like Wing Chun, has numerous spellings and representations, and one commentator even claims that such variance and confusion might have led Taijiquan to be far less popular and recognised than Yoga, which is nearly always spelt the same way. Taijiquan is now a common academic spelling approved by ardent sinologists, but it is far better known as "Tai Chi" in the Western world, and this omits the "Quan" or "Chuan" suffix referring to the martial element (literally, "fist") of the art.

The two words "Tai Chi" are likely to conjure up images of old people practising gentle movements in a park, keeping a safe distance as in times of the pandemic, or even clinical populations undergoing an experimental exercise regime. This is true in many cases in today's world, as very few Taijiquan practitioners train it as a martial art for combat. Some notable exceptions include the late Dan Docherty and his Practical Tai Chi Chuan association, which teaches students the self-defence applications of the movements in the form. Again, this reflects the peculiarity and particular nature of body lineages, as Docherty, like his fellow Scot up in Edinburgh, Ian Cameron, both learned the Wudang style of the art.

Ryan (2008) notes that the Wudang and Wu style under Gary Wragg are the only styles to incorporate all aspects of the art, including fighting applications and Neigong. This is likely to have changed since the time of publication in 2008, and many young teachers have travelled to China and South East Asia in search for a deeper understanding of the art.

The Taijiquan school in which I am conducting an ethnographic study, the School of Internal Arts (pseudonym), is such an example of a new generation of what could be described as "martial arts influencers." Like social media influencers of the 2020s, these influencers make use of various forms of video streaming platforms and technology such as YouTube, podcasts and professional websites with pay-to-access online distance learning courses. Led by Malcolm Reeve, a relatively young British teacher of 40 years of age now based in another European country, the School provides classes in Taijiquan, Neigong, Baguazhang (another internal Chinese martial art) and other internal arts such as meditation, along with courses in medicine and even Chinese astrology. My own teacher in the UK, David (one of Malcolm's senior students), comes from a background in Shotokan Karate, although he does not teach the latter art in our classes, he does use Taijiquan to inform his Karate training – as does his senior in the organisation, Barry. There are evening classes, a morning meditation class (online) as well as a Saturday morning class taught through Zoom, which continued even after the easing of COVID-19 restrictions. We will examine David's life in the martial arts in Chapter 10.

Based in Devon, England, but now expanding across the UK and Europe, Tai Chi Nation is another notable example of an ambitious Taijiquan organisation that wishes to reach as many people as possible (see Tai Chi Nation Official Website). In fact, it wants to be the first Taijiquan group to connect with one million people. In order to achieve this, it tries to make its classes very accessible through its main product of simplified 24-step and 48-step forms. These are modalities of Taijiquan that were developed in the 1950s during a period of sweeping reforms in China. Traditionalist styles were shunned for being feudal, private or bourgeoise, so the Chinese Communist Party wanted a standardised approach to the art that could be taught and disseminated to a wide variety of people in a short period of time. It does not take ten years to complete the two forms mentioned here, although it might take ten years to learn the Short and Long forms in the School of Internal Arts. Nevertheless, over the years, the Tai Chi Nation group have worked closely with more traditionalist instructors in the Zheng Manqing / Huang Shansheng lineage who offer a deeper level of training in the art as the lead instructors themselves continue to seek guidance and mentoring.

At this point, it is important to note the fact Taijiquan instructors – and martial arts instructors on the whole, for that matter – are almost exclusively practitioners. It would be rare to find an instructor of a martial art who does not train or practise themself. Much of the class involves live demonstration for prolonged periods of time, and its expected for the teacher to be the most skilled person in the room. This is quite unlike the world of sport, in which a football coach might have hung up their boots many years ago, now being slower and far less fit than the athletes he or she directs. The martial arts instructor is normally an artist: someone seeking the impossible quality of perfection through years of graft that might even be stimulated by their teaching. As someone who has had the privilege of teaching Wing Chun in different countries, I found my regular classes extremely motivating for my own personal practise – especially of the fundamental techniques and movements such as the stance, guard, punch and first form of Wing Chun.

Organised sports of all kinds eventually have a governing body with committees, sets of rules and record keeping for activities within specific countries. As with painting, singing, sculpting and other forms of art, there is no overarching governing body for the Chinese martial arts at international, national or regional levels. Many people can sing on stage, at home or even teach singing lessons without the need for a government-backed scheme. Likewise, martial arts are still taught in semi-formal and even informal environments through family systems and vernacular approaches to the martial arts (Green, 2020; Ryan, 2017). However, with the continuation of the sportification and rationalisation of the Chinese martial arts, there are now established attempts to regulate the teaching, learning, practice and dissemination of a plethora of arts. In Britain, the British Council for Chinese Martial Arts (BCCMA) does attempt to prepare new generations of teachers, with first aid courses specialised for the martial arts, the all-important safeguarding courses for working with youngsters and vulnerable populations, multi-staged coaching courses akin to football coaching badges and even courses for judges in competitions. The BCCMA even stress the value of accountability, with a route for complaints against qualified coaches (see the BCCMA Official Website). This is certainly great value in this, as older forms of martial arts training would not have external regulation, safeguarding and room for complaints to other professionals.

It is important to note that many Kung Fu schools operate outside its remit, preferring their independence. This is partly due to the influence of lineage and real Kung Fu families operating between cultures and continents (Partivoká & Jennings, 2018) over the more bureaucratic approach to legitimacy – despite the BCCMA advertising itself as a 'family' of sorts (www.bccma.com). Politics, money and ego might also be the cause of splinter groups forming once senior students are capable of running their own schools. Many of my research participants in my ethnographies of Wing Chun and Taijiquan have either worked closely with these kinds of organisations and similar bodies such as UK Sport, or they have had a negative experience to report. In the latter case, instructors commonly find another organisation to affiliate themselves with such as cross-disciplinary bodies offering insurance. A case in point in the British Combat Association (BCA), which is co-founded by a Karate and Wing Chun exponent Peter Consterdine, who like his fellow chief instructor Geoff Thompson (featured in the chapter on martial arts as self-help), adopts a very combative, practical approach to dealing with self-protection (https://www.britishcombat.co.uk/).

The close relationship between Taijiquan and Qigong has led the originally named Tai Chi Union for Great Britain (TCUGB) to be recently renamed as the Tai Chi and Qigong Union for Great Britain (TCUGB) (https://www.taichiunion.com/). This is despite the fact that some Taijiquan practitioners do not follow Qigong sets, seeing the two arts as distinct entities. Nonetheless, they perhaps constitute a minority share of the world's Taijiquan practitioners today, and the TCUGB's very own long-running, in-print magazine for its members is actually called *Tai Chi Chuan & Oriental Arts* – again stressing the pluralism of arts surrounding Taijiquan.

Further governance of these art forms is emerging through the efforts of the Chartered Institute for the Management of Sport and Physical Activity (CIMSPA), which has an increasingly important role is shaping degree programmes in British universities – to the pleasure and disdain of my colleagues. CIMSPA is focusing on the use of Tai Chi (without the martial fist / Chuan element) as a form of exercise for health and fitness within the wellness sector. While some Taijiquan instructors would welcome the guidance from a centrally organised body, others might be concerned that their international lineage might not be recognised in the narrowly defined framework using a more Western logic of science and training. The consultancy was launched by CIMSPA in conjunction with the TCUGB and the BCCMA, and it now has a position statement (CIMSPA, 2020) following a wide-scale survey of practitioners and experts. Shortly after this first stage in which I took part as a survey participant (thanks to my PhD student Daniel Jacklin, an advisory member of CIMSPA), I discussed the matter of regulation with two Taijiquan practitioners of different lineages. One did not like the idea of teaching Chinese medical theory and terms such as Qi, which he regarded as "an ephemeral thing." Meanwhile, my current instructor "David" (pseudonym) was concerned that his own instructor and his close ally in another organisation – who are based in Europe and Australasia respectively – would not be recognised by the framework.

Recent ethnographic work by Giovine (2021) has shown the union of Taijiquan and other arts to be within specific lineages. In his study of "Daoist Internal Arts (DIA)" of Neigong, Qigong and Taijiquan, Giovine examined the specific approach taken by students of the renowned American Taijiquan and internal martial arts expert Bruce Frantzis. Using metaphors of the energy gates of the body as proposed in his numerous books (e.g., Frantzis, 2003), the students in the London branch of this association learned non-dualistic perspectives on the body that united cognition with embodiment. This connection to texts shows how many notable martial arts instructors are also prolific writers and speakers, as seen across the decades. His research is a useful snapshot of cosmopolitan Taijiquan making use of Internet resources, regular classes and detailed intellectual discussions on the art among a demographic of largely middle-age, white British adults interested in enhancing their health and wellbeing. However, it is interesting to note the gender shift in terms of predominantly female students, which differs to the groups I have observed over the years in more rural areas of England and Wales, which tend to be male-dominated (see Chapter 8).

Discussion

Despite its small size, Britain is a complex nation that has great regional variation and complex geopolitics. In my doctoral research in South West England, it was interesting to note the gradual dissemination of Chinese martial arts to rural areas such as Devon and Cornwall, with satellite schools being set up in allegiance with notable instructors based in London. This illustrates the power of internal migration and continued mobilities, with a new generation of instructors travelling far and wide – most commonly in private transport - to learn from the handful of available (and sometimes questionable) teachers in their home county until they find their main Sifu ("teaching father") further afield. Some of these Sifus can be found in Chinatowns in London, Manchester and other metropoles, while others have settled in seaside towns away from the hustle and bustle of the big city. Many Sifus today are not from China, Hong Kong or Asia or even of that ethnicity, as there are now a great number of white British, South Asian and

Afro-Caribbean teachers of Wing Chun and other Chinese martial arts who have attained a high degree of skill and understanding despite not speaking Cantonese in the vast majority of cases. Shaun Rawcliffe's Midlands Wing Chun, James Sinclair of the UK Wing Chun Association and Brian Desire are all examples of this generation, and slightly younger innovators such as Kevin Chan show how Wing Chun might be mixed with other martial arts to offer a complete combat system. However, like Taijiquan, Wing Chun remains male dominated in its leadership and is actually now more associated with the white British demographic than the original generation of Chinese migrants.

In a similarly coastal and rural area, Wales is one of the four countries of the United Kingdom that can boast of a rich heritage in the Martial Arts and Combat Sports (MACS). Despite it having a population of only 3.4 million people, it has contributed much to the history of boxing, from the bareknuckle matches on mountains around industrial towns like Merthyr to the heights of elite boxing seen in the undefeated Joe Calzaghe (Stead & Williams, 2008). Lesser known are the rare styles of Chinese martial arts in Wales, from Feng Shou "Hand of the Wind" and Dragon style Kung Fu to Lee family Taijiquan – the latter two taught by London-born Chee Soo, choreographer for the Avengers series, who later settled and died in Ebbw Vale, South Wales in 1994. Despite only a few final years of his life in Wales, these forms of Chinese martial arts are very widespread in the south of the country. This approach to the Chinese martial arts avoids sporting competitions and its associated will to win, and instead emphasises the union of mind, spirit and body to follow a pacifist neo-Daoist philosophy.

In North Wales, there is even a branch of the Shaolin Temple, Hafan Shaolin Cymru, led by an ordained monk and native Welsh speaker Dol Wong (https://hafanshaolincymru.com/). Although a project in conjunction with the Welsh Government fell through, Dol Wong still has the grand vision to restore a hotel for a new purpose: a dedicated Shaolin Temple centre outside China. Chinese communities are still noticeable in terms of their martial artistry with the festive Lion and Dragon Dance displays during the Chinese New Year. Indeed, some noted Kung Fu Sifus are associated with the restaurant and takeaways businesses in South Wales. Over time, these groups have included non-Chinese students, although I have met some longstanding disciples who recall times when they were first ignored by their Chinese peers unaccustomed to white people learning their martial art.

The notion of non-Chinese people teaching Chinese martial arts outside China is an interesting one when it comes to questions of cultural appropriation. It is perfectly acceptable for a Brazilian to dazzle people with their football skills, even though the game was first codified in Victorian England. To use a very British analogy, we can conceive of the martial arts like fish and chips (another Victorian invented tradition): Although the external presentation might differ in terms of numerous kinds of curry sauces, condiments in mushy peas and the laws preventing the use of real newspaper to wrap the dish. The "traditional" fish and chips would actually be wrapped in local newspapers, but now boxes show prints of such papers to offer a sense of nostalgia. Meanwhile, the white British families have handed over businesses to newer communities of Muslim British people now operating as fish and chip specialists with halal dishes offered alongside the British pies and sausages. Yet the core essence of fish and chips is still the nation's favourite dish, along with curry. The same can be said for the Chinese martial arts in Britain. There are still some Chinese groups operating in secret, but many overt businesses are run by people of other ethnicities who still offer the rich flavour of the Chinese martial arts with their forms, stances, sets and philosophy. They are still Chinese martial arts, but with influence from British culture, law and policies including first aid, safeguarding and injury prevention. Some aspects such as traditional Chinese medicine might be lost, while other practitioners might seek to re-embed them into the daily practices of a school. The Chinese arts continue to be reconstructed for different purposes in specific contexts by a multitude of pioneers and leaders operating in small schools and franchises – just like fish and chip shop owners!

Conclusion

This chapter has extended the idea of conceptualising the martial arts as *arts* through a case study of the Chinese martial arts taught and studied in Britain. Taking Wing Chun Kung Fu and Taijiquan as exemplars, I have shown that the Chinese martial arts differ from the Japanese martial arts in terms of their relative lack of central governance. As such, the Chinese martial arts are more arts that sports, with each generation of students offering their own interpretation and "take" on a given art. Some arts become hybrid through the mixture of Chinese and other fighting systems while others reflect the biographies of their founders. The Chinese styles can express Chinese culture as in the New Year celebrations with the Lion and Dragon Dance, but they more commonly express ideas from specific lineages of families that resist a unifying governing body. These lineages reflect new insights but also the filling of gaps in knowledge and ability with supplementary training in things such as ground fighting and Western fitness training. As in other forms of art, the artist or artisan is given much room for manoeuvre in terms of creativity, passion and hard work alone without much hope for external funding, sponsorship and universal recognition seen in sports. This comes with micro-politics of lineage with judgements on weight distribution in stances, training methods, specific techniques and the verified knowledge of lineage holders. The martial artist becomes both an artist and a connoisseur, and many go on to be arts educators through their roles as instructors, coaches, Sifus or Shifus – whichever term suits their social status and their approach to the art and its origins in northern or southern China. The next chapter continues to examine the creative aspect of martial arts through the trajectory of founders of new systems. In what follows, I consider the martial movement systems used for health, rehabilitation and athletic performance that adapt the core building block of the martial arts: their techniques and methods. We will see the core influence of Asian martial arts mixed with hybrid approaches to human movement and discovery in Western contexts.

References

Bowman, P. (2021). *The invention of martial arts: Popular culture between Asia and America.* Oxford: Oxford University Press.

British Combat Association (BCA) official website. Available at: https://www.britishcombat.co.uk/. Last accessed 4 October 2021.

British Council for Chinese Martial Arts (BCCMA) official website. Available at: www.bccma.com. Last accessed 4 October 2021.

Brown, D., & Leledaki, A. (2010). Eastern movement forms as body-self transforming practices in the West: Towards a sociological perspective. *Cultural Sociology, 4*(1), 123–154.

Charted Institute for the Management of Sport and Physical Activity (CIMSPA). Position statement on Tai Chi and Qigong. September 2020. Available at: https://www.cimspa.co.uk/standards-home/professional-standards-and-consultation-guidance/position-statement-for-tai-chi-and-qigong. Last accessed 4 October 2021.

Frantzis, B. (2003). *The big book of Tai Chi: Build health fast in slow motion.* London: Thorsons.

Gee, G., Ming, B., & Loewenhagen, R. (2004). *Mastering Kung Fu: Featuring Shaolin Wing Chun.* Champaign, IL: Human Kinetics.

Gibson, A. (2001). *Why Wing Chun works.* Chichester: Summersdale Publishers.

Gibson, A. (2012). *Beginning Wing Chun: Why Wing Chun works.* London: New Generation Publishing.

Giovine, V. (2021). Embodying Daoist internal arts: Walking the line between the reification and instrumental use of cognition. *Sociology* (online early). DOI: https://journals.sagepub.com/doi/10.1177/00380385211044319

Green, T. A. (2020). Vernacular martial arts: Culture, continuity and combat. In S.-Y. Park & S.-Y. Ryu (Eds.), *Traditional martial arts as intangible cultural heritage* (pp. 230–240). Jeonju: ICM and ICHCAP.

Hafan Shaolin Cymru official website. Available at: https://hafanshaolincymru.com/. Last accessed 4 October 2021.

Jennings, G. (2019). Bruce Lee and the invention of Jeet Kune Do: The Theory of Martial Creation. *Martial Arts Studies, 8*, 60–72. https://doi.org/10.18573/mas.84

Kernspecht, K. (1997). *On single combat: Strategy, tactics, physiology, psychology, philosophy and history of unarmed self-defence*. Berg: Wushu Verlag Kernspecht.

Kornhaber, S. (2017). Did Meryl Streep misrepresent MMA? *The Atlantic*. Available at: https://www.theatlantic.com/entertainment/archive/2017/01/meryl-streeps-misrepresentation-of-mixed-martial-arts-mma-trump-kerry-howley-thrown-interview/512564/. Last accessed 28 May 2022.

Lee, B. (1975). *Tao of Jeet Kune Do*. Santa Barbara, CA: Ohara Publications.

Martial Arts Studies Research Network official website. Available at: www.mastudiesrn.org. Last accessed 28 May 2022.

Partivoká, V., & Jennings, G. (2018). The Kung Fu family: A metaphor of belonging across time and place. *Revista de Artes Marciales Asiáticas, 13*(1), 35–52.

Ryan, A. (2008). Globalisation and the 'internal alchemy' in Chinese martial arts: The transmission of Chinese martial arts to Britain. *East Asia Science, Technology and Society: An International Journal, 2*(4), 525–543.

Ryan, M. J. (2017). *Venezuelan stick fighting: The civilizing process in martial arts*. London: Lexington Books.

Stead, P., & Williams, G. (Eds.). (2008). *Wales and its boxers: The fighting tradition*. Cardiff: University of Wales Press.

Tai Chi and Qigong Union for Great Britain (TCUGB) official website. Available at: https://www.taichiunion.com/. Last accessed 4 October 2020.

Tai Chi Nation Official Website. Available at: https://www.taichination.com/ Last accessed 13 November 2022.

Tse, M., & Ip, C. (1998). *Wing Chun: Traditional Chinese Kung Fu for Self-defence & Health*. London: Piatkus.

3

Martial Arts as the Basis for Mixed Movement Systems

Movement, Technique and Mixed Methods

One of my PhD participants (in Jennings, 2010) once recalled his eloquent instructor's justification for the rigorous training in Yiquan, Baguazhang and Taijiquan: "We do internal martial arts so that our bodies work as well as they can in everyday life." This was despite the fact that his relatively young, athletic instructor of 27 years was heavily involved in sporting competitions in the form of Chinese kickboxing (sanshou) and pushing hands (tuishou). Nonetheless, due to their history in military and civilian combat, martial arts are undoubtedly systems for learning to fight in an effective manner, but they can also be regarded as systems for learning to move in new and different ways. A practitioner of Ninjutsu can learn to roll, jump, crawl and sneak around like the Ninja of their 1980s and 1990s childhood films, while an advanced exponent of the South Indian martial art Kalarippayattu can wield numerous weapons while leaping extraordinarily high into the air (as I saw when first reading Zarrilli's 1998 monograph on the art). A Brazilian Jiu-Jitsu fighter will learn to bridge their body against that of their training partner and opponent, while an Olympic sport fencer will understand the depth and length of specific lunging techniques.

Taijiquan players often focus on holding postures for long periods of time, and they focus on standing and bodily awareness – although, as we have seen in the previous chapter, this emphasis will vary from lineage to lineage, from teacher to teacher and from school to school. The list could be exhaustive, as each martial art tends to focus on specific aspects of human movement and moments of stillness, with a blend of dynamic action and static postures. The practitioners' minds are drawn into the movement as experienced in the moment, and this involves honing an awareness of specific parts of their bodies, which is why they are often classified as bodily arts akin to Asian forms of dance (Downey, Dalidowicz, & Mason, 2014), modes of mindful fitness or mind-body practices – often referred to as bodymind practices to reverse the hierarchical dualism between mind and body in Western civilisation. Some classification focus on the body, while others tend to stress the mind(ful) aspect of martial arts, but all of them would probably concur that the martial arts are concerned with complex and gross movement skills.

Following the pioneering work of Marcel Mauss on techniques of the body, the ways in which humans learn to move their bodies in different socio-cultural contexts (1970[1935]), Ben Spatz (2015) has argued for the study and theorisation of technique in society. Technique can be regarded as the smallest and most basic unit of analysis in society, as it forms the basis of all society, from the embodied nature of written and spoken language to the construction of technology. Spatz (2015) regards technique as a genuine, yet understated form of knowledge while also perceiving the practice of such techniques as a form of research. He also notes that techniques take a long time to learn and master, and once known, are not easily unlearned. Moreover, techniques can be perceived as cross-cultural forms of knowledge, as in the punching, sitting and standing techniques seen in the Mexican martial art of Xilam that are akin to the postures and movements of many East Asian martial arts (Jennings, 2021; see Chapter 7). Following Spatz's (2015) thesis, the martial artists honing and refining technique and even developing new angles and varieties for these techniques could then be understood as undertaking research in their practices of forms, shadowboxing and sparring. In fact, many martial arts consider their methods as laboratories for experimenting with techniques and the practices composed of them, as in the *Chi Sau* (sticking hands) of Wing Chun.

The focus on specific techniques and practices can lead us to appreciate both the "light" and "dark" side of the martial arts in terms of how they might be (un) healthy practices composed of specific practices (Jennings, 2017). The light side can be increased mobility, muscle mass and control of specific parts of the body built up from repetitive training of a technique or specialist exercises designed to cultivate specific mind-body dispositions. Shadowboxing can develop the speed of one's punches and the medicine ball can help to condition the abdomen for dealing with such punches. Notwithstanding these benefits, taking these techniques and micro-practices to the extreme can lead us to the dark side of overtraining specific parts of the body, leading to an imbalanced physique, poor posture, chronic pain and even long-term injury or disability. Each martial art has its characteristically problematic body regions, such as the knees and hips for fencers (from the excessive, explosive movement of lunging), hands and brain for boxers (due to hitting hard things and repetitive brain injury) and the shoulders and elbow in Wing Chun (from too much anterior movement and air punching in class). I have suffered grazed knuckles from excessive work on the heavy bag as well as a swollen elbow from too many press ups in one guest seminar from a noted Kung Fu master. In a recent seminar (featured in the Preface), my knuckles became so damaged that they now have small scars on them. This was due to the continued counting of ten among a large group of students hitting heavy, water-based bags using mitts. I, however, came ill prepared, and a classmate could only lend me their under-mitt wraps. From the side sword in HEMA, my typically pain-free knees started to flare up thanks to the dynamic lunging motion used alongside the thrusting technique used with this single-hand sword – a precursor to the modern style of fencing. In a Kung Fu seminar led by a well-respected teacher and presenter, my right elbow flared up, meaning I could not eat with that hand for an entire week – all due to an excess of push ups beyond my capabilities.

In the 20th century, several pioneers started to establish their own systems of movement training and personal development as inspired by the lighter side of martial arts techniques and supplementary training methods. A notable example of this is the Israeli Judoka and electronic engineer Moshe Feldenkrais, with his Feldenkrais Method designed in the 1950s to enhance one's way of moving in a more efficient, effortless manner. Feldenkrais began his martial arts training in Japanese Judo and Jujitsu, and used the basis of these grappling arts in his movement system, which was popularised thanks to him becoming the private teacher of the then Israeli prime minister. Years after his passing, the Feldenkrais Method is well established in many countries around the world, and TedEx (2012) and YouTube videos (for example, https://www.youtube.com/watch?v=0FUlRjBcGGE) abound on the wisdom learned from this system in terms of is alternative to strenuous training to become stronger, larger and faster. In these videos, claims are made around Feldenkrais's original theory: that the way we move is reflective of the way we think and therefore act in life. Following this logic, changing the way we move will change the way we react to problems faced in work and everyday interactions. The official International Feldenkrais Federation (IFF) website (www.feldenkrais-method.org) advertises its services to a wide variety of people, from children and elderly people to athletes and artistic performers such as actors and violinists.

In this chapter, I shall examine specific cases of where contemporary 21st century martial arts and movement innovators have created their own martial movement systems for enhancing human performance: in terms of everyday life and health as well as elite athletic performance for people such as competitive fighters. I first turn to another Israeli progenitor, Ido Portal, who has built on his foundation of Capoeira to develop a complex and ever-expanding human movement system named after him, Ido Portal Movement Culture. Accompanying this notable case study is another celebrated trainer of celebrities and martial artists: The American Cameron Shayne, whose timely arguments around the danger of extended sitting in contemporary society have brought him to practise and preach a lifestyle around diverse movement systems combining martial arts training with yoga, gymnastics and dancing. I am grateful to one of my Taijiquan research participants Andrew (pseudonym) for introducing me to these fascinating case studies through YouTube videos watched and shared during our lively discussions. A Russian Systema instructor, Jeff Faris, whom I trained with in the fightingandspirit project (see Chapter 5) also advocated learning about Cameron Shayne, who he quoted as saying: "there's nothing worse for you than sitting." We first turn to the dynamic and charismatic Ido Portal, whose videos were first shown to me by Andrew as we sat in my local pub during an evening out. "He's got the perfect physique!" Exclaimed Andrew, while we noted some similarities of Portal's training methods with those seen in Taijiquan spinal wave as the man moved in a spiral motion while revealing a ripped physique shown in various techniques and practices hailing from different cultures all combined to make one culture.

Ido Portal Movement Culture

"Nowadays we have become overly technical; people are trying to study techniques of movement. But the real techniques that they need to learn, the techniques that originated the techniques that they want to learn, are the techniques of the body. These real fundamental basics." (Ido Portal, in The Ultimate Health Podcast interview, https://www.youtube.com/watch?v=se4kHm0TLCg)

In the above interview, Ido Portal explained how we can aim to become better than today through movement. Instead of using a fanciful or mysterious name, Portal's system is simply called the Ido Portal Movement Culture, as he argues that human need a culture to move in. Like many founders, he works with a close following that support the growth of his system, and he considers this group to be his "tribe" (as shown on his website www.idoportal.com). His own mother Haviva became one of his students in her late fifties, and videos of her moving in her sixties and seventies have been commented on in highly emotive and positive terms (unusual for the often negative environment of YouTube), with viewers reporting that they shed a tear over her accomplishments, which include hanging on the gymnastic rings, and performing unassisted chin ups and press ups. Portal is highly creative and flexible with his repertoire of exercises, which includes catching a broomstick held upright and then dropped in different directions by a partner. Portal often works with members of his inner circle for videos, and this includes Odelia, his right-hand woman and close friend. Odelia's tale is one of recovery from a car accident in which she suffered a spinal injury. Now, she is his most prominent assistant instructor with a high degree of strength, poise and mobility. Various videos portray them using relatively simple, everyday items such as the aforementioned broomsticks, which Portal uses to aid people's mobility. In a video with the podcast London Real, Portal shows the American host Brian Rose how a stick would enable a person to develop their movements according to rules such as: "you can't bend your spine" or "you can only move from to side" as he gently pushes and swipes with his stick. Later in their conversations, Portal warns viewers about "high tech shoes, low tech feet", echoing earlier warnings of the sportswear industry leading to running injuries (McDougall, 2010). He is also keen to stress the need to connect with the floor each day, which is now very rare due to modern Western furniture such as seats, desks and beds.

In an effort to bond with the ground beneath us (often forgotten about while sitting and wearing shoes), animal movements such as the lizard crawl routine are prominent features of the Ido Movement Culture pedagogy. For Portal, the species of homo sapiens are seen as *homo ludens* – literally, "playing [hu]man." Inspired by the classic 1930s text (Huizinga, 1949[1938]) arguing toward human playfulness as the essence of humanity and for the formation of human cultures, Portal is passionate about continuing joyful movement and physical games throughout one's lifespan in order to "pass the time" before meeting our inevitable deaths. He aims to "cultivate the weird" as a self-confessed "weirdo." In fact, in one interview, Portal claimed the loss of playfulness in modern industrialised societies is "a serial killer." At the same time, he is quick to remind people that "we are animals!" Like Karl Marx and his notion of species-essence, he sees the need for a rich variety of joyful, fulfilling activities for the human being to engage with (see Eagleton, 1997). This is in sharp contrast to the commercial gym, which shuns creative and playful movement in its spaces or attempts at linear movement in organised, competitive sport. Crawling, jumping, rolling and squatting "are all human patterns", as Ido stresses again and again in his various workshops, talks and interviews. In his youth, Portal travelled the world seeking out various movement teachers in countries with representative systems (e.g., China for the Chinese martial arts and Brazil for Capoeira) until he felt that there was no specialist honestly dedicating themselves to human movement. With characteristic confidence, he then decided to become that person: the world authority on human movement. Early videos of his moving through a wet patio and spiralling and inverting his muscular body evoked comments from registered YouTube users such as "poetry in motion" and "the poet of gravity."

Growing up in a coastal area of Haifa, northern Israel, Portal began life just like everyone else: as what he calls "a mover." Following a physically active upbringing connected to the outdoors, he later entered the world of Chinese martial arts after being inspired by the Kung Fu movies of Bruce Lee and Jackie Chan, and then, at the age of 15, began his prolonged engagement with Capoeira. It is encouraging to learn this as a martial artist who began training at 14 (see Chapter 10 for my story), as many people might believe that one needs to start training from early childhood. In fact, much or Portal's development and learning has occurred as a mature adult in his 30s and 40s. His main message is a simple one: "Live dynamically. Move…more. If you don't, one day you won't be able to [move]" or simply the mantra: "move, move, move." So the ethos of his movement culture is about the prevention of immobility, personal growth and the creation of movement culture in what Portal deems to be the absence of an honest community. Ido Movement Culture still retains a solid base in Capoeira, although the dynamic movement of bringing the hips and buttocks to the floor for kicks would be regarded as poor technique in the martial art.

Capoeira is of course an Afro-Brazilian martial art with roots in West Africa (around what is now called Angola) and an evolution in the slave communities in the then Portuguese colony of Brazil. However, many people without African ancestry have attained a high level of skill and understanding of the art, with their ability to flip, make a handstand, walk on their hands and many other feats. In fact, many scholars and practitioners call Capoeira a dance-fight-game due to its merging of genres of dancing, martial arts and play. Israeli Ido Portal is one such person reflecting the global appeal of this hybrid physical culture who possesses a seemingly high level of athletic achievement through diligent training, along with impressive levels of creativity and vision. Portal travels regularly to research other martial and movement systems, such as a recent trip to China to explore Baguazhang circle walking (albeit from a Western, non-Daoist perspective). Portal's website for the Ido Movement System (www.idoportal.com) greets the viewer with the message of "meet the tribe." The terms "tribe" and "community" used in the website might be appropriate, as is the family for Chinese martial arts, due to the strong leadership, core membership and the charismatic nature of the founder. Ido believes humans might survive alone, but they can only thrive with a like-minded tribe. As his surname suggests, Ido has created a portal for others to willingly enter this world of movement and personal growth. Indeed, Portal claims that the system is not just about physical growth, but intellectual stimulation through movement patterns. Instead of focusing on the outer look of the body, Portal emphasises the need for more patterns, and his impressive musculature is a by-product of such training. He aims to build a culture around human movement, as "we are humans first, and movers second", rather than follow specific, narrow traditions that restrict movement patterns for their practitioners, noting that all of the traditions "have a price", as in yoga, which has no pulling technique. Portal uses the term "movers" for human beings to emphasise the mobile nature and potential of our species that have evolved from aquatic species in the oceans.

"We are all human first, movers second and only then, specialists" is a common quote from Portal. In fact, Ido believes human became the dominant species on the planet due to their movement capabilities. As a generalist in human movement, Ido has observed and worked with circus performers, athletes, martial artists, parkour practitioners (*traceurs*) and many other specialists he has sought out during his travels. He acts as both as a student as a teacher, believing that all humans simultaneously adapt these roles on a daily basis. Portal's movement system operates along three phases: (1) isolate specific body parts, (2) integrate those body parts and (3) innovate with creative movements and methods. Specific parts of the body such as the spine are first exercised and opened by specific practices such as the spinal wave, which appears to be adapted from Taijiquan – albeit in a more physical manner sometime making use of a wall to press against, testing the person's range of motion, with the head pressing against the surface, followed by the chest. Portal advocates isolated movements like this, as well as 5–7 minutes hanging from a bar and repeated low squatting for up to 30 minutes a day (accumulated in short bouts of static squatting). Such movements are intended to counter the sedentary lifestyle in today's society that have limited the range of motion in activities such as sitting on chairs, where there is very little flexion of the leg joints. For Ido, "everything is connected" as far as the body is concerned, and he often uses the analogy of him pulling on his t-shirt, whereby every atom of the t-shirt is affected.

Portal is adamant that his method is about movement rather than health, although health can be a positive by-product, he admits to having damaged himself through excessive movement training (such as sitting in the resting squat for four hours). Many viewers would like to see Portal's condition when he is in his 80s. Now in his 40s, with a more slimmed-down physique than the earlier videos, Portal tries to overcome the early hyper-specialisation of technique seen in youth sport. In one interview, he claimed: "If you specialise, you will pay a price…yoga has a price, gymnastics has a price, everything has a price." His approach could be regarded as an attempt to attain a great level of physical literacy: the lifelong ability to competently move in different ways. Margaret Whitehead (2010) first coined this term, which she defined in the blurb of her book as: "The motivation, confidence, physical competence, understanding and knowledge that individuals develop at an appropriate level throughout their life." (ibid.) Jumping, rolling, crawling, flipping, squatting and kicking are all such potential movement patterns in the martial arts to develop physical literacy. Portal is particular keen on developing the squatting technique for human beings, which he claims is the natural sitting posture for eating and digesting. Many Asian and Pacific cultures such as in some Indian and Indonesian communities squat while eating or using the toilet, as Mauss (1970[1935]) remarked in his insightful early theory based on his extensive observations in Europe, Asia and Australasia. Writers in physical cultures such as running have also noted this technique in Japan, which might account for lower leg injuries among team runners. The resting squat is becoming more recognised in Western societies. One of my own university students, an international basketball player, demonstrated this low, static squat in one of our theoretical (seated) classes in order to emphasise the importance it was playing on his new exercise routine. Like the basketball player, Portal's own legs are toned, but extremely flexible, springy and durable, as he explained: "I don't want tree trunk legs; I want bamboo legs."

"Can you flip? Can you move? Can you invert? Or is it just…aesthetics?" Following viral YouTube videos of his incredible physical abilities (https://www.youtube.com/watch?v=0JMlXg4XP4E), memorable quotes and intelligent arguments (https://www.youtube.com/watch?v=W0Wr7HsylE0), Portal's reputation

was enhance with his collaboration with no other than the (in)famous Irish UFC celebrity Conor McGregor, well known for his exploits outside the octagon such as the attacking of a bus full of other MMA fighters (see Channon, 2018) and sadly, an old man in his pub. Newspapers and media articles (e.g., Skipper, 2019) shared images of McGregor moving through techniques on a beach, and this added a level of intrigue on his possible secret weapon: a unique movement system allowing him to be so fast and powerful across different weight divisions. Like Bruce Lee before him, with basketball great Kareem Abdul-Jabbar and Hollywood legend Steve McQueen, Portal's professional profile has benefited from famous student-athletes, and as with Lee, he charges a very high fee for private tuition with his team. Top athletes such as Cristiano Ronaldo (37) and Robert Lewandowski (33) now have sleep coaches and strict diets to give them extra edge to maintain peak performance while managing longer careers well into their thirties (and even to 40 in yoga advocate and Manchester United great Ryan Giggs's case). The martial movement systems might be appropriate supplements for combat sport athletes with their attacking and defensive movement patterns, loosening their bodies and training new planes of movement. The martial artist might be able to offset pain and injury through softening of the body, increasing their flexibility and mobility and new mind-body connections through neurological pathways. However, the research on efficacy of such interventions is limited, despite the advocacy of Portal and his contemporaries from noted martial artists.

In 2015, Ido's life changed forever. Conor McGregor spent his final week of training with Portal in his headquarters in Tel Aviv, Israel, and this preparation focused on non-contact mobility and reaction training. Then, after this tutelage in lizard crawling, spinal waves and beam walking on beaches and seaside apparatus (see https://www.youtube.com/watch?v=91NWZKkhMkU), Conor was fortunate to gain a renowned knockout victory against champion Nate Diaz in an impressive 13 seconds. Some fans put this smooth triumph down to this apprenticeship with Portal, while others believed he would have been able to knock out his adversary without this preparation. It is probably impossible to actually determine the degree of success aided by such martial movement coaches, and there is a lacuna of empirical scientific research on the matter. McGregor has learned new dimensions of movement along with peripheral vision training from Portal. Indeed, Portal repeatedly uses the term so often contested by researchers: "paradigm shift." For him, the movement culture offers a collective perspective on how to use our bodies from an open-ended movement perspective rather than a single-culture, disciplinary perspective (as in Indian yoga or Chinese Baguazhang), with their narrow identities around being a yogi, gymnast or Judoka. As I mentioned earlier, Portal believes that movement has enabled the evolution of the human brain in order for us to be the dominant species on the planet. Thanks to our bodies, we humans can share knowledge across the generations as form of a collective knowledge. Right now as I type, I am making the use of the dexterity of the fingers. I am using a standing desk in order to avoid the compression on my spine from excessive sitting – something Portal would consider a self-induced, preventable disability. Moreover, after watching and analysing the numerous video interviews and talks, I have taken to the low squatting to blend my standing and regular sitting throughout the day. This routine and lifestyle approach to physical activity was reinforced during the COVID-19 lockdown in the UK, which restricted my ability to train in the martial arts classes. Now I am expanding my training to the local park, where I am hanging from a chin-up bar to help square my shoulders rounded from years of anterior Wing Chun movements.

Ido's dedicated studio is, in his words, "a playground for adults." It even has a bold slogan written on the wall: "Let them dirty the walls, motherfuckers!", which refers to parents' typical complaints about their children making their houses dirty when putting their feet against the wall. This is one of many platitudes that reflects the Israeli's direct and often brash approach to speaking (which he admits can be common in his nation's culture), but also his key vision for humanity. Portal is adamant that children already know how to move their bodies, and he argues that society starts to disable its citizens through rigid modes of sitting on sofas and chairs. Indeed, he stresses the fact that children are not taught to walk, as they teach themselves to walk, along with other key movement patterns. He regards physical inactivity – or the lack of movement – as the means to disability, which he refers to a lack of mobility. Despite being our most mobile joints, the scapula are particularly prone to tightness from long hours in front of desks and computers, and our knees rarely gain the full flexion offered in a deep squat. All of these movements are seemingly natural to humans, unlike the concept of the workout ("I've got to work out now"), which stems from late modernity and its fitness industry. Portal admits to having been kicked out of commercial gyms for playing around in their clinical, organised and compartmentalised space.

Despite the heavy influence from Capoeira (the martial art that Ido is clearly adept at), one can see some elements of Asian martial arts and philosophies in the Israeli's system. The body of the martial artist is one of functionality, although aesthetics can be a pleasing by-product (as in the case of Bruce Lee). For one, Portal often stresses the Japanese Zen Buddhist notion of Shoshin (the beginner's mind explained in Suzuki, 1970) as a key attitude to approach movement: our own personal craft. He explained this in his characteristically articulate manner common among such influential and successful figures: "I practise like a madman, but with complete detachment from the result." Portal also draws on quotes from Bruce Lee such as "*I don't hit; it hits*" when referring to trained instinct in martial arts striking technique that bypasses direct consciousness in action. Like Lee, he is keen to move beyond the constraints of traditions, as summarised by statements such as: "I want the contents, not the container." Ido also draws on notions such as the Zen koans mentioned by a friend, which he adapts in the form of movement puzzles or physical riddles. However, Portal wishes to distance himself from labels such as "guru" or "master" which are often bestowed on him from commentators, interviewers and followers praising him such as McGregor. At the same time, some of these viewpoints actually resonate with many martial arts instructors' analogies, with my own Taijiquan teacher also speaking of being concerned with cultivating the content of a glass (the water, being the internal principles of Taijiquan) rather than the glass itself (the externally visible Taiji form). We will learn more about this teacher in Chapter 8.

McGregor and Portal have since drifted in different directions, with some fans of followers of the Ido Portal method asking Ido to call Conor in order to resume their working relationship and bring back success to the UFC fighter and sometime boxer. McGregor has since lost several fights (including the boxing match against Floyd Mayweather in 2017), and some commentators claim that his movements are now more rigid. Nevertheless, critics are keen to point out the similarity between the exercises of the Ido Portal method and those seen in the Russian martial art of Systema, which its relaxed, flowing exercises using the breath as its driver for technique and power. The distinctive aspect of breathing might make Systema stand out, alongside its reality-based training for street survival. Other viewers have pointed out earlier progenitors of martial arts-inspired movement systems, such as Cameron Shayne. Some believe Ido moves better, although Shayne's system outdates his own by ten years.

Budokwon Yoga

"The Budokon Yoga style recognises tradition while innovating and leading the way for what is possible. We recognize that postural yoga does not look the same as it did 5000 years ago or even 5 years ago, therefore, we continue to press the boundaries of creativity while maintaining the crucial therapeutic application of asana. Cameron Shayne has been a pioneer in the field of therapeutic movement through yoga and martial arts beginning his personal practice in 1983. Budokon Yoga is the culmination of 30 years of research, development and practical application. Simply put, Budokon Yoga heals, strengthens and changes lives." (www.budokon.com).

Budokon style yoga is a modern yoga style which unites the ancient tradition of self-inquiry with modern mixed movement. Budokon Yoga was codified and popularized by Cameron Shayne in 2001 (Budokon, 2019). Considered a science, art and philosophy which synchronizes classical yoga with martial arts, calisthenics, animal locomotions and life science, the physically demanding style reshapes modern yoga by reflecting the qualities of a yogi as defined by the yoga sutras, in place of more contemporary constructs of morality, spirituality and discipleship. The style was created as a condition practice for movers of all types seeking the highest level of agility, mobility, stamina and strength. (www.budokon.com).

With the above quote from the Budokon official website (www.budokon.com), we can see the deep vision of its founder, Cameron Shayne. Budokon Yoga has seven levels, just like many martial arts such as Wing Chun (with its three empty hand forms, one dummy form and two weapons sequences). This structure is supposed to develop a balance between the two elements of the human being: the warrior and the peacemaker. Shayne is clear in his modernising principle that retains some of the essence of Yoga but acknowledges its continued reinvention. And like Yoga, the martial arts are not traditions per se, but really "a tradition of invention" that (Bowman, 2020), flipping the words of Hobsbawm and Ranger (1983), notes in terms of the traditionalist Chinese martial arts.

The term Budokon is composed of three Japanese terms: *Bu* (the warrior), *do* (the way) and *kwon* (spirit), which combine to form "the way of the warrior spirit." Despite Shayne not being from Japan or of the Japanese ethnicity, the Japanese influence is also seen in this system organised around coloured belts and black belts of varying degrees (dan grades). Shayne's own training background is in Taekwondo, which he started as a teenager before discovering Karate, which he practised into adulthood. He encountered yoga in his 20s, and decided to blend martial arts, yoga and what he calls "living arts." These living arts are primarily forms of bodyweight training using both the hip and shoulder girdles. Shayne was one of the pioneers of animal locomotion that follows the movements of our distant relatives, the quadrupedal primates. While some viewers of archive and recent footage have accused Shayne of copying Capoeira, he has explained that the two systems are distinctive.

The U.S. innovator Cameron Shayne, hailed in some circles as "the father of mixed movement arts" is now well in his 50s, but prides himself in his impressive muscular physique, mobility and bodily control, which is akin to that of a man in his twenties. In online interviews including the *Becoming Budokon* Documentary (https://www.youtube.com/watch?v=SVo1kRQsS8I), he squats on the floor rather than sits on a chair – the mainstay of Western working and living environments that he regards as "bad behaviour." Sitting on chairs is now seen in almost all cultures as societies become more Westernised and homogenous. Shayne has a background in the East Asian martial arts, and like many highly skilled exponents, he has worked as a personal bodyguard to celebrities, namely Hollywood actor Charlie Sheen in his heyday as a star, followed by work as a personal trainer to actresses Meg Ryan, Courtney Cox, Jennifer Anniston and Renne Rousso.

Shayne's main argument is around the dangers of modern sitting for hours and hours each day, and he warns that an hour's stretching at night will not be enough to offset the damage of 8–10 hours of sedentary working, sitting and travelling. Like Ido Portal, he advocates the squatting technique of feet planted firmly on the floor, with the pelvis tilted down for the buttocks to rest near the floor. This squatting technique is not part of conventional Western culture, but it is known to be common among many Asian and African cultures such as Japan. Indeed, in his immersive project on Japanese running, investigative journalist Finn (2015) points out the potential role squatting has in injury prevention among runners. Some of my own students have also taken to use this squatting technique in sports such as basketball, where knee injuries are prevalent. My own Taijiquan instructor has identified my tight pelvis as a major obstacle to my mobility and the dropping of my tailbone to better straighten the spine. I have therefore taken to use these squats in my personal training routine. They are present in our repertoire of exercises in the School of Internal Arts, alongside many other dynamic stretches.

Interestingly, Shayne does not call his system a martial art – even though it drawn from martial arts training and attracts martial artists interested in cross training. In fact, it is registered as a form of yoga, such like Odaka Yoga in the Italian city of Milan, which is inspired by the Japanese Samurai philosophy of Bushido (way of the warrior) and the flow of the ocean. Originally co-founded by a male martial artist (Roberto Milletti) inspired by the film *The Last Samurai* and a female yogi, Francesca Cassia (DiPlacido, 2020), this example illustrates the dual importance of hybrid movement coupled with a distinctive philosophy around mastering the flow of mental and physical movement that makes the style unique or distinctive in a saturated market of mind-body practices. Shayne's followers include actress Jennifer Aniston of *Friends* fame, along with notable martial arts champions and competitors (as in BJJ world champions). Shayne's younger Brazilian wife Melayne Shayne tries to add a Latin American ambience and family feeling to their full-time academy. Together, they can be seen as a power couple in the martial arts movement world, just as Portal works with his own athletic female training partner and assistant in his early videos.

In the 21st century, such pioneers flourish in certain societies that value a return to human movement, with its outcome in aesthetics, health and wellbeing. Shayne and his Brazilian wife Melayne have their very own Budokon University on Miami Beach, Florida. Within its badge are the words: "Martial arts – Yoga – Living Arts" to give this threefold path a balance in terms of its three elements. The couple also host retreats in their customised centre in Colorado, where participants can also enjoy a snowboarding trip. Involvement in such activities is of course costly, as Miami Beach the mountain resorts of Colorado are renowned for the global elite. On one wall of their dojo is a mural of Shayne with a fist, which is beside a painting of a gorilla with a Zen symbol – one of the images of Budokon seen in the "BDK Beast" t-shirts sometimes worn by the teachers.

Shayne's system has clearer Asian roots, and indirect Asian techniques are being incorporated through Brazilian Jiujitsu, which derives from Yoga. All of these systems are concerned with increasing the mind-body connections through movement, as "movement is a way of exploring mind." As with Portal's movement culture, Shayne wishes to increase people's mobility which will in turn facilitate longevity for the professional fighters he is working with. However, when viewers of his official videos started to make comparisons with Ido Portal, Shayne responded to one YouTuber: "I am a veteran martial artist, not a dance fighter. I've been a black belt since I was 16. I've been fighting all my life. I don't train to move, I train to fight. Ido Portal has about as much chance of beating me in a fight as I do out dancing him. Apples and oranges, young man." It is interesting to note that although Shayne positions his own art as a Yoga system, he identifies as being a fighter. His response to the YouTube user reflects the sense of rivalry to his contemporaries, with Cameron noting that he began experimenting with martial arts and movement training "when Ido was in kindergarten." As with traditional martial arts, one's generation, the time one started training and one's pedigree as a fighter give a teacher a certain kudos. We can see the rivalry between Portal and Shayne, even though they live on different continents and have their own clientele. It is the rivalry for their message to the global public that is at stake.

Like the majority of martial arts, both of these martial arts-inspired movement systems as led by charismatic male founders and a team of supportive people such as female life partners, close friends and family members. No founders really form and maintain a sustainable system all by themselves. These men are often regarded as "masters" or "gurus" by their (largely male) followers, and like Bruce Lee, their appeal might be aided by their good looks, physique, worldly outlook and articulate manner. Funnily enough, the MMA commentator and comedian Joe Rogan (featured in Chapter 6) once quipped how so many of these movement coaches look like Jesus, with beards and long hair (see www.sportsjoe.ie). More importantly, the two founders possess the visibly appealing yet highly functional bodies that their followers aspire to attain. Moreover, these progenitors live enviable lifestyles involving regular international travel to give workshops and seminars to spread their martial movement systems across the world. Celebrity endorsements add to the credence of the arts, as does the possibility of promotion through ever-popular forms of 21st century media such as YouTube. The flips of Capoeira and the twists of BJJ have been combined with handing from rings, dancing and dynamic postural yoga to make two well-rounded human development systems. Like Portal, Shayne wishes to distance himself from the title of "guru", even launching his own podcast and clothing brand called The Guru Killer.

Would Portal and Shayne be so successful if they did not possess the physiques that many other men desire to possess? My Wing Chun training partner George (seen in Chapter 9) once remarked how MMA builds the body that most people want to have: "ripped", "toned" and "shredded" might be apt words for this kind of body, unlike some of the bodies of noted Wing Chun masters who have evident pot bellies (as in Wong Shun Leung) or are very slim (like Ip Chun or Chu Shong Tin). In the 21st century neoliberal society, a successful man is often seen as one in control of their weight, body fat and muscle mass as well as their posture and movement. This successful kind of man is also youthful and sexually desirable, moving against dominant Western narratives of decay and decline with age. While some of the Chinese martial arts explored in the previous chapter have been adapted to work with people's postural control and refined movement across the life course, they do not offer a particular aesthetic bare torsos seen in *Men's Health* front cover models. As my own Taijiquan instructor commented in one class in relation to the body idealised in his art: "This doesn't develop the six-pack body, unfortunately. You'll have to go to the gym for that." Another factor in the success of these influencers is charisma. Cameron Shayne and Ido Portal are also very articulate men who present convincing arguments around human nature being deeply connected to movement. In today's sedentary society, such movement systems can offer cultural change at work, home and leisure environments by minimising the hours spent sitting or without movement. However, in an interview in The Atlantic with Hayes (2018), Portal admitted to sitting in front of his laptop to do research on other movement cultures and training methods, and he wholeheartedly embraces technology such as Facebook, even mocking the ideologies calling for a return to the wilderness (although he admits to following the paleo diet of meat and broths during his evenings and regular snacks throughout the day). Research is beginning to explore the importance of exercise snacking using Tai Chi and Western exercises to break up long periods of immobility, especially during COVID-19 (Liang et al., 2021). An interest in the fascia as the connective tissue linking the different muscles and limbs together is also identifying the role of regular movement rather than the standard of 30 minutes moderate to rigorous exercise done five times per week.

Summary: Movement Cultures and Body Culture

Brown (2011) has noted how modern martial arts founders and leaders are almost always charismatic figures, and his charisma is aided by their potent bodies capable of incredible movement, tricks and feats that overcomes some genetic weaknesses, as in Bruce Lee (Brown, 2020). Founders of systems such as Budokon, Ido Portal and Odaka Yoga are all charismatic figures that attract a large following of loyal devotees who are in awe of their bodily control, poise and their articulate storytelling and philosophising. As Brown (2020) has shown, this charisma extends from the body of the bearer to the affective reactions of the viewer, listener and fan. These charismatic yet enigmatic founders often mix movement, meditative and martial arts systems by drawing on specific techniques and practices that match their core philosophy. Students do not learn an entire Capoeira system under Portal, as the musical aspect is completely lacking, nor do they master Taekwondo and Karate under Shayne, who makes use of yoga and grappling arts. Instead, they learn part of the prototype mixed systems that these men – and they are normally always men – have created out of pre-existing techniques.

    The techniques of martial arts are rich in their diversity and express cultural knowledge developed over many generations. Outside the realm of combat, the practices used to learn and train these techniques can be used to challenge people's movement capacity and general mobility for health and performance. Martial arts have a definite influence in the mixed movement systems examined in this chapter; however, it would not be fair to describe them as pure martial movement systems due to the continued use of external movements, techniques and methods in their classes and workshops. For future studies, Eichberg's (1998) study of movement cultures or body cultures can help us in understanding these new systems, which offer alternatives to linear movement, restrictions in use of space and the competitive nature of modern sport. This theoretical perspective also sees the immense value of play for human beings, who can form democratic communities concerned with laughter, joking and joy rather than a narrow focus on winning, record keeping (and breaking) and economic production (Eichberg, 2010). Training out in the open air as a tribe, family or community are alternatives to the restricted membership of a 22-person squad or a gendered division seen in many sports. They might offer the "paradigm shift" (frequently mentioned by Ido Portal) to the dominant paradigms of achievement sport and health-related, individualistic fitness exercises seen in modern commercial gyms.

These founders of the martial arts inspired movement systems have a loyal following of students alongside devoted partners or family members who support them financially and emotionally. Quite often, these systems are created in countries where founders have migrated to, or in places with influence from such migration, as in the United States and Israel. Space between the founder and their various teachers might also facilitate greater creativity, as the pioneer has space to find their own path among the martial arts and related practices. It will take years for a system to develop, mature and be ready for public dissemination. My own fledgling Martial Movement Method seen later in this book was created at a time when I was living the flexible expat life working as a freelance English teacher in Mexico. Nevertheless, it is a stalled practical research project that could easily become a lost ethnography: an idea set up with people and places in mind that was never to be fulfilled (Delamont & Smith, 2019). To make the blueprint of the Martial Movement Method successful, I would probably have to give up my full-time academic job to be able train and teach full-time. With that time and freedom, I could sculpt the body that other martial arts enthusiasts would wish to develop themselves. However, I would need to cooperate with a team of specialists helping me with websites, social media, professionally produced videos and other essential ingredients of a thriving business or social enterprise that we see from the branding of Budokon and Ido Portal Movement Culture alongside Odaka Yoga. Moreover, I might even have to give up my career as an academic research, as to become an innovator, I would spend more time on promoting my brand, using social media and working with clients far and wide.

Nevertheless, the systems of Ido Portal and Budokon are physically demanding, with an optimal background in yoga, mixed movement arts and fighting disciplines needed to excel at them. Their videos might offer a portal to their world of motion, as technique is best understood through motion. However, they have yet to commit their more theoretical knowledge to the stiller medium of texts, unlike the earlier innovators of the 20th century such as Moshe Feldenkrais. There is also little published, pee-reviewed scientific research on their methods and the effectiveness of them in transforming human movement, performance, cognition and postural control, which makes them very interesting case studies for the exploratory qualitative study that is this book. A more accessible approach to self-improvement and personal challenge might be reached through the self-help genre of books, which include texts by noted martial artists among the shelves under items of personal growth. Might these be a more economical and physically accessible route to martial arts knowledge? We examine the reimagination and reconstruction of martial arts as self-help literature in the next chapter.

References

Bowman, P. (2020). Martial arts: A tradition of invention: On authenticity in traditional Asian martial arts. In D. Lewin & K. Kenklies (Eds.), *East Asian pedagogies: Education as formation and transformation across cultures and borders* (pp. 205–225). London: Springer.

Brown, D. (2020). Embodying charismatic affect(if): The example of Bruce Lee. *Corpus Mundi, 1*(3), 14–52.

Brown, D. H. K. (2011) La concezione weberiana del carisma: il caso delle arti marziali. *Religioni e Società, 7*, 42–60

Budokon. (2019). Becoming Budokon documentary with Cameron Shayne. Available at: https://www.youtube.com/watch?v=SVo1kRQsS8I. Last accessed 23 October 2021.

Budokon official YouTube channel. Available at: https://www.youtube.com/channel/UCVffZOcRLHX59Wh4VD5HIHQ. Last accessed 17 October 2021.

Budokon Yoga official website. Available at: http://budokon.com/what-is-yoga. Last accessed 17 October 2021.

Channon, A. (2018). The madness of King Conor: Athlete hubris, promotional culture, and performative violence. Unpublished conference paper. Available at: https://www.academia.edu/36390763/The_Madness_of_King_Conor_Athlete_Hubris_Promotional_Culture_and_Performative_Violence. Last accessed 17 October 2021.

Delamont, S., & Smith, R. (Eds.). (2019). *The lost ethnographies: Methodological insights from projects that never were*. London: Routledge.

DiPlacido, M. (2020). Blending martial arts and yoga for health: From the Last Samurai to the first Odaka Yoga warrior. *Frontiers in Sociology* (online), https://doi.org/10.3389/fsoc.2020.597845

Downey, G., Dalidowicz, M., & Mason, P. H. (2014) Apprenticeship as method: Embodied learning in ethnographic practice. *Qualitative Research, 15*(2), 183–200.

Eagleton, T. (1997). *The great philosophers: Marx*. London: Weidenfeld & Nicholson.

Eichberg, H. (2010). *Body democracy: Towards a philosophy of sport for all*. London: Routledge.

Eichberg, H. (1998). *Body cultures: Essays on sport, space and identity*. London: Routledge.

Feldenkrais Method official website. Available at: https://feldenkrais.com/. Last accessed 23 October 2021.

Finn, A. (2015). *The way of the runner: A journey into the fabled world of Japanese running*. London: Faber.

Hayes, S. (2018). The viral video star behind the fitness fad that may replace Crossfit. The Atlantic, August 7, 2018. Available at: https://www.theatlantic.com/health/archive/2018/08/ido-portal-the-player/566687/. Last accessed 23 October 2021.

Huizinga, J. (1949[1938]). *Homo Ludens: A study of the play-element of culture*. London: Routledge & Kegan Paul.

Ido Movement Culture official Facebook group. Available at: https://www.facebook.com/portal.ido. Last accessed 17 October 2021.

Ido Portal Movement Culture official Instagram page. Available at: https://www.instagram.com/portal.ido/?hl=en. Last accessed 17 October 2021.

Ido Movement System official website. Available at: https://www.idoportal.com/. Last accessed 17 October 2021.

Ido Portal Movement Culture. Available at: https://www.youtube.com/channel/UCPCiBMarvDiTx-lknzt934g. Last accessed 17 October 2021.

International Feldenkrais Federation (IFF) official website. Available at: https://feldenkrais-method.org/. Last accessed 26 May 2022.

Jennings, G. (2021). "A punch has no paternity!": Technique, belonging and the Mexicanidad of Xilam. Ethnography (open access online), https://doi.org/10.1177/14661381211035482

Jennings, G. (2017). Pursuing health through techniques of the body in martial arts. *Journal of the International Coalition of YMCA Universities*, 5, 54–72.

Jennings, G. (2010). Fighters, thinkers and shared cultivation: Experiencing transformation through the long-term practice of the traditionalist Chinese martial arts. Unpublished doctoral thesis, University of Exeter.

Liang, I. J., Perkin, O. J., McGuigan, P. M., Thompson, D., & Western, M. J. (2021). Feasibility and acceptability of home-based exercise snacking and tai chi snacking delivered remotely to self-isolating older adults during COVID-19. *Journal of Aging and Physical Activity*, 30(1), 33–43.

Mauss, M. (1970[1935]). Techniques of the body. *Economy and Society*, 2, 70–88.

McDougall, C. (2010). *Born to run: The hidden tribe, the ultra-runners, and the greatest race the world has never seen*. London: Profile Books.

Odaka Yoga official website. Available at: https://odakayoga.com/en/. Last accessed 23 October 2021.

Skipper, C. (2019). Conor McGregor's movement coach, Ido Portal, on the power of weakness. *GQ Magazine*, 21 January 2019. Available at: https://www.gq-magazine.co.uk/article/ido-portal-movement-culture-conor-mcgregor

Spatz, B. (2015). *What a body can do: Technique as knowledge, practice as research*. London: Routledge.

Sportsjoe. VIDEO: Joe Rogan and Brendan Schaub arguing about movement coaches is comedy gold. Available at: https://www.sportsjoe.ie/mma/video-joe-rogan-and-brendan-schaub-arguing-about-movement-coaches-is-comedy-gold-63600. Last accessed 26 May 2022.

Suzuki, S. (1970). *Zen mind, beginner's mind*. Boulder, CO: Shambhala Publications.

TedEx (2012). A Feldenkrais lesson for the beginner scientist: Professor Dorit Aharonov at TEDxJaffa. Available at: https://www.youtube.com/watch?v=0FUlRjBcGGE Last accessed 26 May 2022.

Whitehead, M. (2010). *Physical literacy throughout the lifecourse*. London: Routledge.

The Ultimate Health Podcast interview Ido Portal – It's Never Too Late to Start Moving. Available at: https://www.youtube.com/watch?v=se4kHm0TLCg. Last accessed 17 October 2021.

4

Martial Arts as the Social Structure for Self-Help

"The medicine for my suffering I had within me from the very beginning. My ailment came from within myself, but I did not observe it until this moment. Now I see that I will never find the light unless, like the candle, I am my own fuel, consuming myself."

Martial Arts, the Self and Social Structures

Martial arts can certainly be concerned with what the individual or, for our purposes in this chapter, a Western notion of "the self" as seen in the common expressions: Self-defence, self-protection, self-improvement, self-realisation and self-cultivation. We see and hear these terms mentioned in martial arts literature, classes and online platforms, as people's initial interest in the martial arts is very often due to their perceived need to work on themselves, their concerns about their ability to defend themselves or to test themselves in competition against a worthy opponent. Like the often related Eastern movement forms, clubs and communities frequently advertise bold claims of how the art in question can transform a person's capacities and therefore change their lives for the better (Brown & Leledaki, 2010). As the twenty-first century continues to focus on the individual and their self-actualisation, the insights from notable martial arts innovators have turned to the genre of self-help books. This is partly due to the discipline, structure and culturally-specific philosophy that underpin each martial art. A martial artist must follow a strict path of learning stances, movements, sequences, drills and free-flow exercises. This focus on the self does eventually and inevitably extend to a focus on others (especially training partners), one's school, lineage and wider society, although this is not necessarily the focus on martial arts self-help books written primarily for laypeople living outside the world of martial arts pedagogies and communities.

The Australian kickboxing instructor Georgia Verry of the Fight Back Project and Trauma-Informed Martial Arts Network has interviewed many people on her exclusive Fight Back Podcast (https://www.fightbackproject.com/podcasts/the-fight-back-podcast). Asking about how martial arts have saved their lives, many people replied with one word: Structure. The forms, rituals, routines and etiquette of the martial arts provide people with a roadmap or a template to live their lives in their daily lives and interactions with others. I also offered "structure" as my response when interviewed by Georgia, as the martial arts have provided me with a life purpose in which I can spend the evenings in a standing posture or the mornings working through some forms. I can also take this structure into other contexts as in a hotel room when standing on one leg or when waiting for someone in the street (with small movements used in the warm up exercises in classes). All of these are examples of how martial arts have been used by individuals to help themselves – be that to structure their lives or simply pass the time.

The notion of self-help emerged in the industrial Victorian period of the late 19th century in which people started to write about human development, quite often from a Christian, moralistic perspective. As cities grew around the imagined communities of strangers, the individual or "self" became more estranged from their neighbours. The self-help industry has been estimated to be an 11 billion U.S. dollar industry, and recent estimates put it at 13 billion dollars. Connecting to themes of personal development, spirituality and popular psychology on the shelves of major book sellers, self-help books fill a void in many people's lives in terms of religion, science and life coaching. As with life coaching, it is an unregulated industry in which anyone can be qualified to write a self-help book. In fact, there are hundreds of thousands of self-help books on the market. Reading such texts can be addictive, with some TED Talks and YouTube videos decrying the industry for its continued repackaging of similar narratives and platitudes (see, for example, TEDx, 2015a, 2020a, 2020b). Many viewers of these videos critique the idea of "self-help" as really just a form of help, as seeking out a book written by another human being is asking for help. However, the relatively impersonal nature of writing and reading (as writers ordinarily write for strangers) a book (or listening to an audiobook) make it appear that we are helping ourselves.

One of the first martial arts self-help books was written by a Korean-American martial arts instructor (1991). A female writer, Dr. Tai Yun Kim (1991) shares tales from her childhood during the Korean War in which she was rescued from a massacre and later learned the martial arts in secrecy from a mysterious master, whose identity is never revealed. Later in the book, this martial art has an instantly recognisable name: Taekwondo ("the way of the foot and the hand" in Korean). In her youth, Kim migrated to the United States with her family, first working as a janitor in school toilets. To the surprise of many people, she reveals that she is very proud of her first job, which tested her drive and resolve in her new culture. Some years after this, she persuaded the principal of the local high school to allow her to teach Taekwondo, which led to great success as an instructor and eventually coach to the U.S. women's Taekwondo squad. After this, she founded her own martial arts and human development system (Jung SoWon) that blends martial arts with meditation training. Her biography and system stimulated the creation of the book (and now audiobook available on Audible), which contains many tales of transformation from both her and her students, from how to become thriftier with money to more in tune with one's life partner.

Continuing with the pioneering efforts of the likes of Kim (1991), in this chapter, I turn to three twenty-first-century examples of martial arts self-help books in which elements of Eastern martial arts and other martial activities have been reimagined in textual form for a wider audience. Written largely by active martial arts instructors, these self-help books share personal insights into not just martial arts, but how to live our lives in a society that is increasingly challenging, complex and uncertain. Interestingly, many of these texts refer to the romanticised ideals of the warrior – even with their title. Renowned bouncer and martial artist turned British Academy of Film and Television Arts (BAFTA) winning writer Geoff Thompson's (2010) text is simple called *Warrior*, while Steve Jones's (2004) book is *The Way of the Intelligent Warrior*. I turn first to the most recent book in my collection – one that makes use of wisdom from the late 20th century Kung Fu icon, Bruce Lee.

Be Like Water: Be Like Bruce Lee

Bruce Lee (1940-1973) is best known for the action movies in the last three years of his life, although this was often the expression of his martial art and philosophical imagination of Jun Fan Jeet Kune Do. As a former university student of philosophy and drama, Lee continued to read the works of influential thinkers, and later indulged in self-help books to inspire him during a difficult period in trying to settle into Hollywood as an Asian leading man. In recent years, Bruce Lee's legacy has passed from his widow Linda Lee Cadwell to his only surviving child, his daughter Shannon Lee. Although Bruce's premature death in 1973 (when Shannon was only four years old) prevented Shannon from directly knowing him and vividly remembering him as a martial artist and rounded human being, the extensive records he left behind through his writings have enabled people such as the loyal editor John Little to construct the Bruce Lee Library series towards the end of the 20th century (as in *Bruce Lee: Artist of Life* collated by Little, 1999), making use of his sketches, photographs, letters and journal entries. I read these books as a teenager, and found them to be immensely stimulating for my personal training in the gym and for home training of specific techniques. Shannon has continued this approach in *Be Water, My Friend* (Lee, 2020), which focuses on Bruce Lee's iconic platitude about how one should strive to be more fluid and open, like water:

> Empty your mind.
> Be formless, shapeless like water.
> You put water in a cup; it becomes a cup.
> You put water into a teapot; it becomes the teapot.
> You put it into a bottle; it becomes the bottle.
> Now water can flow, or it can crash!
> Be water, my friend.

Her father Bruce Lee's own writings offer the source of this water metaphor in his teenage annoyance with being chastised by his teacher Ip Man. Hitting the water in a lake, he saw the water reverberate as it absorbed the power of his fist. Some explanatory videos (e.g., Sisyphus 55, 2021, https://www.youtube.com/watch?v=rpI9putqbg8) argue that he had an epiphany at that very moment, which was enabled by him keeping his cup (mind) empty for new ideas. Recent biographical research by Polly (2019) has pinpointed this oft-quoted extract to Lee's interview with Pierre Burton, when Lee was actually acting out his role of his namesake "Lee" in the one-off episode of *Longstreet*. Since then, the words have been used for commercial advertisements on television, and even by my friend and colleague David Aldous to inspire my colleagues in the Physical Health Education and Lifelong Learning (PHELL) research group that he lead at our university.

For more many people – a teenage me included – Bruce Lee has been their hero as a youth. In 2015, Shannon Lee was invited to one TEDx talk as part of a series on superheroes. These TED Talks have now set a world standard for public speaking, as Gallo (2014) explains in the blurb of his book on the genre: "ideas are the true currency of the twenty-first century". In its characteristically bold manner, the TED Talks company explained the role of real-life superheroes in society:

> Superheroes exist. They live among us. They put on their capes every day. In offices, in labs, on the sports track, in garages. Creating, designing, educating, entertaining, informing – making a true difference. To a true hero, every detail matters, every second is important, every inch counts. They lead by example driven by their own targets. They are the ones that will not conform, willing to face challenges and to set out on journeys to uncertain endings. Yet, they do not know how to give up. And once they succeed – because they like any hero they always succeed – change is created. (https://www.youtube.com/watch?v=QOKKUSwEaxg).

Shannon's speech "Be an action hero: The philosophy of Bruce Lee" (TEDx, 2015b) was 75 years after the birth of Bruce Lee. Arguing the case for Bruce Lee to be recognised as an innovator in fitness, films and the martial arts, as well as breaking barriers in white-dominated Hollywood. Shannon called people to become "practical dreamers" like her father, whose words around being an authentic human begin help to close the message to the audience:

> This is why we are still talking about Bruce Lee 42 years after his death. This is why there will never be another Bruce Lee because he started from the very route of his being as he asked 'how can I be me?" And he operated form that place of his heart and what he wanted to create out in the world. And he gave it to us – he expressed that out into the world. What people care about, what people are passionate about – and they are looking to make an impact… (Lee, 2015)

The impassioned TEDx talk resulted in 417 largely praising comments – particularly from men who held Bruce Lee as their idol while growing up. There is even another TEDx talk on "the hidden power of Bruce Lee that we all have" by Mary Cheyne (2020a), a public speaking coach, who calls for listeners to follow our intuition, which she regards as our overlooked superpower. Many of the famous scenes from Bruce Lee's films – such as "Lao's time" in *Enter the Dragon* (1973) – are used as lessons for life, and there is even the influence of Shannon Lee, whose The Bruce Lee Podcast episode on the self-inquiry approach of intuition inspired Cheyne to create such a talk.

Like Cheyne and other TEDsters braving the crowd to talk about the philosophy and legacy of Bruce Lee, Shannon is not a renowned martial artist or instructor herself, although she does detail lessons learned from the unbeaten, world champion American kickboxer Benny "the Jet" Urquidez and his wife, who is a native American healer. Shannon reveals that she has also learned Jeet Kune Do under Ted Wong, one of Bruce Lee's closest students and dear friends. However, due to his premature death during her infancy, Shannon never directly trained under Bruce Lee, but she does recall his rare essence and love for her, which she sums up as his energy. And it is the energy of water that Shannon is able to examine in great depth, with useful examples from how water always finds a way through obstacles (as noted in the flooding of her office building!).

Indeed, Shannon is very confessional and humble in her writing style, offering insights into her own bad habits (such as excessive consumption of sweet food and her chronic lack of self-confidence), which are analysed in depth. For example, the indulgence in sweet food was put down to the day of her father's funeral, in which a kindly old man offered the four-year-old Shannon some candies to make her feel better. Shannon does not have the incredible confidence of her father, and besides her shyness, she admits that he would never expect her to be like him. Instead, readers are encouraged to discover their own Kung Fu, which does not have to pertain to the martial arts. The compound term Kung Fu, when broken down into their Chinese characters mean "skill achieved over time and effort", which means that academics can have Kung Fu in writing and teaching and chefs can have Kung Fu in cookery. In *Be Water, My Friend*, we are encouraged to develop Kung Fu of ourselves in order to truly understand our limitations and how to overcome them. This reflects the "my friend" aspect of the reassuring utterance, and the book takes an informal, relaxed and friendly tone to follow suit.

Like many of the martial arts self-help books, Shannon Lee encourages the readers to start small, first beginning in one's mind, bodies and homes. Martial artists very often sweep the floors of the studios in which they train, and they almost always put the crash mats and their equipment away after the class – something my own HEMA instructor noted as being a distinction between a martial artist (someone how lives and breathes the martial arts and their virtues) and a martial arts practitioner (someone who just turns up for training). Lee therefore encourages the reader to start changing their lives by tidying their apartments. We can move onto using affirmations (a technique in both Christian and secular self-help) to develop positive thinking habits that might lead us to follow a more fulfilling life. Much of this water metaphor relates to the mind and the habits we develop over a lifetime: "My father bids us to cultivate 'a mind that has no dwelling place but continues to flow ceaselessly and moves beyond our limitations and our distractions.'" (Lee, 2020, p. 170). Throughout the book, Shannon makes use of her father's original words written in his journals and notes:

> We are always in a process of becoming and nothing is fixed. Have no rigid system in you, and you'll be flexible to change with the ever changing. Open yourself and flow, my friend. Flow in the total openness of the living moment. If nothing within you stays rigid, outward things will disclose themselves. Moving, be like water. Still, be like a mirror. Respond like an echo. (Bruce Lee in Lee, 2020, p. 156–157)

However, self-help books do tend to over emphasise the potential for individual to change their lives through their unique avenues for agency. The first self-help book – literally called *Self-help* (Smiles, 1859) – blamed poor people for their socioeconomic status due to laziness, which of course ignored the working conditions and poor pay of the time. Like the vast majority of self-help books, *Be Water, My Friend* put the onus of responsibility almost entirely on the individual. They do not adopt the sociological imagination (Mills, 1959) to consider the social structures that might restrict people in achieving their life aims, as in nationality, gender, sexuality, social class and disability. There is little consideration of partners, family members or wider communities, neither. However, it is reassuring to know that not even Bruce Lee was perfect (Shannon notes his fiery temperament), while observing that the warriors also face fear:

> Warriors also feel fear, but what they don't typically feel is insecure or unsafe. They don't feel unsafe because they know they have the tools and the skills and the confidence to solve their own problems or to meet failure with grace; they know they are in cocreation with their life and all the lives around them. They choose when to act and when to stand down. They are deeply in touch with their abilities, and so they can move swiftly over the gap and move definitively within the void to take action in the face of a beautiful flowing stream or a raging storm, whatever it is that shows up. (Lee, 2020, p. 187)

This is perhaps a romantic ideal of a warrior and man, who will undoubtedly feel insecure and unsafe at some point in their lives. Bruce Lee, for example, had a fear of drowning as he could not swim (Thomas, 1994). In terms of the research theme of the Eastern stimulus and Western response, the attractive packaging includes golden Chinese dragons on the front cover and black dragons at the start of each chapter. Bruce Lee was both Western and Eastern in terms of his heritage, residence and education, and Shannon Lee (2020) blends both sides of this legacy in her writings. She has trained in Western kickboxing and enjoys jogging like her father, and while she has an Anglicised Chinese surname, she uses modern American slang to convey her message to contemporary readers. The recent 2019 Martial Arts Studies conference on Bruce Lee's cultural legacies revealed numerous legacies as an icon, actor, writer and founder of Jeet Kune Do.

For Shannon (Lee, 2020), one of Bruce Lee's overlooked legacies is his status as one of the underrated philosophers of the 20th century. Some argue that Lee's crucial legacy was that of anti-racism, with his acceptance of Black and ethnic minority students among his fold, which was followed by a cult following of people from all walks of life. Shannon Lee (2020) emphasises the unique nature of Bruce Lee, who never sought to emulate another fighter, leader or actor:

> Bruce Lee was so quintessentially himself that no one else would ever close to truly imitating himself. The way he moved, the sounds he made, the way he spoke, his handwriting, his musculature, it was all artisanal – crafted by his own hand and through his own effort. He didn't seek to create himself in anyone else's image. He sought only to be *himself*. And that he did magnificently. I think this is the thing we sense in him when we see him - that he is somehow this heightened version of what is possible in a human being, and it feels extraordinary and exciting. (Lee, 2020, pp. 188–189, my emphasis)

The book closes with realistic advice on how to live in a genuine fashion as a true individual:

> Maybe, in the cultivation of you, you become someone who does what they say they are going to do, someone who is real and fully present, someone who is skilled because they have put time and effort into practicing something important to them, someone who has great energy that uplifts everyone they come into contact with. It doesn't have to come with a name attached – such as greatest martial artists of all time, Nobel Prize winner for literature, employee of the month, best mom ever. Remember, names create limitations. Those labels only describe one aspect of your total humanity. But if we have to have a name, then perhaps it can be "human, fully expressed." (Lee, 2020, p. 224)

Shannon Lee has continued to manage Bruce Lee's legacy and estate, adding to the literature and knowledge on the martial arts icon through the Bruce Lee Podcast and her writing of *Be Like Water, My Friend* along with her TEDTalks. In one of the more recent public talks (TED, 2019), she positioned herself as a student of Bruce Lee and a student of her own life (https://www.youtube.com/watch?v=TSDOXxlT0U0). Shannon explained in the video that her mother noted that there were not multiple Bruce Lees (e.g., on and off the camera), but one genuine Bruce Lee expressing himself and having faith in himself. She stressed that her father's philosophy was an evolving one that he lived. She asked: "Do you get there as an amateur? Are you sloppy? Are you wild, are you chaotic? Sometimes you do get lucky, sometimes you're not lucky. Or, are you a warrior? Are you confident? Are you focused? Are you skilled? Are you intuitive? Are you expressive, creative, aware? Such virtues of the warrior are also promoted by Geoff Thompson in his martial arts self-help text examined next.

Warriors of the 21st Century

The white Englishman Geoff Thompson is quite a different figure from Shannon Lee, although he is proud to be compared to her father Bruce Lee for his influence on the martial arts, often quoting the claim from Black Belt Magazine U.S.: "The most influential martial artists in the world since Bruce Lee." *In Warrior: A path to self-sovereignty*, Thompson (2010) is similarly frank and unapologetic in his writing style, and he recounts tough experiences as a doorman in his hometown of the post-industrial city of Coventry in the West Midlands of England. Although retired from this profession of the night-time economy, Thompson often used door work as a metaphor for life. For instance, when working outdoor a club with a trusted colleague, several local gangsters wanted to enter the club. However, Thompson was adamant that this would not be possible, for once the gangsters had entered the establishment, they would start to set up their home there. He likens this to vices such as addictive behaviour, which once instilled in the person, will be very difficult to extract from their brains. Neurological research has looked at gambling addiction and how the brain is activated by images of gambling. Thompson (2010) wishes to help people avoid these temptations by instead working on their bodies as the basis for all that they do in life. As a pioneer in reality-based martial arts training, Thompson suggests readers to train in boxing, Judo and wrestling clubs because these combat sports typically uphold high standards, rather than other systems in which there might be brilliant teachers and schools in one city, but a poor one nearby. The Chinese martial arts examined earlier in this book are generally overlooked – quite possibly due to the immense variety of styles and interpretations in systems such as Wing Chun.

Thompson (2010) views the warrior as the archetypical perfect human being – far removed from the modern sedentary and overweight person that he disdains. This contrasts to the Thompson's idolised masculine, lean, muscular and attractive figure. In the beginning of *Warrior*, Thompson harks back to our roots as early human hunter-gatherers fighting against sabre-tooth tigers. As a working-class man with an abusive childhood, he sees traumatic experiences as being the fuel for his own excellence as a writer. Negative emotions such as fear can be channelled as energy, as he admits to being sexually abused a seven-year-old boy, which became the reason for him being so prolific. Indeed, Thompson does not hold back in his discussion of tough topics such as people's addiction to pornography on the Internet, which he sees as a major problem in society. He even advocates avoiding the popular press, which he classifies as forms of pornography or "filth." Like the other martial arts self-help writers, Thompson (2010) urges us to return to the present moment – being attuned to the people with whom we are dealing with at the time. Like Shannon Lee (2020), he urges readers to maintain a tidy home as a basis for one's life projects. Moreover, he considers the vital role of hygiene for the person's development. Using stories of his own students, he explains how some of them issue a terrible smell that reveals poor self-care, while other students was able to beat cancer through controlling his diet – what Thompson (2010) explains as "his palate." Thompson's own palate has been tempered after years of alcohol abuse, and he now averts from drinking fermented beverages and unhealthy foods, and is moderate in his sexual activity after being a self-confessed sex addict.

However, Thompson (2010) does connect with many of the self-help gurus in his pursuit of wealth, fame and spiritual authority. He even sees money as an extension of energy, and through that, an extension of God. With more investment of energy, the more we are returned with in terms of ideas and rewards from these. Thompson's (2010) vision is a bold one, as he perceives the way of the warrior – a physically active, health human being – as possibly the only route to our survival as human beings. This is especially evident in the blurb of the book:

> We are no longer at the bottom of the food chain. The tigers and the lions and the Man-enemies of antiquity are safely caged and emasculated in public zoos and national parks. But new enemies have emerged and they are insidious masters of stealth: the illnesses, viruses and diseases that largely exist in contemporary society because of man's penchant for excessive consumption and his lack of physical activity. With the need for hunting and gathering and living off our wits rapidly declining, the under-used physical body is becoming less of a sinewy working tool and more of a cumbersome liability. We have lost not only our desire for the warrior mentality; we have lost our reason for it. Infirmity is kicking sand in all our faces, and this has to change if we are to survive as a species.

There are some contradictions between Thompson's vision of our hunter-gatherer ancestors and the accumulation of luxury goods such as his Jaguar XR car mentioned in the book. It is also important to point out that Thompson's is a distinctly male voice and audience in this book, which differs to the two books written by women that I have explored in this chapter. Following this argument, we can note how viral diseases are being replaced by neurological ones, although COVID-19 has shown how viruses could still be deadly even in technologically advanced societies. In *Burnout Society* – originally published in the same year as *Warrior* – the acclaimed Korean-German philosopher Han (2015) examines the global order left by late modern capitalism, also known as neoliberalism – a system in which the individual is given greater credit and responsibility for their achievements as long as they fit within the logic of the market. In such a burnout society – named as such because people tend to burnout within it – we become our own commodity to be sold and branded.

Self-help books and the related courses, talks and retreats fit this model, as individuals seeking ways to help themselves buy numerous texts and subscribe to podcasts and other forms of social media in order to receive pearls of wisdom from the modern martial arts gurus – a term often shunned by these experts, who prefer terms such as "teacher" or "guide." We can listen to these self-help books while exercising on a treadmill or bicycle or while relaxing in the bath, as I often do. However, Han (2015) notes that such multitasking puts us back into survival mode, as all other animals multitask when they eat, watch out for predators and keep another eye out for their mate. For him, we have turned from disciplined subjects of the 19th and 20th centuries (as posited by Michel Foucault) to achievement subjects concerned with building our CVs and continually self-promoting ourselves. This is certainly relatable in academia, with serial tweets and an obsession with publishing more and more.

Notions of the warrior do of course follow cultural conventions (as we will see in a later section on the Mexican martial arts in Chapter 7), and Thompson's own version is a predominantly Western one, as evidenced by the front cover of his book, with the shadow of a man lifting what appears to be a medieval longsword. His ideal of self-sovereignty has its benefits in how might help people become more assertive, but it of course has its limits as agency always does. The next book explored before adopts a Chinese framing of the warrior, albeit written by another Englishman who learned Kung Fu from a Welshman.

A Traditional Chinese Warrior Archetype

Another martial arts self-help book based on a warrior ideal is *The Way of the Intelligent Warrior* by Steve Jones (2004). Like Thompson, Jones is also a competent martial artist who has worked as a doorman – this time in the larger metropolis of London. As a practitioner of Wing Chun Kung Fu, Jones continued the Body Mind Spirit system of his late mentor Derek Jones (no relation), the Welsh Wing Chun innovator who was inspired by none other than Bruce Lee – as seen in a 2017 documentary available on YouTube. Sifu Derek Jones moved to London to learn under one respected senior Sifu (Victor Kan), until he found a later mentor in William Cheung in Australia (Traditional Kung Fu, 2017). This singular devotion to his teacher's legacy differs to Geoff Thompson's electric approach of mixing Western combat sports with Japanese arts, as Steve Jones considers Chinese medicine as the guiding point for his interpretation of Wing Chun. Indeed, in his text (Jones, 2004), he admits to feeling that the focus on combat sports or reality-based combat overlooks the more holistic side of the martial arts. However, he points out that both Eastern and Western medical paradigms are united in their consideration of a healthy spine and nervous system as being the basis for good health. From this foundation of sound posture and balance of physical, mental and emotional faculties, Jones (2004) claims that one can command "personal power." On the cover of his book, with Jones in a calm and poised Wing Chun position, several such claims include:

> Win at work
> Sharpen mental focus
> Be socially confident
> Strengthen your health

However, the changes in the individual's body and mind move to the realm of social competence, which might appeal to those shy, socially awkward people struggling to make friends or form relationships, while even the avid martial artist would be tempted to enhance their health – something that is often preventative (rather than curative) in the Chinese martial arts. These supposed social skills and emotional intelligence complements the self-defence and awareness skills that the martial arts training offers. Nevertheless, with many self-help books, these transformative claims are of course hard outcomes to exactly measure, especially if we take the holistic approach of Chinese medicine and philosophy. On the back cover, potential readers' inner desires and concerns are highlighted with the following three questions:

> Do you want to feel confident and balanced every day?
> Do you want to focus on your goals and achieve them?
> Do you want lasting physical, mental and emotional health?

There is a focus on longevity required to achieve such lofty objectives, and this begins with correct alignment and posture in order to avoid problems later in life. Jones (2004) gives everyday examples such as using a backpack to balance one's shopping rather than using carrier bags, which can lead to imbalances and stress on the vertebrae. Moreover, the reader is encouraged to avoid excessive emotion such as angry outbursts while remaining calm in the face of adversity. However, it is important to note that Jones does not present any credentials as a qualified psychologist, counsellor, negotiator or meditator. This is common in self-help books, whose authors often claim to have the knowledge and skills to write and teach about these topics. As in many how-to martial arts books akin to the *Bruce Lee's Fighting Method* series (cf. Lee & Uyehara, 1977), Jones's text offers several clear images of him and his senior students working on core drills and self-defence scenarios. These photos show the normal human reflexes involving visible tension across the face and neck, which contrast sharply with the calm responses seen in the expert execution of technique within the book and its front cover. Like many Wing Chun instructors mentioned previously, Jones (2004) combines the martial art with Qigong (what he calls Chi Kung) training to help develop a calm and ready disposition for listening inside the body and mind while being alert to one's surroundings.

The Intelligent Warrior, like the other two books examined in this chapter, demonstrates how the underpinning philosophy, training methods and specific techniques of the martial arts can be used to offer structure in people's lives. A single, affordable and accessible book that can help a person become successful in their career while having greater mental clarity and emotional control will no doubt interest many readers who are fans of popular psychology books such as Goleman's (1995) *Emotional Intelligence*. My own Taijiquan instructor (David), the former owner of my copy of *The Intelligent Warrior*, kindly handed Jones's (2004) book to me after a clear-out of his old martial arts library. Having moved from a strong background in Karate, David had briefly flirted with training in other martial arts until he found the art for him, Taijiquan and broader Daoist internal arts. However, he, like me and many other martial arts aficionados, have found solace and enjoyment in reading about other people's martial arts journeys – especially in terms of the positive transformation that these martial artists perceive their art to offer them and other people.

Discussion: The Commercialisation of Self-Help over Collective Help Communities

Although now associated with New Age spirituality and non-European religious traditions, self-help initially developed in the more religious climate of Victorian Britain – with Smiles's (1859) first-ever book on the topic using that very name for its title. The influence of the British imperial reach was accompanied by the wider commercialised and more secular industry that really developed in the United States in the early-, mid- and late-twentieth century as the U.S. became the world's dominant superpower. As stated earlier, this self-help industry is worth as much as somewhere between 11 and 13 billion dollars, with no signs of abatement. Estimates on the value of the self-help industry vary, but the calculations are in the billions of dollars. Katz (1993) noted that the very definition of self-help suggests a person's autonomous effort to solve a problem. The term self-help did actually involve a sense of social action, as in self-help housing movements.

Other authors in the late 20th century advocated self-help as understood by individuals being able to gain strength from a community of people who share common experiences through self-help organisations. Sectors such as education, health care and human service fields were such possible avenues for shared human flourishing. However, this is rarely the case with literature, with gurus, influencers and movements making self-help being about advice to an anonymous reader (of books) or listener (of audiobooks). This individual uses self-help in their search for meaning, although writers in the 1990s, such as Simonds (1992) alerting to the fact that the genre tends to recommend individual change rather than social change. The structure is set out for the individual in terms of how they slowly but steadily progress through a martial arts system, and how they can organise their day through pre-existing routines. This suits out increasingly individualised and often isolationist society, with many people living alone or remaining single, and with many others feeling the sense of loneliness. Such issues have only worsened due to the COVID-19 pandemic, leading many people to feel frustrated and alone.

As an unregulated industry, self-help is becoming increasingly varied in its medium of transmission, with Schueller and Parks (2014) raising concerns about issues of motivation and engagement, the variety and flexibility of the exercises and the fit between the person and the activities most suitable for them. These psychologists predicted that "the future of self-help involves spreading these practices through classes, workshops, books, and increasingly prevalent technologies such as Internet sites and mobile applications" (p. 145). We have seen this with martial arts as self-help, with books and audiobooks being downloadable and mobile – all accessible from a device as one multitasks, reading a PDF while on a treadmill or listening to the wise words of an author while in the bath. I know some martial arts classmates and students who listen to audiobooks during their travels as delivery drivers and busy professionals, texts which then stimulate their storytelling and inspiration during informal conversations in class. Some critics, such as the celebrated philosopher Byung-Chul Han (2015) in *The Burnout Society*, highlight the fact that this multitasking is in fact a characteristic of animals in the wilderness: eating while looking and listening for predators while also checking on their mates and offspring. New technology might inadvertently lead to greater stress on the neurological system, with Han arguing that we live in the age of such widespread illnesses as achievement subjects. It is increasingly difficult to access the authors of martial arts self-help books, but can always tune into The Bruce Lee Podcast co-hosted by Shannon Lee or watch an inspiring and dynamic TED talk with her or Geoff Thompson.

In her poignant critique of self-help, McGee (2005) notes that self-help books help to reproduce "the figure of the reasoning, self-inventing, and self-mastering individual[…]a self-interested, rational and calculating subject maximising her individual opportunities through a regimen of time management" (p. 4). There is most certainly a gendered theme, as this trope therefore reinforces the American ideology (and myth) of "the self-made man" seen from the time of Benjamin Franklin. McGee asks the question: what about women and people of colour? "The ideal of self-invention and self-mastery that hails from a culture where someone else's labours (that of wives and enslaved persons) would provide for the necessities of daily life." (p. 9). Similarly, Riley, Evans and Anderson (2019) rightly pointing out that the early self-help books were written by men for men wishing to be more reputable and prosperous. However, the example of Shannon Lee shows how the words of a powerful male figure such as Bruce Lee can be used by a woman to improve the wealth of her family. Nevertheless, it is important to point out that Bruce Lee's success can also be attributed to his widow Linda Lee Cadwell's devoted work as a wife and mother of his two children. In fact, in an interview with Thomas (1994), Linda confessed that Bruce Lee did not know how to even boil water, as she would always cook for him. Kim's

(1991) earlier self-help book pointed the way to a new genre of women writing about martial arts wisdom and personal experiences, although there are far fewer autobiographical accounts in the marketplace (e.g., Fox, 2007 on a vicar's wife's journey through Judo).

This focus on minimising perceived problems and strengthening desirable attributes continues, as they Riley et al. (2019) note: "Self-help offers us the promise of becoming "better": Better people with fewer character flaws, or with more desired characteristics such as charisma, confidence and self-assurance" (p. 3). The martial arts texts and writers explored in this chapter certainly follow this ongoing trend in terms of eliminating habits perceived as "bad" and improving qualities seemingly far removed from fighting, such as the personal financial management and the control of vices. One critique of self-help is its continual identification (and perhaps fabrication) of the person's potential flaws, which might lead to mental health issues through an image of endless insufficiency. McGee (2005) develops an evocative understanding of the consequences of this:

> The literature on self-improvement defines its readers as insufficient, as lacking some essential feature of adequacy – be it beauty, health, wealth, employment options, sexual partners, marital happiness, or specialized technical knowledge – and then offers the solution. The resulting contagion of insufficiency constitutes the self-improvement industry as both self-perpetuating and self-serving. While the purchase of a commodity – mouthwash or dandruff shampoo – was once the route of some interpersonal social security, today the simple purchase of a commodity is insufficient: altogether too easy. Instead, one must embrace a lifestyle, a series of regimes of time management or meditation, of diet and spiritual exploration, of self-scrutiny and self-affirmation. (McGee, 2005, p. 8).

Martial arts have a key structure, as in the way to stand, move and hit, as well as the temporal aspect of daily and weekly routines. Many practitioners of martial arts have made bold statements around "martial arts saved my life", as seen in Georgia Verry's Fight Back Podcast mentioned in the introduction to this chapter. In a recent Taijiquan class, my instructor admitted to going through a period of work-related stress and anxiety in which Taijiquan was "quite literally life saving for me." However, those voices represent people's experiences under the tutelage of a teacher among a wider learning community in a physical space, rather than an isolated individual reading or listening to a book. The martial arts helped the person, rather than the person truly helping themselves (which self-help is supposed to be). The structure of martial arts is therefore beneficial to the self-growth, self-development and self-discovery because it is part of broader social structures of lineage, family, governing bodies and comradeship.

Concluding Comments

We have already seen how, in a short space of time, the Chinese martial arts such as Wing Chun and Taijiquan (as with wider forms of art) are varied in their interpretation and delivery in real-life classes in Britain, and this includes the merging of Asian martial arts with (largely Western) therapies and even the creation of bespoke martial arts therapies around the world. This chapter has turned to the expanding sub-genre of martial arts books as representatives of the more established division of self-help books. These books have existed since the late 20th century, but they have expanded in scope and format in the last two decades. Geoff Thompson's various texts all draw from his biography as a former bouncer (and streetfighter) and experienced martial artist, while Shannon Lee's recent book makes use of the friendly words and 1960s counterculture discourse of her father, Bruce Lee, to teach us to flow (and be) like water. Steve Jones's one-off and lesser-known book follows a similar Chinese philosophy through its pursuit of balance in the body, mind and spirit – crucial to his own style of Wing Chun Kung Fu of the same name. The more commercially successful texts are now supported by podcasts, audiobooks and TED talks and YouTube videos that reach out to wider readers, viewers and listeners. All three books draw on the notion of a warrior being a perfect (and perfectible) human being (man!) that we can strive to emulate and become.

As with Eastern movement forms such as yoga and qigong intending to reduce stress and build better mind-body integration (see Brown & Leledaki, 2010), there are many transformative claims of the martial arts in flyers, posters and now self-help books and audiobooks emerging from the 1990s to the present day. Some organisations claim their arts to be about the unification of mind and body, while others focus on the mastery of movement and character development among children. The individual self can be protected, nurtured and cultivated through actively participating in martial arts training alongside reflection, introspection and theorising about this. However, this is rarely achieved alone, as people will talk about self-help books with others, and might try out new routines such as jogging with their partner, friends or family members. Self-help is perhaps an oxymoron, as even reading a book written by another person is a way of seeking or receiving help.

Although self-help has been associated with cooperative self-help groups (Riessman, & Carroll, 1995), research has begun to critique the latest approach to self-help through individualist literature (Rimke, 2010). An excessive focus on the self can lead to self-obsession and unrealistic expectations and pressure to be positive and happy all the time. Humans have the right to be angry or sad about an event in their lives, and they are welcome to question their identities and test new ones are they move through the life course. Critics of self-help, as in the TED talkers (2020a, 2020b) mentioned earlier, point out that self-help preys on supposed weaknesses in a broken person who needs to be fixed. Future analysis of these sources might provide descriptions of how such self-help narratives are created for specifics genders (or non-genders!). The martial arts self-help books are a more holistic approach to self-help that is not so concerned with financial power and the reproduction of the capitalist system, although they cannot be removed from it, as the self has become our most valuable commodity in contemporary in which we are encouraged to increase its value, think positively (through positive psychology) and develop that all-important "great personality." As such, the values of the marketplace are taken into the values of the person.

However, the books examined in this chapter do share common aspects of the self-help genre through the authors' impressive credentials, accessible and relatable writing style and confessional tales about their own struggles with issues such as other people's harmful behaviour and toxic relationships that they needed to end. As martial arts are the product of many people's hard work, the principles and strategies of these fighting systems can be reimagined and repackaged and accessible human development manuals at very affordable prices – without the insurance, membership fees and physical pain of entering a gym or dojo. However, the actual subscription to verified martial arts schools remains the norm, for good reason: We need a regular, qualified teacher to guide through a legitimate martial art. Yet the martial arts are still an unregulated industry that is more policed by internal critics and trolls online. We turn next to the continued commercialisation of the martial arts through what is now known in a pejorative yet comical fashion as the "McDojo" phenomenon: a grass-roots critique of hyper-commodification and the perceived dilution of martial knowledge and applicability in real combat.

References

Brown, D., & Leledaki, A. (2010). Eastern movement forms as body-self transforming cultural practices in the West: Towards a sociological perspective. *Cultural Sociology, 4*(1), 123–154.

Fox, C. (2007). *Fight the good fight: From vicar's wife to killing machine.* London: Yellow Jersey Press.

Gallo, C. (2014). *Talk like TED: The 9 public speaking secrets of the world's top minds.* London: Macmillan.

Goleman, D. (1995). *Emotional intelligence: Why it can matter more than IQ.* New York: Bantam Books.

Han, B.-C. (2015). *The burnout society.* Redwood: Stanford University Press.

Jones, S. (2004). *The way of the intelligent warrior: Command personal power with martial arts strategies.* London: Thorsons.

Katz, A. H. (1993). *Self-help in American: A social movement perspective.* Woodbridge: Twayne Publishers.

Kim, T.-Y. (1991). *Seven steps to inner power: How to break through to awesome.* Mountain Tiger Press. Available on Audible: https://www.audible.co.uk/search?keywords=seven+steps+to+inner+power&ref=a_hp_t1_header_search

Lee, B., & Uyehara, M. (1977). *Bruce Lee's fighting method: Basic training.* Santa Barbara: Ohara Publications.

Lee, S. (2020). *Be water, my friend: The true teachings of Bruce Lee.* London: Penguin Random House.

Little, J. (Ed.). (1999). *Bruce Lee: Artist of life.* North Clarendon, VT: Tuttle Publishing.

McGee, M. (2005). *Self-help, inc.: Makeover culture in American life.* Oxford: Oxford University Press.

Mills, S. W. (1959). *The sociological imagination.* Oxford: Oxford University Press.

Riessman, F., & Carroll, D. (1995). *Redefining self-help: Policy and practice.* San Francisco: Jossey-Bass.

Riley, S., Evans, A., & Anderson, E. (2019). The gendered nature of self-help. *Feminism & Psychology, 29*(1), 3–18.

Rimke, H. M. (2010). Governing citizens through self-help literature. *Cultural Studies, 14*(1), 61–78.

Schueller, S. M., & Parks, A. C. (2014). The science of self-help: Translating positive psychology research into increased individual happiness. *European Psychologist, 19*(2), 145–155.

Simonds, W. (1992). *Women and self-help culture: Reading between the lines.* New Jersey: Rutgers University Press.

Sisyphus 55 (2021). BE LIKE WATER: The Philosophy of Bruce Lee. Available at: https://www.youtube.com/watch?v=rpI9putqbg8. Last accessed 31 May 2022.

Smiles, S. (1859). *Self-help.* London: John Murray.

TED. (2020). Shannon Lee. What Bruce Lee can teach us about living fully. Available at: https://www.youtube.com/watch?v=TSDOXxlT0U0. Last accessed 31 May 2022.

TEDx Talks. (2020a). Mary Cheyne: The hidden power of Bruce Lee that we all have. Available at: https://www.youtube.com/watch?v=Sq7FxNyKURY. Last accessed 28 May 2022.

TEDx Talks. (2020b). Marianne Power: Why self-help with not change your life. Available at: https://www.youtube.com/watch?v=YWO-NbYmmFg. Last accessed 14 November 2021.

TEDx Talks. (2015a). Shannon Lee: Be an action hero: The philosophy of Bruce Lee. Available at: https://www.youtube.com/watch?v=QOKKUSwEaxg. Last accessed 21 November 2021.

TEDx Talks. (2015b). Suzanne Eder: The dark side of self-improvement. Available at: https://www.youtube.com/watch?v=wljRiAofFJ8. Last accessed 14 November 2021.

The Fight Back Podcast. Available at: https://www.fightbackproject.com/podcasts/the-fight-back-podcast. Last accessed 14 November 2021.

Thomas, B. (1994). *Bruce Lee: Fighting spirit*. London: Pan.

Thompson, G. (2010). *Warrior: A path to self-sovereignty*. Oxford: Snowbooks.

Traditional Wing Chun Kung Fu. (2017). Wing Chun Master Derek Jones documentary. Available at: https://www.youtube.com/watch?v=jB8S8R2nSII. Last accessed 14 November 2021.

5

The Restructuring of Martial Arts as Therapy

Introduction: Situating Martial Therapies

After situating martial arts as art forms open to the artist's interpretation and re-creation, I examined how aspects of the martial arts might be utilised for movement systems and self-help. This leads us to consider the potential for martial arts for human development, wellbeing, health and therapy. Martial arts and therapy have a longstanding and close relationship, and this topic is now coming to the attention of scholars in various disciplines, from anthropology to sport science. Fuller (1988), in his oft-cited review, was one of the first scholars to propose that martial arts might act as forms of self-help and therapy for psychological disorders. Martinková and Parry (2016) make a brief mention of the "martial therapies" in their taxonomy of martial activities. As a "minor category" in their interesting system focusing on more widespread activities consisting of categories such as martial sports, martial arts, martial paths and martial games, I thought that these therapies, with their international diversity and practical dimension deserved a chapter in itself.

In the first chapter of the book, I demonstrated how the broad church of Chinese martial arts, and Wing Chun Kung Fu in particular, acted, quite literally, as arts. I offered various examples of how martial arts are continuously reinterpreted by individual practitioner-instructors who, over decades of practise as research, develop their own unique approaches to teaching, training and performing martial artistry. My analysis thereby showed how martial arts are in fact artistic endeavours harnessing people's creative talents and biographies, along with their preferences and interpretations. One such interpretation of the martial arts from China, Chinese communities and other cultures, is the turn to health, wellbeing and healing seen in the aforementioned popular texts such as Ip and Tse's *Wing Chun: Traditional Chinese Kung Fu for Self-Defence & Health* (1998) and Chen and Yue's *Tai Chi for Health* (2005), which take a holistic Chinese medical view on the martial arts, viewing an inextricable link between emotions such as anger with the health of organs such as the liver. Perhaps these arts, like painting, dancing and poetry, might act as forms of therapy as has been promised in the equally broad spectrum of arts therapy. In this chapter, I seek to interrogate the idea of using martial arts as a form of therapy in the broadest sense of the word. In particular, I will explore the re-structuring of established martial arts systems to become therapies for specific populations and problems within the framework of philosophical pedagogies as established by pioneers and their partners within the specific context of a place in question.

I begin by outlining the longstanding relationships between martial arts and various forms of therapy across cultures, but most notably Asia, where there is a tradition of martial medicine. This demonstrates how martial arts can correspond with specific forms of therapy, but might also act as a customised therapy alone. Following a brief discussion of early writings on the links between martial arts and psychological and emotional wellbeing, I then turn to the noteworthy but often overlooked efforts from pioneers of distinct martial arts therapies in different cultures and contexts. These considerations are explored in detail through two personal case studies of emerging martial arts therapies in the West: fightingandspirit (where martial arts meets psychotherapy) and the Martial Movement Method (through which martial techniques are modified for physical health). I offer a local example of one initiative in South Wales: fightingandspirit (deliberately written as one word, as we shall see), developed by psychotherapist and counsellor, Stephen G. Thomas (see www.fightingandspirit.com). I am fortunate involved in this project as an academic collaborator, as we are currently planning an action research project for working with different forms of martial arts for specific issues in people's lives. The second case study is the blueprints for a more physical form of therapy that can act as exercise rehabilitation or a supplement for a physically active lifestyle: what I have called the Martial Movement Method. This leads me to introduce the Theory of 8Ps of the Martial Therapies (pioneer, population, problem, philosophy, pedagogy, people, product and place) in order to indicate how and why a person and their team of specialists might modify the martial arts for helping alleviate a particularly pressing issue in society.

This chapter offers an early summary of this work in progress, which is followed by a theoretical assessment of how and why Asian martial arts (and other martial arts for that matter) can be harnessed for people's mental health and/or physical condition – also relevant to the chapters on movement systems and self-help in this first part of the book (on Reimagining the Martial Arts). It is also supported by more recent examples of martial arts initiatives through the Trauma Informed Martial Arts Network led by Georgia Verry, an Australian innovator and leader of the Fight Back Project (see Verry, 2022a), a trauma-informed kickboxing project.

Martial Arts *as* and *alongside* Therapy

Rather than one relationship, we can actually conceive of three main relationships between martial arts and therapy: (1) A martial art conceived as a therapy in its own right; (2) martial arts medicine; and (3) martial arts adapted as therapies. To follow this order, the first relationship is that martial art *is* therapy. Branding and clever products such as t-shirts with this slogan "martial arts is therapy" are readily available for order online, as can be seen from a quick Google Images search. Some scholars contend that martial arts like Brazilian Jiu-Jitsu, although potentially injurious, hyper-masculine and competitive combat sports, can act as therapies for various forms of existential suffering for experienced male martial artists (Farrer, 2019) or even exceed them in terms of health benefits. Practitioner-oriented magazines such as *Tai Chi Chuan & Oriental Arts*, the journal of the Tai Chi Union for Great Britain (TCUGB), always contains articles communicating research on the mental and physical health benefits from a Western scientific perspective (such as for countering lower back pain and spinal degeneration) as well as more holistic viewpoints from the guise of Chinese medicine (cf. Langweiler, 2019). Taijiquan is by far the more obvious example of a martial art turned to physical (and sometimes psychological) therapy. Its focus on grounding and body unity as well as its characteristic controlled, steady movement, makes it ideal for older people with a multitude of health problems. The art has been used in rehabilitation and also as a form of preventative medicine.

Taijiquan is undoubtedly the most studied martial arts in terms of health, which leaves room for a great deal of empirical research examining how other "harder" martial arts might be adapted for health, healing and rehabilitation. Mixed methods research on a variety of martial arts and their connections with wellbeing are now emerging, as in Fuller and Lloyd's (2019) recent monograph, which draws on a large-scale international survey and local interviews with adult practitioners of numerous martial arts styles (albeit mainly in Taijiquan), offering a largely positive perspective on subjective wellbeing. Research in Europe and the U.S. by the Italian Danilo Contiero (2019) is now being conducted on Japanese Karate-do and Korean Taekwondo in terms of how older adults engage with their movements and exercises. Meanwhile, a special issue around the themes of "Martial Arts, Health and Society" (Jennings, Pedrini & Ma, 2022) explores these various studies and opportunities for applied projects.

The second relationship can be seen in *martial arts medicine*. Sometimes martial arts are trained alongside the receival of therapies, while Zarrilli's (1998) acclaimed ethnographic study of the South Indian martial art of *Kalarippayattu* in the region of Kerala shows an integral connection between a unique form of massage to prepare and restore practitioners of this "exercises in the pit" (the actual meaning of this martial art). In the chapter "To heal or to harm", Zarrilli (1998) charts how exponents in the *Kalari* (pit) are groomed to enter their apprenticeship through oiling and softening the tissues to make the body pliable and dynamic. These students are eventually trained to become both healers and fighters, and this is actually a common progression in their career in the martial art, with veteran *Gurukal* (literally, gurus or teachers as part of a lineage) working full time in their own clinics. The holistic knowledge of health is thereby passed onto the community, as these *Gurukal* also provide medical services to the local villages and towns, offering case for infants and the elderly among their young, athletic students. In rare archive footage from the 1970s and 1980s, Zarrilli (2006) has documented unique forms of massage and bone setting including those of one elderly *Gurukal* using his feet rather than his hands – another example of the artisanal nature of martial arts. These kinds of examples demonstrate that the relationship between massage, medicine, therapy and martial arts might vary within a given style and region of a country.

Even in the West, there are those Western exponents of Asian martial arts who specialise in particular forms of healing. In Victorian-Edwardian London, Edward Barton-Wright coordinated his hybrid form of self-defence, Bartitsu (an early combination of Japanese Jujitsu with pugilism, French Savate and Swiss wrestling and stick fighting), while trialling a variety of novel electrotherapies for the management of painful conditions that continued long after his experimentation with the martial arts (www.bartitsu.org). Indeed, Loeb (2010) argues that the combination of alternative medicine and consumerism intensified the growth of a therapeutic culture that is central to modern Western society (see also Madsen, 2014). Chinese migrants to Britain, for example, have brought with them a plethora of healing and medicinal practices from acupuncture and herbology to specific forms of massage. All of these kinds of clinics are now very common to find in cosmopolitan centres in the Western world. Many of the clinics, practices and courses are often culturally and philosophically aligned to a specific martial art. It is quite common for Taijiquan practitioners to train as Tuina massage therapists as they both follow a Chinese Daoist medical view of the body (Chen & Yue, 2005).

It is also common for people to practise additional forms of Qigong alongside or within Kung Fu systems such as Wing Chun (as seen in Ip & Tse, 1998) while it is not unusual for martial artists to engage in the better-known Japanese Shiatsu following years of studying the body from an Eastern perspective, even if they as people are not Asian in nationality or ethnicity. Indeed, as I have demonstrated in the UK (Jennings, 2015), there are various health paradigms competing and contrasting among the Chinese martial arts alone. Within the Japanese styles, Cynarski (2012) offers some examples of veteran martial arts instructors, such as the German Lothar Sieber, in his native Poland who are also advocates of alternative and natural medicine – an approach the author terms "martial medicine", a term translated from the Japanese *Bujutsu Ido*. He offers some reflections on his own engagement in such practices, which are an eclectic blend of therapies designed to enhance good health rather than cure serious disease:

> *Shihan* W.J. Cynarski's method contains [...] *ki-keiko* (breathing and energizing exercise), *shiatsu* massage, rules of first-aid help (including *kuatsu*), relaxing techniques, rules of healthy eating and supplements, methods of athletic renewal as well as methods of diagnosis and natural therapy medicine. The last ones are realized in cooperation with doctors and specialists of natural and oriental medicine. The rest of the elements directed mostly to a healthy person who practices martial arts; they result from a long-time experience and comprise a sort of loans from different sources. (Cynarski, 2012, p. 57).

However, Cynarski and Sieber (2015) later contended that this notion of martial arts (alternative) medicine is limited to a few channels from East Asia to Europe, while the practice of such healing is also restricted to a few institutions. In addition to medicinal and healing practices used in conjunction with fighting systems, these martial arts themselves might be reinvented in order to function as effective therapies for a variety of ailments.

The third relationship is *martial arts adapted as therapies*. To date, there has been some empirical research and writing about these therapies in more specific martial arts – as opposed to the umbrella term "martial arts" – although a relative shortage of theoretical analysis or mapping of them. These martial therapies have no unifying governing body, and are the result of pioneering efforts and experiments from inquisitive and entrepreneurial martial artists. In Spain, now the country with the greatest longevity, the Japanese martial art and combat sport of Judo had been adapted for elderly populations at risk of falling to become Adapted Utilitarian Judo (Del Castillo et al., 2018). In the southern city of Seville, practitioner-researchers of Judo have used their knowledge of sport science and exercise rehabilitation to adjust the dynamic, fast-paced wrestling art to a systematic approach to gripping, falling, rolling – even tying the belt is taken as an exercise in manual dexterity. All of these adaptions facilitate the improvement in the quality of older adults' lives. I was fortunate to learn more about this with a presentation by two of the team: a father and daughter, both Judo black belts who are even aiding their mother and grandmother through this therapy. Alongside the physical health benefits in terms of autonomous movement (mobility), the research team have examined the aspects of socialisation among people who might normally be isolated, along with the elderly participants' reduced fear of falling (Campos-Mesa, Del Castillo, Toronjo-Hornillo, & Castañeda-Vásquez, 2020).

The notion of martial arts acting as a therapy might be a strange claim given the relatively combative nature of the activities. Some scholars such as Arseny (2011) claim that this paradox is especially evident in the West, where the therapeutic ethos (of cure and revitalisation) is seen at odds with the martial arts ethos (or mortality and demolition). Yet researchers have postulated the potential for the fighting arts to be used in conjunction with verbal psychotherapy for 25 years (Weiser et al., 1995), considering them useful supplements to formal guided therapy due to their useful engagement in internal conflict with the self and others in a dynamic and engaging set of movements. For these therapists, even sparring could be regarded as a non-verbal conversation.

Following the more recent writings of Finlay (2011), one can assert that phenomenological research into mind-body connections and the lived world of practitioners is required in greater depth. This takes us to the first in-depth case study of fightingandspirit, a therapy and training programme developed not just for psychological wellbeing, but for the professional development of therapists themselves.

The fightingandspirit Project: Where Psychotherapy Blends with Martial Arts Workshops

One example of a psychotherapeutical approach to martial arts training is fightingandspirit. Stephen Thomas saw the rich potential of martial arts when working with a group of gay British men within a rural therapy retreat with them. He worked with grappling and close-range exercises to explore the men's ideas of trust and intimacy. This led Thomas to envisage a broader notion of fightingandspirit for a wider population in which in-person, physical martial arts training could be adapted according to three distinct considerations: (1) Specific fighting styles could be harnessed as a tool or stimulus for therapy; (2) a particular psychological issue prevalent in society (such as stress and anxiety) for the general public, and (3) patients/clients and even for the training of therapists and counsellors themselves.

Thomas evoked the concept of spirit in terms of the psyche, which he felt always accompanied the action of fighting in the martial arts context, and the journey through life – in terms of attitude, self-concept, confidence, awareness, anxiety control and relaxation. The ideal of the warrior is also evident in the mission statement of the pioneering project:

> Fightingandspirit believes in the psychological potential of martial arts training. We combine the two disciplines at regular training events to help participants find their inner warrior. (www.fightingandspirit.com)

This claim is repeated later on in the "About" page:

> Our training events utilise teachings and physical drills from different martial arts and explore how these can be applied to personal and interpersonal problems to help you find your inner warrior. (www.fightingandspirit.com)

Like much of the popular self-help literature explored in Chapter 4, the fightingandspirit ethos is one of discovering the inner warrior within all of us. The warrior in this context is not someone who is an overt warrior in society – one who yearns for military combat, a mesomorph who engages in street fighting or an athlete who earns money from prize fighting - but a brave, courageous and honest person who faces up to the fears and troubles that plague them and many other people: anxiety, low self-esteem, distorted self-concept, among a plethora of problems now readily identifiable in contemporary society. In this sense, an unemployed man in his 50s or a housewife in her 30s could be a warrior as could a retired pensioner in their 60s or a university academic or student with low physical fitness or a form of disability. The website stressed the inclusive nature of the workshops as well as the focus on health and wellbeing rather than fitness and performance:

> Fightingandspirit training events are designed to enhance the health and wellbeing of all participants. As such, we welcome all skill levels and no previous martial arts experience is necessary. (www.fightingandspirit.com)

The warrior is therefore tied to a mindset rather than physique, a system of values and behaviours that guide them on and off the mat. It is also open to a ranger of cultures, as the martial arts workshops include classes on Chinese Wing Chun Kung Fu, Russian Systema and the Italian school of Historical European Martial Arts (HEMA) explored in Chapter 7. Within the confines of small dojo, students connect through ice breaking discussion, volunteer their experiences and ideas through an informal circle and help to theorise about specific concepts on a white board. The conceptualisation of topics such as self-confidence are thereby co-constructed and confirmed by all participants.

The project began with the training of a trusted group of local counsellors and psychotherapists, making us of Stephen Thomas's professional network to gather together eight participants based in England and Wales as part of their own Continued Professional Development (CPD) expected of them several times a year in order to remain qualified. Entitled "Martial Arts and the Therapeutic Alliance", this was initially tested by learning the building blocks of one martial art: Russian Systema. Although Systema was supposedly developed for an elite branch of the Soviet (and now Russian) special forces (although there are controversies surrounding this claim), its focus on breath control, bodily and spatial awareness and mind-body relaxation made it a pertinent starting point for the exploration of a topic: the relationships between martial arts and therapy, and kinds of relationships (e.g., with the floor, with one's body, with other bodies) in general. It also possesses a clear warrior ethos, with its logo and key images of a burly, bearded Cossack warrior in battle. Although in the modern era of warfare far removed from the feudal imagery (and at the time of writing two years since that workshop, a period of Russian aggression in Ukraine), Systema is believed to develop strong survival skills for people in emergency situations, and is therefore highly pertinent when dealing with topics such as stress and anxiety, which are simultaneously embodied, cognitive and affective.

The workshop leader is a seasoned martial artist, Systema instructor, close security expert and psychotherapist himself, with a research interest in survival psychology. He also has a particularly strong knowledge in Russian and Soviet psychology in this regard, and he frequently refers to Russian scientists and pioneers of Systema within training sessions, as many of them are among his personal contacts. As with regular martial arts classes, a storytelling approach is also employed in this regard. The session began with a conceptualisation of therapy, which resulted in key words. One repeated and agreed upon is "relationship." Interestingly, this is a term highlighted in the official website of the fightingandspirit initiative designed by Stephen Thomas. In his words:

> We believe the *and* is a crucial element in our philosophy here at fightingandspirit. Martial arts have always offered participants an amazing opportunity to learn to trust and develop as part of a group. Equally, as experts in the field of counselling and psychotherapy, we recognise the mentally transformative potential of the mat room. (www.fightingandspirit.com, original emphasis)

The word "and" is deliberately written in red to highlight the interconnections between seemingly unrelated things such as individual human beings and martial arts and therapy. It is also why, beyond innovative branding through various outlets on social media, the word fightingandspirit is written as one phrase without spaces between words. This can be seen from the standpoint of relational sociology, in which researchers can study the interconnections between people and also constructs such as fear, pain, danger and memory: linking the past, present and future as well as the body and mind.

Following calls from sociologists like Crossley (2012), the project would follow a continued tradition in sociology that is not to focus on studying either abstract concepts of "society" or the so-called "individuals" within them, but the relationships between people in terms of networks of interactions. Such interactions exist within the mat room through partner training, demonstrations between the instructor and a volunteer and in social gatherings at the end of training sessions. Networks of interactions and relations also occur outside the safe confines of the community dojo, such as the family members mentioned in the group discussions, the teachers of the instructors who are so often revered. Real, imagined and hypothetical (and momentary) relationships with potential assailants and gangs in the street have been mentioned in specific workshops with the trainer, while the relationship between patient and therapist has been interrogated within the CPD sessions. Stephen Thomas neatly summarises the structure of the sessions as follows:

> We deliver regular public-access training events as well as workforce and professional development sessions. These sessions and events offer a combination of martial arts instruction, physical training, teamwork and discussion groups; and are delivered from either our dedicated mat space or on site. (www.fightingandspirit.com)

The fightingandspirit project has expanded to reach charities and companies in the UK. Thomas has negotiated with Bernardo's Wales, a leading children's charity, to offer events for their staff. This was not the initial approach of the therapy, which was first based on a close network of individuals, but it would enable fightingandspirit to become more financially sustainable over time and to teach people with working relationships and the issues that have been identified in today's working environment: work-related stress, anxiety and depression. To date, finance has been the major obstacle for fightingandspirit to take off from being a fledgling initiative to a movement that can have impact beyond South Wales and the Bristol region (South West England). Also, the unanticipated COVID-19 pandemic impacted upon the project by preventing the in-person, physical and interactive training to be possible. We, as a team, did not plan for online classes because of the importance of human interpersonal touch in the fightingandspirit ethos, and the project remains to be reopened at the time of writing. This differs from the more regular communities of martial arts groups that had to quickly adapt to online teaching and socialising, as seen in the Preface of this book.

The Martial Movement Method: A Hybrid System of Human Mobility

One proposed workshop for fightingandspirit was the Martial Movement Method (MMM) – the skeleton of a slowly emerging intercultural, holistic martial arts system that I had imagined several years ago in Mexico. Like many embryonic creations in the martial arts and other areas of human endeavour, this came about at an unexpected time. I was working as both an independent researcher and a freelance English teacher. One day, my business English student, a busy executive, did not show up to class. This was actually quite common among such directors and senior managers, and I always tried to maximise the opportunities in waiting to pen my ideas pertaining to the martial arts. I waited outside his office in a peaceful garden area, with my trusty small notebook at hand.

As a student of the Mexican martial art of Xilam at that time (see Chapter 7), I had started to combine various solo exercises in order to improve my posture, which had been slumped from early weight training as a teenager and an over-emphasis on anterior movements in Wing Chun. My postural health was further hampered by the fact that we live in a right-handed world in which we students of Wing Chun trained to excess on the right side, thereby neglecting the left side (actually my dominant side). This was detected in a free testing of my weight distribution and spinal alignment by a chiropractor, who then offered me a consultation. I had limited range of motion for someone my age (then 28), and sclerosis visible from an x-ray. However, the proposed treatment was expensive at the time, as I was earning a relatively low wage per hour as an English teacher and university lecturer, which necessitated me to travel across Mexico City to give classes at various establishments. So could I heal myself in some way on the move and at home during my leisure time? In my free time over that past year, I had already combined Xilam with some fundamentals of Taijiquan that I had learned through some fieldwork in one school during my PhD, plus some exercises from Wing Chun. This aimed to increase my bodily awareness, and work specific joints, tendons and ligaments as well as the postural support muscles. The variety of movements included spiral exercises from Taijiquan, circular movements from Wing Chun and low, controlled stances and dynamic warm ups from Xilam.

I had the time within my flexible schedule to map out the fundamentals of a movement and human development system. This Martial Movement Method would draw on different martial arts (hence the Martial), focus on human Movement and would be based around specific practices (Methods) that could be beneficial for health. I had found that several martial arts had a relatively small number of levels that were built upon. Wing Chun, for example, normally involves three empty hand forms that require the student to begin with the first form before moving onto the second. That fundamental form focuses on the static, standing posture in the basic stance for the Siu Lim Tao sequence. However, in order to promote verticality and posture, I envisaged focusing my first stage on sitting exercises. My experience in Xilam and other arts led me to discover that many people focused on sitting to deeply into painful stances without having the proper alignments. This Early Stage could include exercises for peripheral vision and listening, and well as postures taken from the *seiza* (Japanese kneeling I learned in Kendo) and other seated positions. The Second Stage would involve standing on two legs using different kinds of martial arts stances as in the Chinese martial arts, which tend to emphasise the practice of standing. Many dynamic exercises could accompany this standing, which would continue to enhance the practitioners' posture that was already developed from the stage of sitting.

As in Wing Chun, stepping and turning would follow the standing to form Stage Three, targeting bipedal motion. Stage Four would involve one-legged postures for balance and control, which could draw on the excellent exercises I had been learning in Xilam and Taijiquan and could also include controlled kicking. Stage Five would involve transitions from sitting to standing and on one leg. Stage Six would take this further to focus on groundwork techniques of falling, rolling and arching to develop core strength. Finally, Stage Seven would utilise objects such as chairs to make use of movements I had learned from Chinese lion dancing and other martial arts in terms of weapons in order to develop whole-body strength and dexterity. The last two stages were still very much a rough sketch, which was in part due to my far more limited exposure to grappling and weapons-based martial arts.

The Martial Movement Method is therefore an example of a martial arts therapy more obviously aligned to physiotherapy than psychotherapy. This is because of my background as a graduate in exercise and sport sciences who has worked in exercise rehabilitation and personal training before becoming a specialist in the social science of martial arts. I was far more interested in the exercise component of my study than the element of elite sport, and as a non-elite martial artist with little self-defence or street fighting experience, the turn to health and therapy seemed logical. I had postural issues that could lead to long-term health problems, and I was not the best person to coach a seasoned prize fighter or MMA athlete.

The system, still in its embryonic state, was created by one person then in his late twenties who had studied Taekwondo, Kendo, Judo, Wing Chun and Xilam with an increasing interest in the health and longevity aspects of the martial arts. This is not to state that the Martial Movement Method could not be harnessed for psychological and emotional wellbeing - far from it. Its rich potential as an open framework could only truly be unlocked through collaborations such specialists such as Stephen Thomas and the continued study of various martial arts in order to learn about techniques and the methods used to hone and harness them. Medical practitioners might see its potential for hospital rehabilitation wards. I had used some of the fundamental movements of Wing Chun and Taijiquan for stroke survivors undergoing exercise rehabilitation at my old university, Exeter. Within the Action After Stroke clinic, a voluntary group led by students that I eventually coordinated during my PhD years, I saw the fertile potential for the diversity of movement and the artistic nature of such techniques as enjoyable to perform and fun to watch – as much as potential science as established art.

In 2018, I later trialled the MMM system within a summer course on "Physical Activity for Health" at Miguel Hernández University, Elche, in Spain. The Spanish students (along with a lecturer and an international student) enjoyed moving around the room, playing interactive games of tag that required good reflexes and defences (drawn from a workshop from the Love Fighting Hate Violence campaign seen in www.lfhv.org), plus balancing exercises taken from Xilam. The seven stages were purposefully mixed in order to challenge these young, athletically gifted and physical active sport science students.

With my formation mainly being in the Asian martial arts, albeit with Mexican Xilam and now Historical European Martial Arts (HEMA), the structure based first on sitting and standing is perhaps unsurprising. If my main martial activity was boxing or wrestling, it might begin with shadow boxing or clinch work as the fundamental stages. Nevertheless, it is these precise practices that would form the basis of the system – a system that is open to permeation from new styles and various techniques. Standing meditation, Qigong, shadow boxing and even sparring could be modified to fit the different patients or clients engaging with MMM. Using this acronym adds to the expanding number of terms like MMA and HEMA in the martial arts world, and perhaps serves at offering a degree of scientific or academic credential so common in the social sciences (cf. Billig, 2016). It is a term in English that might be readily understandable and translatable into other languages. Although I have imagined the system in Mexico and was tempted by using an Indigenous language such as Nahuatl, I thought to use an English name to give it a detailed title that most people in the Anglo-American context could understand. However, unlike with fightingandspirit, the MMM lacked a coherent philosophical framework. One way to understand its purpose is through theories on bodily technique.

In between text and martial arts philosophies are the techniques that constitute martial art systems. For Spatz (2015), in his thesis of *What a Body Can Do,* technique is a form of distinct yet overlooked knowledge, while practice is a mode of researching this knowledge for academics and innovators alike. Martial arts therapies can be formed from technical knowledge in these systems that are adapted in modified practices to make them more accessible, safer or less overly combative. I have previously argued that there is a rich diversity of "techniques of the body" (Mauss, 1970) in the world's fighting systems, and these can be utilised for a holistic approach to movement beyond the original intention of learning to fight (Jennings, 2017). These movements can not only harm but also heal injuries and possibly heal people in a more integral sense. However, as noted in Jennings (2019b), attention still needs to be paid to the practices involved, such as forms, striking the air or pads and external training methods to have balanced examination of both the light and dark side of what can be (un)healthy practices. Technique, then, as a basis of analysis along practices, can help us understand the building blocks of martial arts therapy. These building blocks can be pieced together through an organisational structure understood through the 8Ps, the Theory of Martial Therapy explored next.

To an extent, both the Fightingandspirit and the Martial Movement Method projects are what Delamont and Smith (2019) called lost ethnographies – projects that, for various reasons, never came to fruition. Ideas were generated from the brief episodes of planning and training in these martial arts workshops, and there is scope for a planned ethnography to turn into an action research project with specific populations using local and international communities.

Moreover, since that time, other initiatives have taken off outside Britain. Georgia Verry is a young Australian kickboxing instructor and exercise scientist who set up the Fight Back Project using a trauma-informed kickboxing curriculum for women (see Verry, 2022b). Expanding this framework to other martial arts and specialists, Georgia set up the Trauma Informed Martial Arts Network in 2020, with the first international conference on the topic. Using their Microsoft Teams and WhatsApp groups, the network share the recent publications on the topic of martial arts, trauma and therapy and have come to the conclusion that martial arts are therapeutic, but not always therapies per se.

Discussion: Theorising the 8Ps of Martial Therapy

The two case studies of fightingandspirit and the Martial Movement Method (MMM) can offer some insight into how and why a pioneer can create a new martial arts therapy. Although different in their theory, structure, context and inspiration, we might see commonalities between them – a union of the personal and social, a crisis with creativity as seen in the Theory of Martial Creation (Jennings, 2019a). The number seven remains an important one for my research, as it is not only the number of levels in Xilam and the MMM, among other systems such as the Chinese internal martial art Yiquan, but also in my analysis of new martial arts health and healing systems. It is a reasonable number in order for most people to recall each of the elements in a list. Alongside the martial arts, the inspiration for the original 7Ps (pioneer, problem, population, philosophy, pedagogy, partners and product) came from academia. This was not from a theoretical framework in martial arts studies, but a methodological guide to conducting qualitative research seen in Markula and Silk's (2011) *Qualitative Research for Physical Culture*. In this text, I found an excellent guide for planning and evaluating research from the problems and paradigms required to understand them to the presentation of the research and the politics of interpreting them. The authors offer a clear comparison between key approaches stemming from the initial problem, which helps both formulate a rationale for the research and to evaluate completed research projects.

Nevertheless, despite the appeal of a seven-layered model, there might be an eighth P in that regard: Place, which ties to the Product. The facilities, space and equipment required will vary according to the therapy. The last P is perhaps the hardest to establish, as the bare bones of a framework can be sketched in a café or in a park with little personal financial investment. Where then, and how can the product be shared with other people in a safe atmosphere? Could the martial arts therapy be transmitted as readily as a martial sport? Judo has spread globally with relative ease, but could the Judo become therapy? Or do martial arts need the vehicle of sport to travel far and fast?

Such an approach could be followed in problem solving and planning in the martial arts, especially with martial arts therapies. Throughout this chapter, I have alluded to numerous circumstances and questions that might lead someone to established their own therapy in a very specific social, cultural and political milieu. The 8Ps of Martial Therapy is a new framework that I am beginning to explore after several presentations on the development of new martial activities, starting with a conference presentation in Naples in 2019. This was well received by scientific experts in ageing, undergraduate students, lecturers in health and several top-level Italian Karate athletes – quite possibly due to its simplicity. My theory is therefore geared towards the general public in order to be understandable to those with even a relatively limited grasp of English. In an attempt to share a comprehensive and memorable framework, the eight Ps can be understood as follows:

- *Pioneer:* What kind of background do they have in terms of professional qualifications and martial arts experience? What do they have, and what do they lack in terms of knowledge and skill?

- *Problem:* Is there a specific problem that these pioneers have encountered themselves? Or have they witnessed this problem among other people in their community or society? How is this problem a social issue?
- *Population:* What kinds of people (with the above problem) might benefit from martial arts training? How could it be adapted to their needs?
- *Philosophy:* What is the ethos behind the therapy? What are its fundamental assumptions about humanity and fighting? How might the founder's dreams link to culture, ideology and philosophy?
- *Pedagogy:* How does the philosophy connect to some kind of teaching and learning system? In what ways can people progress within the system? How must the training be adapted according to the population?
- *Partners:* Besides patients, what kinds of people does the pioneer need to collaborate with? Could they help ensure the project becomes sustainable for future generations?
- *Product:* Following all of the six stages, what is the product? How might it be sold, marketed or promoted? Could the pioneer make a living out of it, or receive some kind of aid? How might it be expanded from their hometown?
- *Place:* Where is this product design to be used? In a specialist dojo or in the open air? Could it be adapted for seated environments?

This framework could be understood as being sequential and relational. The founder might be examined first, but the list could quite understandably be jumbled to put the pioneer with their partners or collaborators. Whatever the order, the 8Ps could offer a comparison of available martial arts therapies for historical analysis and comparison or for policy and decision makers to decide on developing or selecting a therapy to trial. Following the logic of the model, we can see that martial arts therapies are thereby very specific, as they are normally created by a long individual collaborating with trusted colleagues, friends and family members. They might be similar kinds of people, such as women healing from the trauma of domestic abuse and sexual violence through a physical, rather than purely mental medium or empowerment thanks to self-defence oriented martial arts training (see, for example, Guthrie, 1995). Individual founders are commonly connected to the population and patients in question (who might be their grandmother or daughter), and they are likely to have experiences beneficial transformations from martial arts training.

Indeed, as Lantz (2002) found, the martial arts are increasingly turning from activities for individuals to those practises by families and couples, who can benefit from self-confidence, self-defence, physical rigour and values such as respect. These visionary people, working together, might be specialists in one art or they might be generalists in several modes of combat. Experts in other fighting systems and realms of human development (such as mindfulness meditation, yoga or Western forms of exercise) might be required to enhance the holistic approach to mind-body medicine outlined in the beginning of this chapter. The Spanish development of adapted utilitarian Judo is one such case, with a family and close colleagues collaborating to help elderly people in their local community of Seville. As Spain is now the country with the greatest longevity in the world, a system to help elderly people's bodily control, balance and ability to fall safely is very fitting. The final consideration is a very practical one in today's capitalist, neoliberal Western society. A therapy might be registered as a charity or civil association depending on the legislation in the country in question.

Conclusions: From Asian Martial Arts Medicine to Modern Therapies

This chapter has provided an overview of the relationships between martial arts and forms of therapy, from longstanding connections in the culturally specific system of *Kalarippayattu* to emerging cross-cultural projects such as fightingand-spirit. The Eastern martial arts have most certainly played a role in stimulating the creation and refinement of martial arts therapies in different contexts. Due to their well-established scenario, Asian arts such as Taijiquan and Judo can form the main or sole basis of a therapy. They might also be combined with Western approaches to fighting such as boxing as culturally and technically hybrid systems. The Asian systems, in particular, are readily translated to health and well-being, especially when removed from full-contact, combative and competitive practices and ideologies. However, some Western approaches to martial arts (as in MMA or HEMA) and Eurasian ones (such as Russian Systema) are now being experimented with through various approaches to psychotherapy.

Chapter 5 has presented two case studies of emerging martial arts therapies in the British context as told in terms of an action research project and some autobiographical reflections. These were used to build a case for the re-structuring of martial arts as therapies as understood through the emerging explanatory framework of the 8Ps of Martial Arts Therapy. I hope that this model is relatable and applicable for scholars, pioneers and practitioners interested in adapting the martial arts for various populations, populations and places.

It should be noted, however, that martial arts therapies are very often fledgling enterprises developed by innovative people with busy family and working lives. Without government support or commercial backing, they will remain local projects benefiting small-scale communities. Videos and documentaries on YouTube can certainly assist the spreading of their message, as can books and audiobooks in which the therapy moves away from the dojo mat and therapy room to the homes of the readers and listeners themselves. This resonates with the previous chapter on how the world's martial arts, and particularly the Asian styles, have been reinvented as forms of self-help to once again reveal and stimulate the inner warrior inside all human beings.

Now that several of the popular reimaginations of the martial arts have been covered, I turn to the second part on Reconstructing the Martial Arts, which aims to examine how martial arts professionals, influencers, commentators and administrators are trying to manage the martial arts industry. This begins with an examination of the McDojo critique, which is an attempt to criticise and to some degree police the poor practices of many martial arts instructors across the world (although most notably in the Western context). It is followed by an exploration of how some pioneering groups are experimenting with reviving lost martial arts and elements of warrior cultures in hope of connecting them with a renewed interest in martial arts as (in)tangible cultural heritage.

References

Arseny, T. (2011). Therapeutic ethos and the martial arts. *Ido Movement for Culture: Journal of Martial Arts Anthropology, 11*(1), 33–36.

The Bartitsu Society official website. Available at: www.bartitsu.org. Last accessed 12 May 2020.

Billig, M. (2016). *How to write badly: How to succeed in the social sciences*. Cambridge: Cambridge University Press.

Campos-Mesa, M. C., Del Castillo, O., Toronjo-Hornillo, L., & Castañeda-Vásquez, C. (2020). The effect of adapted utilitarian Judo, as an educational innovation, on fear-of-falling syndrome. *Sustainability, 12*(10), 4096.

Chen, Z., & Yue, L. (2005). *Tai Chi for health*. Manchester: Chen Style Tai Chi Centre.

Contiero, D. (2019). Dojo and traditional martial arts: A social community for physical activity and health prevention in later age. *Journal of Science and Medicine in Sport, 22*, 82.

Crossley, N. (2012). *Towards relational sociology*. London: Routledge.

Cynarski, W. J. (2012). *Martial arts phenomenon – Research and multidisciplinary interpretation*. Rzeszow: Rzeszow University Press.

Cynarski, W. K., & Sieber, L. (2015). Martial arts (alternative) medicine – Channels of transmission to Europe. *Ido Movement for Culture: Journal of Martial Arts Anthropology, 15*(3), 8–21.

Del Castillo, O. A., Toronjo-Hornillo, L., Toronjo-Urquiza, T., Cachón Zagalaz, J., & Campos Mesa, M. C. (2018). Adapted utilitarian Judo: The adaptation of a traditional martial art as a program for the improvement of the quality of life among older adult populations. *Societies, 8*(3), 57.

Farrer, DS. (2019). Brazilian Jiu-Jitsu is therapy: Shifting subjectivities on Guam. *Ethnografia e Ricerca Qualitativa, 3/2019,* 407–428.

Fightingandspirit official website. Available at: https://www.fightingandspirit.com/. Last accessed 19 April 2020.

Finlay, L. (2011). *Phenomenology for Therapists: Researching the lived world*. Wiley-Blackwell.

Fuller, C., & Lloyd, V. (2019). *Martial arts and wellbeing*. London: Routledge.

Fuller, J. R. (1988). Martial arts and psychological health. *British Journal of Medical Psychology, 61,* 317–328.

Guthrie, S. R. (1995). Liberating the Amazon: Feminism and martial arts. *Women & Therapy, 16*(2–3), 107–119.

Ip, C., & Tse, M. (1998). *Wing Chun: Traditional Chinese kung fu for self-defence and health*. London: Piatkus.

Jennings, G., Pedrini, L., & Ma, X. (2022). Editorial: Martial arts, health and society. *Frontiers in Sociology*. https://www.frontiersin.org/articles/10.3389/fsoc.2022.1032141/full

Jennings, G. (2019a). Bruce Lee and the invention of Jeet Kune Do: The theory of martial creation. *Martial Arts Studies, 8,* 60–72. https://doi.org/10.18573/mas.84

Jennings, G. (2019b). The 'light' and 'dark' side of martial arts pedagogy: Towards a study of (un)healthy practices. In C. L. T. Corsby & C. N. Edwards (Eds.), *Exploring research in sports coaching and pedagogy: Context and contingency* (pp. 137–144). Newcastle: Cambridge Publishers.

Jennings, G. (2017). Pursuing health through techniques of the body in martial arts. *Journal of the International Coalition of YMCA Universities, 5,* 54–72.

Jennings, G. (2015). Transmitting health philosophies through the traditionalist Chinese martial arts in the UK. *Societies, 4*(4), 712–736.

Lantz, J. (2002). Family development and the martial arts: A phenomenological study. *Contemporary Family Therapy, 24*(4), 565–580.

Loeb, L. (2010). Consumerism and commercial electrotherapy: The medical battery company in nineteenth-century London. *Journal of Victorian Culture, 4*(2), 252–275.

Love Fighting Hate Violence campaign official website. Available at: http://lfhv.org/. Last accessed 24 May 2020.

Langweiler, M. (2019). Editorial: Another year. *Tai Chi Chuan & Oriental Arts: The Journal of the Tai Chi Union for Great Britain,* No. 55, Page 5.

Madsen, O. J. (2014). *The therapeutic turn: How Psychology altered western culture*. London: Routledge.

Markula, P., & Silk, M. (2011). *Qualitative research for physical culture*. Basingstoke: Palgrave Macmillan.

Martinková, I., & Parry, J. (2016). Martial categories: Clarification and classification. *Journal of the Philosophy of Sport, 43*(1), 143–162.

Mauss, M. (1973). Techniques of the body. *Economy & Society, 2*(1), 70–83.

Spatz, B. (2015). *What a body can do: Technique as knowledge, practice as research*. London: Routledge.
Verry, G. (2022a). What does it mean to fight back against trauma? Available at: https://www.fightbackproject.com/about. Last accessed 31 April 2022.
Verry, G. (2022b). Fight Back Project. Available at: https://www.fightbackproject.com/. Last accessed 31 April 2022.
Weiser, M., Kutz, I., Jacobson-Kutz, S., & Weiser, D. (1995). Psychotherapeutic aspects of the martial arts. *American Journal of Psychotherapy, 49*(1), 118–127.
Zarrilli, P. B. (2006). *Kalarippayattu: Composite introduction* [DVD]. The South Asian Ethnographic Performance Archive. University of Exeter Arts Documentation Unit: Exeter Digital Archives.
Zarrilli, P. B. (1998). *When the body becomes all eyes: Discourses and practices of power in Kalaripayattu, a South Indian martial art*. New Delhi: Oxford University Press.

Part II
Reconstructing the Martial Arts

6

Regulating the Martial Arts Industry: The McDojo Critique

There is no other physical activity where you can claim to be proficient at without actually doing that thing. You cannot say you are proficient at basketball until you get a ball, get on the court and play a game of basketball. You cannot say that you're a proficient mountain climber unless you actually go climb mountains. You cannot say you are a proficient swimmer unless you actually get in the pool and go swim laps. For some reason in the martial arts, we have the myth of doing Kata and forms and partner drills and you'll become a skilled fighter, a skilled technician without actually doing the thing you say you're going to do. (Jerome, the Barbarian Philosopher Podcast, 2017, YouTube video)

(Bruce Lee, in Lee, 2020, pp. 154–155).

Commercalisation and the McDonaldization of the Martial Arts

The above quote by an African-American martial arts YouTuber Jerome from the Barbarian Philosopher Podcast (2017) reflects a well-established criticism from Western martial arts experts of what are normally non-Western martial arts – and what are often called "traditional Asian martial arts" in particular. These Eastern martial arts teach the practitioner the specifics of certain aspects of fighting, but they rarely fight full contact – or even semi-contact for that matter. In might be fairer to say that these arts teach people to become proficient in the specifics of the art that the totality of armed and unarmed combat. From a Western logical perspective, the martial arts are not synonymous with fighting, but slow and graceful forms (in the case of Taijiquan), dynamic weapons sequences and acrobatics (in the case of Wushu) or sticking hand (chi sau) exercises with a relatively cooperative partner (as in Wing Chun). Interestingly, in an interview with podcast host Joe Rogan, one UFC fighter explained his dislike of the term martial arts being associated with these kinds of activities, which are really about "martial skills" rather than "martial arts." This former champion claimed that to be a martial artist, one must spar and fight – when the creativity and individuality can shine through.

Whereas other people would argue that martial arts are vehicles for self- and shared cultivation or human betterment, many people consider martial arts as merely tools for fighting rather than human development, and consequently, the teacher as a technician with a narrow skillset to be treated with a more realistic set of expectations – as opposed to a mentor, guide or even a parental figure in some cases. The martial – derived from war – is emphasised of the human expression of the art in something my HEMA instructor contrasts between a *martial* art (perhaps something like most forms of Krav Maga, with little consideration of spiritual development) and a martial *art* (something like contemporary Aikido or Taijiquan). The instructor is therefore a professional paid for the class or course and nothing like a Mr. Miyagi of Western popular orientalist imagination. This teacher should not feel the need to take students under their wing, teach people about a culture, provide them with a life philosophy or take them on travels to the origins of the martial art. As we have seen with Geoff Thompson's (2010) writings in the self-help text *Warrior*, this contrasts to Western combat sports such as boxing, fencing and wrestling, which are synonymous with their activities due to these nouns deriving from self-evident action words (the verbs to box, to fence and to wrestle conjugated to the gerund or -ing form). Although there might be styles of boxing and wrestling connecting to schools of thought, Indigenous cultures or fencing masters, they are all doing the thing their name suggests. As such, there is rarely an accusation against a boxing, fencing or wrestling academy being a McDojo due to them continuously testing themselves in sparring and competition, although this will of course depend on one's definition of what a McDojo is in the first place.

In terms of etymology, the "Mc" of McDojo, is not in relation to a clan in the Scottish or Irish Gaelic sense of a clan or family (Mc or Mac meaning "the son of…"), but is in reference to the globally successful yet infamous American food chain, McDonalds, which is no longer under the control of the original McDonald brothers (as seen in the well-regarded Hollywood film *The Founder*). The Dojo suffix, meanwhile, makes use of the Japanese concept of "a place to practice the Way (Do)." The compound concept of the McDojo would in theory mean "a family-based place to practice the Way", but it in fact a pejorative term that is not respectful of the teacher's business acumen or their artistic approach to a system. According to many online definitions, a McDojo is a highly commercialised school of martial arts that is more concerned with profit than the performance of its teacher and students. It is a fitting term in as much as the McDonalds fast food chain is a very American brand that has spread around nearly all countries in the world. Indeed, back in 1993, the influential U.S. sociologist George Ritzer identified similar trends in many aspects of social life following distinct organisational and business principles – a process he labelled as the McDonaldization of society. At its heart, McDonaldization is an expression of the rationality of modernity, ironically, slowly starts to become irrational in what Weber (1904) warned of as the iron cage of our own creation. As a whole, this process of McDonaldization involves four specific principles of:

1. *Efficiency* – things are done as quickly and with little effort as possible;
2. *Predictability* – we can expect the product to be exactly the same elsewhere;
3. *Calculability* – everything is made to exact, quantifiable measures;
4. *Control* – quality control ensures the standards of the product.

As Ritzer (1993) explains, a McDonalds burger or meal is the perfect example of these four processes, as the food is constantly being prepared in order to arrive to the customer in two to three minutes. The taste of the burger patty and the bread is also predictable, giving the distinct McDonalds flavour and texture. The fries are also the same dimension and thickness everywhere, despite which city or town you might pick your happy meal up from. This is something manifesting in the 21st century in many avenues of life (see Ritzer, 2010), with talk of impersonal yet plush McGyms offering 24/7 facilities in metropolises around the world – with the same equipment, contracts and rules to enable customers to move around facilities in an increasingly mobile world. The market-driven McUniversities churn out a specified number of graduates for new industries while appeasing governmental demands will remove the need for a charismatic lecturer teaching in a personal manner with a small group of students they know well. For instance, online Multiple-Choice Quiz (MCQ) tests for research methods modules is rapid and highly efficient way to assess hundreds university students. It is very predictable, as little can go wrong (as in staff illness or absence). Moreover, and rather worryingly, staff can easily be replaced once they have created their content and tests. However, through its computational calculability, there is a focus on quantity (large numbers of students taking the test in the droves) over quality and human interaction where the lecturer / professor gets to know their students. This is particularly evident post-COVID-19, as universities continue to teach and deliver material through Zoom and Microsoft Teams, saving money on heating rooms. Many of my own students have complained about this form of learning online, even requesting face-to-face teaching and meetings with less predictability and control. However, there are no market standards and consensus among university senior managers that this is the way to go for teaching a vast array of academic subjects.

We can try to apply the McDonalisation process to the martial arts and combat sports. In terms of fighting, efficiency is a key principle in most martial systems, whether it be about being able to strike to the nearest target (as in Jun Fan Jeet Kune Do) or to flow with the opponent's force (as in Aikido or Systema). However, it is the efficiency of the business model that is open to critique. There are certainly numerous global martial arts brands that prioritise money over quality martial arts instruction and realistic self-defence training. Their founders run the business like a conglomerate and have often accrued an impressive personal fortune. These chains of martial arts produce hundreds – sometimes thousands – of black belts who are often contracted to teach through a system of pyramid selling. As a culturally recognised symbol, the belt has become fetishized. "What belt are you?" is a very common question from non-martial artists when one reveals their identity as a martial artist. The black belt did one receive a great deal of respect, although this has changed since the advent of mixed martial arts and the Ultimate Fighting Championship (UFC), which rocked the public image of traditionalist martial arts. These systems have lost their mystique, as my colleague David Brown once remarked, although they have also turned to more mystical and perhaps questionable methods and esoteric claims – something examined later on in this chapter.

The McDojo critique is largely a grassroots idiomatic expression that developed in the late 20th century United States as the Asian martial arts (then mainly Karate-do, Kung Fu, Taijiquan, Japanese Ju Jitsu, Judo and hybrid styles) became more commercial, inclusive and, as a consequence, seemingly less about realistic combat training. In a male-dominated, even patriarchal industry, it is largely spread by experienced Western male martial arts practitioners, instructors, bloggers, influencers and now those who utilise the social media of the 21st century to expose poor teaching and discredit fraudulent practices. Although the critique is largely situated in the West, this is not to say that McDojos are a Western phenomenon, as there are hyper-commercial and fraudulent martial arts schools in Eastern societies and all parts of the world. Similarly, the teachers in question (sometimes called McSenseis, joking using the Japanese term for teacher or "the one who has been before") are ordinarily middle-aged to elderly men who seem to be the target of many jokes for their quirky characters, eccentric self-presentation, rotund figures, bizarre claims and unsafe practices. In this chapter, I examine the contemporary spread of the McDojo critique against hyper-commercialised, low-quality martial arts training and education. This begins with a consideration of the humorous aspect of the critique before turning to the more serious matter of abusive teachers – those McSenseis operating in unlicenced McDojos in a highly unregulated, potentially dangerous industry. As with other chapters, I use numerous case studies including Joe Rogan of Spotify (in)fame and the YouTube influencer Ramsey Dewey, but one case is used at length due the quality of its analysis and dedication to the cause of critique: the influential McDojoLife channel seen on Instagram and YouTube.

The McDojo Critique: Between Humour and Genuine Concern

One way to instantly see the ridicule that martial arts schools labelled McDojos face is by searching on Google Images. Making reference to the high number of child black belts, some images show tiny children gearing a white gi and a black belt that is far too big for them. One meme shows a Lego figure of an old man's face on top, with a real-life photograph of a martial arts school lined up for their official group photograph, with the text reading: "I don't believe my lego eyes. 19 black belts in one school under the age of 16." Other images mock the identity politics around self-identification (e.g. in terms of gender), with one showing a woman in a uniform, with the text "I IDENTIFY AS A BLACK BELT." Memes are particular popular in contemporary society, and memes about McDojos include one of Willy Wonker from the original Charlie and the Chocolate Factory in a funny expression: "SO YOU GOT YOUR BLACKBELT IN SIX MONTHS? YOU MUST HAVE STUDIED 'THE WAY OF THE MCDOJO.'" Another meme is of a quiz show host smiling with his thumb up in agreement, with the text reading: "WELCOME TO A MCDOJO. WHERE THE STANDARDS AREN'T ENFORCED AND THE FORM DOESN'T MATTER." Other images available show a higher level of creativity, as in a made-up book "How to avoid enrolling into a McDojo for Dummies", which has aims to help the reader learn to: "Save you money; spot a fraud, and avoid grandmasters." A final example is a meme mocking the believe some people have in their "traditional" style. The text reads: "I'm so thankful that I don't belong to a McDojo. Our style is 100% traditional", which is followed by a picture of a very young man covered in medals and badges to the degree that it is ludicrous and more than likely fabricated for the sake of humour.

The martial arts world is highly divisive and political, and this is particularly evident on social media between "keyboard warriors." A short video of someone demonstrating their skills can quickly become critiqued or even turn into the butt of jokes or curt comments. I recall a short video of a dragon and lion dance event being attacked on YouTube by someone critiquing what he viewed as something of poor quality. This was quickly rebuked by one of the parents of a child in question, who asked the social media user to write to him on his private channel. The example of McDojo jokes above can of course upset those represented in them without their consent, or those who might feel connected to a particular style or organisation. A small child might not be aware that the photograph of them and their classmates might be used by a stranger in another country for their and others amusement. Some memes can be even more aggressive in terms of people's physical appearance, with images of overweight martial artists lining up corresponding with the text: "McDojos: A martial arts school full of lazy, unathletic black belts." Many videos and chat fora share an extensive list of key characteristics of what the writers or creators (the critics) see as being typical of a McDojo (e.g. with the comical Martial Arts Journey video from 2019). In numerous YouTube videos, there are shorter, more memorable lists, which include the following warning signs that a martial arts school might be a McDojo:

- Instructor stepping away (they are not actively engaged in the class, and thereby make the environment unsafe);
- There is a primary focus on children (which lowers the standards to the combative training);
- The group operate through a sheltered ideology that is narrow minded and dismissive to other forms of martial arts;
- There is an overemphasis on belts, and high charges for grading;
- There is no sparring.

Some videos and websites list up to ten or even over 30 features of a McDojo. Other videos channels, such as the one from Art of One Dojo, explain that the McDojos are characterised by excessively large classes and unclear lineage. The instructor and podcaster clarifies that arts cannot be McDojos, but the schools of those arts that are concerned with making money than the quality of its content are not (Art of One Dojo, 2020). One of its videos does not present numbered lists, but ask questions of the viewer in order to actively reflect on their own experiences of a martial art school more concerned with the quantity of students than the quality of tuition:

> Are students being corrected and monitored?
> Are they required to buy merchandise?
> Do they (the instructors) spar or physically interact with their students?
> Do people fail tests? Why are being getting promoted?
> Does the instructor disregard cross-training?
> Are many students advancing so quickly?
> Is the grandmaster only in their thirties?
> So children have adult black belts?
> Does the instructor date students? Do they behave inappropriately?
> Is the style clear? Is it named after the founder?
> Does the instructor answer or divert your questions?

I have witnessed and experienced some of these defining features in some of the martial arts schools I have learned in. My own Wing Chun Sifu has left senior students to take the warm ups and first form while making a cup of tea. However, this does not mean that the school is a McDojo, as the teacher delegating some responsibilities to their students is a common practice in the Chinese martial arts. The final indicator of no free sparring (or rolling or wrestling) is a common aspect noted by numerous commentators on social media. One video commentator noted that "you have to spar, you have to wrestle, you have to roll" in order to develop timing, range, how to set up a technique, and how to roll with a punch. This returns us to the issue of martial arts not being equated to actual fighting. However, a counter argument can be made around the fact that not all people begin and continue martial arts with the motives of learning to fight, compete or defend themselves. In an apparently safe society, people's motivations might include expressing their culture, learning about a different culture, enjoying human movement, having fun, forging a new identity and develop a strong sense of belonging. Moreover, sparring is a cornerstone of Western martial arts such as boxing, fencing and wrestling now recognised as combat sports.

Other lists of characteristics of McDojos are exhaustive, and lack any depth of analysis making them less trustworthy. There are more stable critical perspectives from martial arts influencers that are well thought out and articulate. Jocko Willick is one man who has been recommended by my dentist (a Wing Chun practitioner and fitness enthusiast) and my HEMA instructor for his presence and experience as a former U.S. Navy Seal and BJJ practitioner. Willick is tired of arguing with other martial artists about the validity of their styles, although he does share a tale on London Real (a show in which Ido Portal has featured) of beating traditional martial artist with 20 years of experience with just one year of BJJ under his belt. For Willick, the most effective martial arts for self-defence are first and foremost a concealed gun, followed by BJJ, boxing, Thai boxing and then wrestling, followed by knife and stick systems. He believes they teach the exponent humility and discipline just like the more traditionalist systems or the "voodoo martial arts that someone made up." This might be due to the real-life combat and constant testing through sparring in which the martial artists are continually humbled after being tapped out or struck – in his words, "controlling the ego so that the ego does not control me."

However, Willick's talks are more related to martial arts, personal development and self-help rather than the McDojo critique. I therefore turn to three case studies of detailed, ongoing critiques of the martial arts from notable influences Joe Rogan, Ramsey Dewey and Rob from McDojoLife. These critiques cut across different forms of social media, from audio material on Spotify to more visual, moving content on Instagram. They have very high numbers of followers, and they sometimes comment on each other's work and accomplishments (as seen in the stories in McDojoShow Episode 24 https://www.youtube.com/watch?v=D_IJNEw-O6Y). I begin with Joe Rogan, a former competitive Taekwondo fighter and kickboxer turned stand-up comedian and UFC commentator. Like many people involved in the martial arts, he took up an art as small, young and vulnerable person to help defend himself from bullies in school, and now uses his passion to become successful in conventional modern terms of fame and wealth.

Exploring "the Ancient Art of Bullshido" through The Joe Rogan Experience

Unlike many of the figures mentioned in this book, Joe Rogan probably requires no introduction for the reader. He is a man with 11 million YouTube subscribers who has a podcast that is estimated to be downloaded 200 million times a month. The charismatic yet controversial American martial arts veteran and podcast / chat show host, is well-known in the martial arts world and popular culture, although he has recently been criticised for providing a platform for the dangerous message advising young people not to get vaccinated against COVID-19. This has resulted in a backlash from famous musicians such as the Canadians

Neil Young and Joni Mitchell who asked Spotify to choose between them and Joe Rogan. With the exclusive 100 million dollar deal with Spotify in 2020 giving them all the profit from advertising, Spotify chose Rogan (BBC News, 2022). Although Rogan has since apologised via his Instagram channel, admitting that he is not a source of authority when it comes to medicine, he is not apologetic when it comes to his critique of "the ancient art of bullshido" – a pun on the feudal Japanese Samurai philosophy of Bushido (way of the warrior) that has been reinvented for different purposes (Benesch, 2014). This is because Rogan has been involved in the martial arts since his childhood, and this began with Taekwondo and has since taken him to the grappling and submission art of Brazilian Jiujitsu (BJJ), commonly referred to Jujitsu. He trains on a regular basis to stay in shape at the age of 54, with no plans on stopping when he reaches his 60s. Indeed, in one episode, Rogan shared images of Sylvester Stallone in his early seventies, showing how "shredded" he was to the other mature male commentators.

Rogan's no-nonsense approach involves him using expletives on a regular basis, with the F-word being a favourite term a la television chef Gordan Ramsay. In one episode I joined, the words "dick" and "shit" were used in the first two sentences! Besides the profanities, the format of the Joe Rogan Experience is unique, as it is all about discussing a wide range of topics with a wide range of people – something that makes it one of the most popular podcasts worldwide, and perhaps the most popular talking-based channel. Rogan's podcast episodes are often in conjunction with guest speakers and collaborators, which enables a rich and funny discussion about many topics pertaining to the martial arts – a theme that crops up in discussions about many other issues. However, the conversation can then stray from fighting to include chats about conspiracy theorists such as the FlatEarthers. Not afraid of the aforementioned profanities, which might even add to his appeal, Rogan has made enemies through his mocking of these groups, and he has undoubtedly angered many people in the martial arts communities. This includes a group of African American Kung Fu practitioners who were inspired by the Kung Fu movies of the 1970s (see Bowman, 2021). In one video available on YouTube, Rogan spoke with another martial artist about Wing Chun, noting that chain punching (repetitive straight blasts) "17 times in the head" would only really work against someone with "no clue" about fighting. "Try that against a MMA fighter" is a common conclusion to this issue, with an image of a MMA fighter being shown in the video version of the podcast. As a Wing Chun practitioner myself, I could point out that the chain punches are normally in successions of three and five blasts at a time – as seen in the Siu Lim Tao form involving three punches – but never high a number as 17!

Rogan's videos enable followers to see what he is laughing about. "The ancient art of bullshido" is often seen in short video clips of strange and ineffective martial arts practice. The video sometimes enlarged in full screen, and on other occasions, Rogan's emotive and comic reactions are at the forefront of the viewer's attention. We see him chuckle, gawp and guffaw at eccentric martial artists performing poor techniques. However, Rogan is less analytic than many of the McDojo critiques who freeze-frame videos, wind them back and zoom into the specific body parts involved in the execution of a technique. In terms of no-touch knockouts, Rogan believes this is a form of mental illness as in FlatEarth believers. One of his guests recalled meeting an Aikido practitioner who claimed: "Once I sink my Ki, you won't be able to move me." It was reported that his teacher was then moved shortly after issuing this statement!

In many episodes, Rogan and his guests debate the legitimacy of specific martial artists, asking the question: "Is so-and-so legit?" or "is so-and-so a legit martial artist?" In one episode, Rogan and a guest began to discuss the Hollywood actor and Aikido instructor Steven Seagal, asking the question: "Is Steven Seagal legit?" Due to Seagal's size and his abilities shown in videos, the men came to the conclusion that Seagal is legit, although Rogan noted "but the martial art [Aikido] is the questionable thing." Using the history of Aikido to help him explain, Rogan revealed that according to his knowledge (which he wasn't totally sure of), Aikido was originally designed to help deal with an opponent wielding a sword. This highlights the limits of the system for combat, as it is based on specific problems in combat (the force and leverage of an opponent) and society (resolving the conflict in a peaceful manner where possible). The men then watched a video of a 90-year-old Judoka, noting, "Judo is way more legit than Aikido" and then, "There are certain aspects of Karate that are applicable, but a lot of it is really limited." This was tied to the evolution of BJJ (Rogan's main martial art) from Judo. The guest was less aware that Judo had both standing and groundwork elements, which highlights the relative authority of Rogan in comparison with his collaborators. At the same time, it also reveals the bias that Rogan holds in terms of BJJ and what makes a martial art legitimate.

For him, legitimacy appears to be about effectiveness in combat in different ranges and environments. He said in one episode: "Jujitsu is all about exposing reality. A lot of martial arts put on a show." BJJ is able to expose such a reality of vulnerability due to the fact that is practitioners get checked on a regular basis – getting tapped out, crushed and squeezed by their peers and competitors. Nevertheless, Rogan admits that the ego is still important for a martial artist, as it is there to keep you alive and move from one day to the next. He sees BJJ as a very tough martial art that really pushes the exponent to their limits. When chatting with one guest, Rogan joked at how he would see the photographs of martial artists of other styles and judged them from their faces, surmising that "he's not a Jiujitsu black belt!" He and his guest both agreed that such people do not have the strong frown lines across their faces, which are caused by the physical and mental strain that the art puts people through. In contrast, they shared a story from a Ninjitsu practitioner where a newcomer challenged the Sensei to a sparring match. The teacher announced at the end of the class: "We have a challenger!" He then blindfolded himself and sat on the floor, asking the outsider to attach him. The outsider was bemused at first, but then crept round the back of the Ninjitsu teacher to put him in a naked rear choke, causing an instant victory.

Rogan holds what might be seen as a modern, Western pragmatist view on martial arts that require constant testing and competition to be deemed effective or legitimate. He often refers back to his days in Taekwondo, which provided him with a solid foundation in the martial arts in terms of sparring and experience in competition against resisting opponents. However, he is quick to point out the rigid rules and etiquette that makes him uncomfortable with more traditionalist martial arts.

Like many martial arts influencers, Rogan has become his own brand known for his unique image, voice, style and approach. His voice is distinctive, as is his image of a shaven head, designer stubble and t-shirts revealing a heavily tattooed torso. The Joe Rogan experience uses an artist's expression of Rogan's intense facial expression to provide a unique logo. While many of his guests are relatively softly spoken and mild-mannered, Rogan is gruff and seemingly more orthodox in his masculinity – giving him the position of the alpha male of the studio. Indeed, the guests tend to be adult males from North America and Britain, with few women or young people involved in the discussions.

Legitimacy is a key concern for many martial arts groups wishing to be recognised by neighbouring martial arts groups and the wider community. It is no surprise that one word is uttered again and again in these podcasts and video blogs (vlogs): Legitimacy, or more commonly, the abbreviated adjective "legit." Common questions I have encountered in my own fieldwork as "do you think he's legit?!" Or "that guy's legit!" Sometimes "legit" refers to a system, but it ordinarily correlates to how a person is interpreting, using and perhaps even appropriating a martial art for their personal gain, which can be shadier that just teaching sloppy technique at a high price. We explore this darker side of the McDojos through a specialist who devotes his time to advising martial arts businesses and exposing frauds and cults around the world. As this is now the central focus on the influencer's life, it makes perfect sense that the channel is called McDojoLife. Before that, we turn to the warnings from Ramsey Dewey.

"Is my gym a McDojo?" Advice from Ramsey Dewey

Many of the martial arts have come to the West from East Asia, having been transmitted by Asian ex-pats, migrants and American ex-service professionals. Now there is a counter flow of martial arts dissemination, with mixed martial arts spreading from the Western world to Asia, bringing with them a combination of Eastern fighting techniques (as in the knees, elbows and kicks of Muay Thai), modified versions of such Eastern techniques (as in Judo techniques adapted in BJJ) and Western combat skills from boxing and wrestling. China now has had its first UFC champion in the form of Weili Zhang, and this number is likely to increase as the People's Republic of China (RPC) continues its sporting ambitions on the world stage – from the Winter Olympics to combat sports and football (see Mangan, Horton, & Tagsold, 2020). Ramsey Dewey is an American former MMA fighter turned MMA coach based in China who has produced a large quantity of YouTube videos on specific martial arts topics. Dewey normally works alone in his videos in order to produce an impressively articulate monologue for his followers, using his smooth, silky voice that some YouTube viewers regard as his special (and perhaps wasted) gift that could be used in professional voicework. Unlike other influencers, Dewey does not use memes, video clips or images to get his point across; his cultured voice and gestures are enough to provide a convincing message. However, he has created videos that joke about topics such as knife defence, with one video showing him getting stabbed by his assistant, Jordan Chow.

Ordinarily, Dewey's videos pertaining to the issue of the McDojo are in the form of a monologue, unlike the interviews that Rogan develops. Dewey is also something of a martial arts agony aunt, taking in questions from viewers and followers who have written private messages and emails about their concerns about the martial arts. One such letter was "is my gym a McDojo?" (Ramsey Dewey, 2020). Dewey summarises this with the following description:

> Viewers constantly ask me if their gyms are McDojos. Well, are they being dishonest with you? Are they trying to teach you no touch knockouts? Are they giving you the services you pay for? Is your sensei a morally questionable person who exploits his/her students? (Ramsey Dewey, 2020a, https://www.youtube.com/watch?v=hd_3d-LdVGc).

The inquiring martial artist had noted that although several champions trained in his gym, he had picked up many injuries in the first few months. Dewey, in his characteristically honest manner, told him "you will pick up injuries in combat sports. It's not a question of if, but when and how bad." However, he was hesitant to label this school as either a legitimate establishment or a McDojo, saying "I don't know, man…" on several occasions in this video. Dewey wished for more details in the letter, noting "you're not giving me much to go on…" Without video evidence or material from the school's website, it was hard to make an informed judgement and not pass unfair criticism of a teacher and their team. Also, without actually meeting the follower in person or online, Ramsey's conversation remains limited, only engaging with the concerned martial artist over email. These kinds of questions are posed in his other videos, such as "Do I belong to a martial arts cult?", which has the icon of an excitable Ramsey with his headset on and "Where are the boxing McDojos?" (Ramsey Dewey, 2020b), where Ramsey concluded that "you cannot fake boxing."

Ramsey Dewey, like the other charismatic influencers examined in this chapter, is an advocate for Brazilian Jiujitsu (BJJ) due to the fact that is techniques are testable or demonstrable, unlike some martial arts techniques involving ripping the groin (explained in McDojoShow Episode 24 https://www.youtube.com/watch?v=D_IJNEw-O6Y). However, he has a background in more "traditional" Asian martial arts such as Taekwondo, the first style that he trained in. Since moving to China, he has also cross trained in Sanda (full-contact Chinese kickboxing) and some exchanges in Taijiquan, which he now understands as a wrestling style. Indeed, when interviewed by McDojoLife, Dewey likened the changing status of Taijiquan by making the viewer / listener imagine "if in 400 years' time, there was no one practising freestyle wrestling. People had a memory of it, but it had become an interpretive dance." He was angry about what had happened to Taijiquan (or Tai Chi Chuan as he prefers it, trying to avoid sounding the mysterios qi word) but he admitted to being impressed by the 80-year-old Taijiquan teacher of the Sanda coach he was learning from, showing his openness to new realities in the martial arts. This avoids the position of a zealot or a fundamentalist who is not open to new ideas or ideologies. Rob from McDojoLife had also admitted in a joking fashion that he would give up BJJ immediately if he was able to knock someone out with his mind.

In the same interview with Rob, Dewey wanted to distinguish between the critique of the person and the critique of technique. He and Rob had both been critical of the technical and pedagogical approach of Master Wong, a colourful character in the British Wing Chun circuit who has created many professional but funny videos on YouTube from the base of his garden. Some of his exercises include training on top of a Swiss ball or grabbing the opponent's groin "and make him eat it" in a street fight. Both Dewey and Rob noted that such techniques would be untestable outside a real fight, unlike a rear naked joke from BJJ. Dewey regarded Wong has putting on an entertaining character for the sake of humour, which does make sense given Wong's commercial success and large following on YouTube. However, he admitted to not disliking Wong as a human being, as the Sifu did have a personal discussion with him to explain his position on street self-defence. Rob concurred, admitting that people could call him out for technique and poor performances in competitions.

Ramsey Dewey has created a successful social media package composing of YouTube videos, Instagram and Twitter to develop his distinctive profile that relies on his powerful, deep voice and articulate speech. Although he no longer competes, his background as a full-contact fighter who has studied the more traditionalist arts such as Taekwondo permit Ramsey to have an informed and balanced viewpoint on different fighting systems, both Eastern and Western. Another character with such a pedigree is Ramsey's compatriot Rob Ingram, simply known as "Rob from McDojo Life."

"Keep the martial arts legit": McDojoLife and the Hunt for Martial Arts Frauds

McDojoLife was set up by martial artist Rob Ingram, simply known as Rob (to protect his identity and safety), a U.S. citizen in his mid-30s who hails from Florida. After being bullied at school, Rob took up Karate to help defend himself, but eventually admitted to matching the cliché of "the arts changed my life." Rob has engaged in the martial arts since taking up Karate at the age of 12, and he boasts of a 3rd Dan black belt in the art as well as a decent record as an amateur boxer and kickboxer, with only two losses that led him away from a path to turn professional. Rob has also studied a rare weapons style enabling him to judge a wide range of martial arts practices. He now practises Brazilian Jiujitsu – an art in which he holds a purple belt, although he admits that they are many people who "could kick my ass." One Podcast, *My White Belt Jiu-Jitsu* (2022), introduced Rob through his prestige given by *Black Belt Magazine*: "Devoted to exposing martial arts frauds as well as criminally dangerous instructors and schools that simply engage in unethical business practices." In another podcast interview with the Whiskey, Beer and Conspiracy Podcast (2021), Rob explained that during one BJJ class, the topic of the McDojos arose, and one newcomer asked Rob to further explain what this strange term meant. After a detailed explanation and set of examples, the beginner exclaimed: "Well, why doesn't anyone do anything about that?!" This provided Rob with the impetus to devote his time to exposing frauds while getting paid for this work via social media followers and subscribers. In the 21st century, martial arts influencers can make a decent living from sharing high-quality, popular content with like-minded people. He asks for financial support in order to help shut down fraudulent gyms – many of which include paedophile instructors preying on vulnerable young people away from the protective eyes of their parents and guardians. One podcast hailed Rob as the main "explosive frauds and shutting down gyms that allow paedophiles to run wild!"

As there is no regulatory body for the martial arts around the world – or even in the United States – Rob is often sent videos and links to information about dangerous, abusive and deluded teachers claiming to teach valid forms of martial arts, combat sports and self-defence. Sometimes Rob is more concerned about the alignment of the claims made by martial arts instructors with the actual product they are teaching. Taking the concept of martial activities (Martinková & Parry, 2016) explored in the introduction chapter, we can see the mismatch between the problematic umbrella term of "martial arts" and the vast number of arts, styles and systems available to the public. Martial fitness is not the same as combat sport, and combat sport is not the same as martial games. According to his episodes, Rob has no issue with cardio kickboxing or Taijiquan as long as the instructors are not claiming to be teaching self-defence or close combat.

Key to the success of McDojoLife is its clear conceptualisation of what constitutes a McDojo. In one early episode, Rob assesses different definitions of McDojos on the Internet. One common perception of McDojos is the pursuit of profit – quite possibly thinking of the Mc aspect pertaining to extreme commercialisation. However, Rob, as a martial arts business consultant, does not perceive the pursuit of profit as being a problem, arguing that profit will help the instructor pay their life bills on time while reinvesting in their martial arts business through new equipment. Rob disputes another claim on the pattern of McDojos as mainly being located in the Western world, as he has found charlatans in all corners of the globe. He also questions terms such as "watered down" and "impractical", considering that many martial arts are more for health, fitness and enjoyment.

As with many sources of the McDojo critique, the McDojoLife channels have their comical aspects that help them gain attention and regular followers. As Rob reflects in an interview: "You turn them into a meme. You make it so people can't take them seriously, and when that happens, people don't want to sign up for those classes with those people." For instance, the McSenseis in question are rated on a Likert scale (1–5) according to what Rob has coined "The Dillman Scale" (named after infamous martial arts teacher George Dillman, famous for his pressure point fight techniques and Kyusho Jitsu system). Dillman's face is used as an emoji, with five faces being the most ridiculous (and ridiculed) art and instructor. Rob explains that Dillman is selected not just because of his fanciful ideas around combat concerned with pressure point knockouts, but his claims to be able to determine – not just predict – the sex of an unborn baby simply by checking the strength of the pulse on each of the expectant mother's wrists. Using archive footage, Rob plays a short video of Dillman making these claims in a guest seminar, with a young female practitioner as standing with him.

One follower of Dillman claims to be able to knock people unconscious by hitting people on their tricep muscle – and even his mind. Coincidently, this teacher is called Grandmaster Paul Bowman, although he is no relation to martial arts studies scholar Professor Paul Bowman! Grandmaster Bowman has founded his own style of Zendroryu, giving himself the grade of 10th Dan. This connects to Rob's comments in a podcast interview: "Anybody – absolutely anybody – can open up a school and invent their own belt system." Rob breaks down videos of these instructors and their dutiful assistants, analysing poor techniques and tricks of the trade that make the audience believe that a real-life knockout has occurred. Sometimes techniques are shared to allow Rob's viewers to laugh (as in the "no handed throw", which involves the martial artist moving out of the way from a compliant partner). In a podcast interview, Rob confided in the hosts that he himself has been hit by a supposed pressure point knockout strike on the neck; however, to the instructor's dismay, this only hurt the recipient as a heavy-handed slap. Rob explained that this Karate instructor – a friend of his own teacher – claimed that the failure was due to incorrect technique. This connects to the critiques from Ramsey Dewey covered earlier.

Rob often investigates instructors who lie about their martial arts resumé. For instance, once Turkish boxing coach called Eroz was renamed as an anagram by Rob as "Zero" due to the coach's abusive and dangerous practices of hitting students in the head. The young men in his club were lined up take several shots without any head protection or defensive techniques which, as Rob rightly pointed out, would lead to concussions and eventual brain damage. Another video showed Coach Zero kicking students in the head while wearing street shoes. The students were getting kicked in the head above concrete, with no safety mats below them (or head gear around their skulls). This instructor claimed to have a very high number of amateur fights that seemed unreal. However, Rob eventually found footage of the man, noting how he was knocked down twice by a flailing, seemingly incompetent fighter in what turned out to be an exhibition fight (where there is no winner) in which both combatants were awarded medals.

In one episode, Rob broke down ludicrous claims from martial arts advertisements. One advert for a mail-order self-defence course held the following claims:

> "How would you like to become a brutally effective fighter…in just a few days?"
> "Find yourself with a gun to your back? Problem solved."
> "Multiple attackers and nowhere to go? Piece of cake."
> "Home invaders got your wife and kids? Easy!"

The course was supposed to be based on the experiences of the pioneer's friend, John, an alleged "special ops guy" who is supposed to have over 600 street fights. Breaking this claim down, Rob joked about the title of "special ops guy", laughing about how this would not be a real title in the armed forces. Sensibly, he seemed worried about if the claim of John's excessive tally of over 600 street fights was true, begging the question why John was not in jail. Rob raised thoughtful questions around topics such as: What kind of person gets into hundreds of street fights? What is wrong with them mentally, emotionally and socially? He then broke down the other claims, noting that it is impossible to become a brutally effective fighter in just a few days. Gun defence is a very difficult area of combat, as is multiple attackers – especially where hostages and loved ones are involved. These videos and their claims show how martial arts and self-defence really do need more regulation to save people wasting money and deluding themselves with an excessive sense of competence.

Another interesting video breaks down the Ron Jeremy School of Martial Arts, a school of American Kempo. As a BJJ practitioner himself, Rob was concerned about the claims made by Jeremy when it came to ground fighting and Jeremy's ability to overcome the BJJ guard. Rob used short clips of Jeremy's demonstration with his student, who lay sprawled on the floor, with his arms in a crucifix position rather than in an effective position to block and strikes to his own head. Rob admitted that Ron Jeremy had made some sound points in regards to the dangers of going to the floor against multiple opponents, although he laughed when Jeremy said "it's the girlfriend who's going to get you" and "mercenaries wouldn't fight like that." Rob laughed, imagining the eccentric Jeremy frequenting with mercenaries.

A key argument in favour of genuine or legitimate martial arts training is "the mats don't lie" and "there's no room for that fluff [invalid technique] on the mat." As Rob says in the podcast interview with Chew Jitsu (2020), noting a lack of honesty in contemporary society, "it's one of the most honest situations with another human being." In contrast, he regarded the McDojos as cults in which the instructor is not teaching the martial arts for the betterment of their student, but for their personal – and often shady – gains. In many videos and interviews, Rob refers to the devout followers of cult leaders as "drinking the coolade" – in reference to the horrific incident where American pastor-turned-cult leader Jim Jones's disciples killed themselves by drinking a poisonous beverage. Comparing the model arts groups to those of religions and cultures, Rob concluded of McDojos: "They are just cults. That's what they are. They are cults run by cult leaders for the betterment of their ego." In another YouTube episode, Rob concluded, "you're giving yourself a false sense of security more than any cult I've seen", advising people to select a different hobby that won't endanger themselves and other people. One his simple mottos is: "the mat doesn't lie," as on the mat, the martial artist can be exposed in terms of any contrast between what they claim they can perform in the guise of technique and what they can actually do against a resisting opponent.

There is a price to pay for Rob's work, as he explained in several interviews that he received threats of violence – and even death threats. However, even Rob joked that he would shut down McDojoLife if he learned to knock people down with his mind. Yet Rob reminds listeners that "you cannot fake being good at martial arts." He is living the 21st century American dream, as stated at the beginning of the interview with the Whiskey, Beer and Conspiracies Podcast: "I'm living the dream, man. I wake up in the morning, expose a fraud or two and get paid for it." Rob has over 400,000 followers on Instagram and 60,000 followers on YouTube. His Channel has been recommended by Ramsey Dewey, who asks his followers to like and subscribe it, concluding "it's a good channel", especially in Rob's relatively unique work on exposing sexual predators and convicted criminals in the martial arts. Another interesting aspect of McDojoLife is its assessment of extremist martial arts schools as "cults run by cult leaders" – something worth examining in its own section to conclude the chapter.

Concluding Comments on the "Culty" and "Creepy": McDojos as Cults?

This chapter has examined the phenomenon of the McDojo, which is being scrutinised as technology continues to develop in the 21st century. Now that high-quality colour videos and archive footage can be combined for a detailed, prolonged analysis by martial arts influencers, fraudulent and deluded teachers of the martial arts can be exposed for their shady business schemes and unethical sales pitches. Although many people outside the martial arts have scoffed at the fanciful characters of the martial arts world, many of my own martial arts teachers and groups have laughed about the charlatans, from Wing Chun Sifus claiming to be the sole inheritor of the original system to the mad exploits of the deluded Charlie Zekanoff who claimed to be an undefeated boxer with over 200 fights under his belt. Videos are often used on people's smartphones to demonstrate silly technique and exposure of fraudulent teachers. Billy Marshall, my own HEMA instructor, is one such teacher who has told me all about the likes of Zekanoff, immediately sharing a video link with me after a one-to-one catch-up via Facebook Messenger. In our socials, he sometimes walked to the end of a dinner table to show a video on his phone of what he called "Slapoeira" – making up a term from the suffix of Capoeira for a series of slaps from a no-touch master trying to defend himself from a challenger.

Notwithstanding the power of social media and video technology, word of mouth can also be a powerful tool of persuasion or dissuasion. Very recently, Billy (head instructor of the Blade Academy) shared a story with me. One friend asked another HEMA practitioner "are you going to the sparring day [which combined several local HEMA schools]?" to which the other man replied with dread, "will the Blade Academy be there?!" Billy's friend replied "yes…why?", to which the other HEMA student responded: "I was told their lead instructor is a cult leader." Billy and I laughed at this short story, and we agreed this might be due to the fact that the young man in question not having a strong martial arts background, leading to be unaware of what a martial art might entail. However, it so transpired that the young man was friends with a student of a rival school, whose instructor has had a personal disagreement with my teacher. Assessing this example, Billy and I concurred that when people think of martial arts, they often come up with images of uniforms, belts, salutes and discipline – with the camaraderie and spirit de corps that goes with it. However, in some arts, teachers do not have this structure in mind, while others go to an extreme in keeping the students controlled at all times. The latter end of the spectrum can be a cult, while the former more of a hyper-commercialised approach that wants to retain students by keeping shockingly low standards. For the hyper-commercialised martial arts schools churning out young black belts with low standards, Ritzer's (1993) McDonaldization thesis can be very helpful. Whereas, in order to understand the more secretive and controlling teachers, anthropological theories on the organisational structure of cults and the charisma of their cult leaders can be extremely valuable. I do not have space to expand on my analysis here, but these two themes could certainly be examined in the near future through long-term studies – something I would relish.

Bearing this distinction between the two forms of McDojos in mind, we can regard some McDojos as direct expressions of McDonaldization, focusing on principles such as efficiency, reliability and calculability in order to maximise profits. These large, transnational associations try to retain a large following by making classes relatively pain-free and tests deliberately designed to be almost impossible to fail. The extensive coloured belt grading scale ordinarily involves very frequent gradings for various tag levels that are significantly incremental in cost – starting cheap and finishing with very expensive exams for black belt level. Some of the McDojos have young children black belts, which shocks and sickens many in the martial arts community. These kinds of McDojos might attract many young families, making the most of the family-friendly image that martial arts can boast of. Indeed, there are many professional schools that do praiseworthy job of integrating adults with children in a highly inclusive physical culture within a wider society that is very age segregated, dividing its generations into age-appropriate activities. However, as we have seen with the cutting-edge analysis by Rob of McDojoLife, some of the lead instructors in certain schools have taken advantage of this extensive contact with young children and vulnerable teens who are repeatedly preyed upon.

Moving on from the often mocked "Taekwondo / Karate and day care" franchise, the other kind of McDojo is the cult, which I would argue to be more common among groups of adults who learn about no-touch knockouts and other fanciful ideas that are, of course, untestable and untested in real combat (or even sparring for that matter). Very often, the teachers promote themselves as master or grandmasters of a style they have created or renamed after themselves. Like some of the other forms of McSensei, they often lie about their martial arts pedigree, lineage and fighting or military experience. They can even become controlling of their members' behaviour, asking for total loyalty as if they were their liege lord. The students in such cult-like McDojos are not permitted to train in other styles or cross train with friends learning within other schools. This is despite the students actually being a customer in a highly competitive consumer market that is the martial arts industry. In the next chapter, we will turn to a rapidly expanding industry that is accompanying the globalisation of Historical European Martial Arts (HEMA) and related activities such as battle re-enactment and Live Action Role Playing (LARP) – the latter coincidentally being an activity equated with the no-touch powers. This case study accompanies an ongoing analysis of the Mexican martial industry that includes an increasing number of recently invented martial arts inspired by ancestral cultures and Mesoamerican philosophy. Both of these movements correspond with a global concern for the survival and revival of Indigenous martial arts now starting to be recognised and protected by UNESCO.

References

Art of One Dojo. (2020). What is a McDojo? Revisited. Available at: https://www.youtube.com/watch?v=rQv-KhNXvbc. Last accessed 27 May 2022.
Barbarian Philosopher Podcast. (2017). 5 signs that you are in a McDojo. Available at: https://www.youtube.com/watch?v=LX2ws87jF6Y. Last accessed 27 May 2022.
Benesch, O. (2014). *Inventing the way of the samurai: Nationalism, internationalism and Bushido in modern Japan*. Oxford: Oxford University Press.
BBC News. (2022). Joe Rogan: Podcast is staying on Spotify say boss. Available at: https://www.bbc.co.uk/news/entertainment-arts-60286699. Last accessed 13 February 2022.
Bowman, P. (2021). *The invention of martial arts: Popular culture between Asia and America*. Oxford: Oxford University Press.
Chew Jitsu Podcast. (2020). Episode 87: Rob from McDojoLife. Available at: https://chewjitsu.libsyn.com/episode-87-rob-from-mcdojo-life-returns. Last accessed 13 February, 2022.
Mangan, J. A., Horton, P., & Tagsold, C. (Eds.). (2020). *Softpower, soccer, supremacy: The Chinese dream*. Oxford: Peter Lang.
Martial Arts Journey. (2019). A sure way to spot a fake martial arts school [funny]. Available at: https://www.youtube.com/watch?v=muSJ20BZmFQ. Last accessed 27 May 2022.
Martinková, I., & Parry, J. (2016). Martial categories: Clarification and classification. *Journal of the Philosophy of Sport, 43*(1), 143–162.
McDojoShow Ep. 24: Ramsey Dewey Available at: https://www.youtube.com/watch?v=D_IJNEw-O6Y. Last accessed 13 February 2022.
My White Belt Jiu-Jitsu (May 2022). McDojo Life's Rob Ingram! Available on Spotify. First aired 18 May 2022.
Ramsey Dewey. (2020a). YouTube Channel. Is my gym a McDojo? Available at: https://www.youtube.com/watch?v=hd_3d-LdVGc. Last accessed 13 February 2022.

Ramsey Dewey. (2020b). YouTube Channel. Where are the boxing McDojos? Available at: https://www.youtube.com/watch?v=mnFuUziMcbM. Last accessed 13 February 2022.

Ritzer, G. (2010). *McDonaldization: The reader*. Los Angeles: SAGE.

Ritzer, G. (1993). *The McDonalization of society*. Los Angeles: SAGE.

Thompson, G. (2010). *Warrior: A path to self-sovereignty*. Oxford: Snowbooks.

Weber, M. (2001[1904]). *The protestant ethic and the spirit of capitalism*. London: Taylor & Francis.

Whiskey, Beer and Conspiracies Podcast. (2021). Episode 97: The Life of a McDojo with Rob of McDojoLife. Available at: https://www.listennotes.com/podcasts/whiskey-beer-and/97-the-life-of-a-mcdojo-with-5g4tJslfBA0/. Last accessed 13 February 2022.

7

The Revival and Protection of Martial Arts as Heritage

Introducing a Modern Renaissance of Martial Arts Lost and Found

The previous chapter on the McDojo critique began Part II on "The Reconstruction of the Martial Arts." This reconstruction of the world's martial arts needs careful monitoring and management in the 21st century, as there are many dark practices occurring in this social world, from charlatans to hyper-commercial chains that take advantage of gullible consumers, not to forget the abusive instructors who are now being exposed by martial arts influencers on their social media channels. This kind of policing of the dark side of the martial arts industry will correspond with the continued enthusiasm and creativity from its many practitioners. In this chapter, I focus on the lighter side of the reconstruction of the martial arts by focusing on historical martial arts that are now being revived and new martial arts inspired by ancestral systems of combat and warriorhood. I draw on the case studies of Historical European Martial Arts (HEMA) and the recently invented Mexican martial arts inspired by pre-Hispanic Mesoamerican warrior cultures. We begin with the European context, taking heed of the concept of renaissance, before finishing with a consideration of cultural heritage, the role of UNESCO and a short example from Wales and its martial heritage.

The 15th century European Renaissance (the Renaissance with the capital R) was a period of inspiration from the much earlier cultures of Ancient Greece and Rome – Western civilisations that eventually died out, leaving ruins, statues, infrastructure and the foundation of languages and academic disciplines derived from Greek and Latin. These cultures did of course shape the region now known as Italy, which still boasts of a rich heritage of these Mediterranean empires and city-states. However, the influence was not just about architecture, but also art and science, with the works of the likes of Leonardo da Vinci and Michelangelo being inspired by stylistics, science and creation from the pre-Christian era. Despite being in a Christian, late medieval society, specific artists and creative people were able to use techniques, styles and products inspired by the world of their ancestors. Greek gods could be painted while nude statues were finally starting to be accepted in influential cities such as Florence and Milan. There were of course critics of this movement, and it was not a smooth, one-directional process (like any cultural and sociological process), as seen with the powerful Medici family in Florence (recently depicted in the Netflix series *Medici the Magnificant*). However, it opened the possibilities for future generations to appreciate art as cultural heritage.

With a similar passion for ancestral wisdom, in the 21st century, there is a more specific renaissance (with a little r) in the martial arts inspired by ancestral culture of medieval Europe and pre-Hispanic Mesoamerica. The Historical European Martial Arts (HEMA) movement extend the longstanding interests of historical fencing enthusiasts that have been around since the Victorian period in Britain, as in the period of Bartitsu taught in Soho, London (1989-1902) – another martial art that has been revived by groups of enthusiastic martial artists eager to experience living history (see for example, The Bartitsu Club Official Website). This movement forms part of a productive (and sometimes cottage) industry of specialists creating weapons, protective equipment and decorative gear that coincides with the historical tourist and entertainment industries.

Meanwhile, other grass roots movements include the revival of Mesoamerican influences on combat and human development as seen in the newly created Mexican martial arts created for a new generation of their compatriots facing fresh and increasingly complex challenges for their health, security and national identities. This chapter examines both of these case studies as examples of renaissance movements making use of surviving evidence of how ancient warriors, knights and mercenaries might have fought, lived and died.

"A whole plethora of things": From Historical Fencing and Western Martial Arts to HEMA

In the late 20th century, there was little evidence of Western fighting systems in martial arts events, which were predominantly about the East Asian styles from China, Korea and Japan – and not even South of Central Asian fighting arts. I recall visiting the British martial arts expo, the *Seni*, in Birmingham with my oldest friend and another former Taekwondo classmate. Wandering around the stalls, we met Wing Chun practitioners demonstrating their homemade wooden dummies, Taekwondo fighters walking around with teammates and even John Saxon (Roper of *Enter the Dragon* Fame) posing for autographs. The *Seni* even has an Asian name, reflecting the influence on this region in terms of combat. In his expansive encyclopaedia, Crudelli (2008) notes that Asia has contributed more martial arts for the world than any other continent. This might be true in terms of their current global dissemination, although since that time, arts such as Brazilian Jiujitsu and Capoeira as well as Mixed Martial Arts (MMA) and other systems have taken a large proportion of the market.

Martial arts are still normally taught by official amateurs and hobbyists who have other working commitments in their lives. However, for some entrepreneurs, martial arts can be big business ventures. We have already seen how the martial arts are being increasingly professionalised, with instructor training courses, governing bodies, specialist insurance policies, consultants (such as Rob Ingram from McDojoLife) and a number of full-time centres emerging in cities in Britain and elsewhere.

Alongside the moving, feeling body of a martial arts organisation comes materials such as uniforms, badges, protective equipment, safety mats, rash guards for grappling and many other relatively recent inventions. The martial techniques might not change so frequently, but fashions do emerge within specific martial arts (such as personalised, funky rash guards for Jiujitsu) and across them. Combat sports have offered insight from full-contact competitions in terms of how safety equipment can be modified and developed, while other martial arts can craft their own equipment with these precautions in mind.

In *Acta Periodica Duellatorum,* an academic journal devoted to the study of HEMA, Jaquet, Sørensen, and Cognot (2015) rightly point out that HEMA operates at a crossroad between academic research, martial heritage re-creation and martial sport practices. They claim:

"Historical European Martial Arts (HEMA) have to be considered an important part of our common European cultural heritage. Studies within this field of research have the potential to enlighten the puzzle posed by past societies, for example in the field of history, history of science and technology, or fields related to material culture."

It is therefore pertinent to point out that martial arts do not exist in a vacuum, but alongside wide range of physical cultures, forms of popular culture and material productions.

When discussing my ethnography of HEMA with one classmate, Liam, he replied to me in an eloquent manner: "It [HEMA] can take you to a whole plethora of things." Alongside events, there are specialist centres of martial tourism for fans of television series, films and military history. Some of these sites include battlefields, but also commercial establishments and cottage industries of material production. For Domaneschi (2018, 2019), the material aspect of martial arts is something missing in the attention of martial arts scholarship so far more concerned with the body alone. Clothing, equipment and realia are all key to daily practice, sparring, competition and special events such as seminars, workshops, training camps and retreats. His own research in Italy examined the disciplines of *Tuishou* (pushing hands) and *Muay Thai* in terms of the clothing, from tunics and shoes to shorts vital to the construction of those specific cultures of combat.

One notable example of a centre of production and dissemination of Western martial arts materials is The Knight Shop in Conwy, North Wales, which is situated right next to King Edward I's fortress Conwy Castle, within the medieval walled town that is recognised as a UNESCO world heritage site. The Knight Shop has become so famous that it is even recognised within tourist guides to Wales, with one Lonely Planet guidebook advertising it as: "Always buying boring, samey souvenirs for your loved ones? Then why not go for a Henry VIII-era replica helmet, a ramshead heavy siege crossbow, some chain mail or perhaps a Viking drinking horn?" (Dragicevich & McNaughton, 2017, p. 279). On the outside, The Knight Shop provides replica weapons wielded by characters such as the Viking shieldmaiden Lagertha (from the hit series *Vikings*) as well as blades from *Lord of the Rings* and *Braveheart*. There are also daggers for those interested in the Knights Templars and other specific warrior orders. I first encountered The Knight Shop as a specialist provider in equipment for HEMA and related activities (see www.theknightshop.com). From its website, one can purchase a synthetic longsword and starter kit before moving onto heavier steel swords and the protect equipment required for that level of combat. Various sections include unique items for re-enactment of various forms and heritage products such as the medieval honey wine, mead.

Behind the façade of the quirky tourist attraction and Hollywood memorabilia is another side of The Knight Shop: A key supplier to the expanding HEMA industry. From their warehouse come their own Red Dragon set of synthetic weapons and safety equipment to protect against them – from helmets and neck protection to padded jackets with specific capacity to absorb a prescribed number of newtons of force to the torso and padded dungarees. This is an apt brand name from a country known for its red dragon proudly displayed on the national flag. Such a variety of equipment is essential because HEMA permits a range of attacks to the entire body (aside from the groin and spine), requiring the practitioner to buy their own equipment to supplement the basic equipment provided to beginners.

Indeed, safety is a key concern for leaders of the HEMA movement attempting to establish a legitimate practice that does not detract from people's long-term health and wellbeing. Starter kits help the HEMA practitioner build their own armoury of longswords, axes, daggers, Viking shields as well as protection from head to toe. Students are not permitted to spar or compete with a Level Two sword (metal blade) with only Level One armour designed for the less dense synthetic (plastic) swords used by beginners and lower-level students.

These weapons are not cheap by any means, and when I teach about the HEMA movement and its corresponding industry, my university students are often impressed by the cost of individual items, with one rugby player and bodybuilder exclaiming, "it's so expensive!" and another rugby player noting, "that is quite an expensive hobby." Despite their expenses on diet, supplements and perhaps also alcohol (as part of the drinking culture in British universities), the cost of £225 for a metal longsword was just too much. Buying a longsword, buckler (a small shield), side sword, dagger and poleaxe would normally cost around £1,000 or more, depending on the quality and the supplier in question. However, there does appear to be a tendency among HEMAists to gather as many swords as one can. During the first lockdown (as noted in the Preface), I noticed the walls of my classmates becoming increasingly saturated with swords as their sword racks (sometimes more than one) started to fill with different kinds of blades – even swords from the Japanese traditions that they do not study in any formal way.

However, suppliers do come in and out of fashion themselves. Over my three years involved in the Blade Academy, I have witnessed talk of numerous companies such as Black Fencer (known for firmer and heavier swords), a supplier to another school nearby. Another supplier is based in Pakistan, creating replica European weapons for aficionados around the globe. When our first-year anniversary came up, the students all contributed to a gift for our HEMA instructor: A beautiful, ornate sword that was shipped all the way from Russia. This took many weeks, as did a Chinese sabre for my Taijiquan instructor's 60th birthday gift (which was accompanied by a special red and white Fu to be displayed in his home).

This brings us to the topic of sustainability. With the use of specialist materials comes a considering of waste, carbon footprint and pollution all to serve what is largely a leisure pursuit for the majority of HEMA practitioners. A sword using plastic created in China or a mail-ordered rapier created in Russia or even an American blade sent across the Atlantic are good for the regional and world economy but perhaps bad for the global environment. The culture of HEMA is becoming richer by the day, with new online groups offering links to the suppliers of the essential materials and perhaps extravagant materials to add to that. One of my HEMA classmates once came to class in a black breast plate and helmet in the Roman tradition while we were all working on 14th century Italian longsword, sword and buckler and dagger of Italian fencing master *Fiore de Liberi*. Many brands are evident in any given sparring day or workshop, and suppliers are mentioned in class announcements and online chat fora. In the Blade Academy Messenger group, students regularly share pictures of their latest equipment orders – especially once they have arrived. Facebook and Instagram profiles commonly show these practitioners in their fencing gear or re-enactment kit – often through action shots that showcase an interesting persona for potential friends and followers.

We are now far removed from a local economy where the blacksmith and other professions would fashion weapons for the warriors living among them. There are, however, some specialists in every community who play such a role. As a professional cobbler, my classmate Alun is a specialist in fixing shoes and watches; he also is the resident leathersmith who has helped to patch equipment together for members of the Blade Academy. Other students have leant out protective equipment, as Templar John kindly did for me in terms of the forearm protection after I suffered a haematoma on my right wrist. I still have his old protectors which I have then lent out to other students who did not have their own. Equipment is redistributed to those in needed, although there is very often a surplus of kit. Dave Bright, a Wing Chun instructor and martial arts pedagogy researcher once reflected on his time in historical fencing: "What do I need two longswords for?"

Nonetheless, in terms of the wider industry, there might be less duty of care for one's fellow practitioners. What happens to waste material from these suppliers? Are they manufactured in an ethical fashion away from sweat shops? These kinds of questions could lead to more critical studies and investigative journalistic accounts of the martial arts industry, which has not undergone the scrutiny that its counterpart in sport (with the giants of Adidas and Nike) have been under over the last few decades due to their use of child labour and enforcement of poor working conditions in developing countries. Again, as in with the McDojo critique, the martial arts could benefit from an industry watchdog looking out for the best interests of workers, animals and the planet as a whole.

With the recent concern for concussion in combat sports (especially boxing and MMA) and contact sports such as American football as well as rugby (both union and league) and football (soccer), HEMA instructors often advocate specific measure to avoid brain damage for their students. My own instructor has suggested a rugby scrum cap beneath the safety helmet, which one student noted of mine: "it can help prevent micro-concussions." I have purchased my own cap from a rugby store opposite Cardiff Castle, and some weeks later, Billy advertised this shop and its excellent deal on the Blade Academy's Member's Private Facebook group. Like the red dragon, Rugby is very important to a popular sense of Welsh national identity (Johnes, 2019), with the national stadium being right in the city centre – a rarity in world sport. The sport of rugby, its connections to sport medicine and its manufacturing industry have an indirect influence on some HEMA practitioners concerned for their brain health, which gives us another example of the interconnected fields of martial arts, sport and manufacturing industries.

One such pioneer of safety in HEMA is Keith Farrell, who carries the message with him in various interviews, visiting teaching and workshops away from his base in Liverpool. Farrell is keen to enable his fellow HEMAists to continue training into their 80s or even older, which is only possible by paying attention to pain within the body and looking to the future (see Keith Farrell Official Website). He, like many influential figures in the HEMA community, has set up his own publishing press and also requests donations in order to help sustain his projects.

We can look to the past and the future in the martial arts, but also to alternative realities. This is because HEMA, like all martial arts, has an imaginative dimension as people relive their childhood fantasies of crossing swords with their friends and living as Conan the Barbarian or Zorro (depending on the version and generation in question). However, degrees of imagination and fantasy are open to scrutiny by gatekeepers to specific organisations. The practitioners of HEMA that I have spoken to seem to distance themselves from Live Action Role Play (LARP), a playful and rather fanciful approach wherein the participants make up rules for fighting, which might include magic powers. This might be acceptable if people admit to LARP just being a game, just as a group of Ninjitsu practitioners admitted to enjoying dressing up and playing as Ninjas when speaking with podcaster and MMA coach Ramsey Dewey.

As we have seen in the previous chapter, there is an ongoing disagreement on the need for a uniform in HEMA academies and their chapters (branches). Some HEMA practitioners snigger at LudoSport – an approach to Lightsabre combat inspired by the Jedi knights of Star Wars. In my own Academy, the group next to us within a large leisure centre was in fact a LudoSport group who used trampolines to bounce around as if they were Master Yoda. Whereas some people might point out that LudoSport is not an actual sport, unlike fencing and historical fencing. However, like HEMA, this kind of martial art might attract the kinds of people not normally involved in organised sports and martial arts. As one devoted classmate told me when I mentioned the Euro 2020 tournament, with Wales playing that very evening, "this [HEMA] is the only sport I follow." Very few of the students follow conventional sports that are popular in the UK besides some interested in boxing and MMA. HEMA tends to attract and retain what one of my interviewees, a practitioner of another academy, explained as "embodied geeks" – people living out fantasies but through their moving, feeling, active and highly trained body.

The intellectual aspect of HEMA is reflected in the efforts of pioneers such as John Clements and Guy Windsor. The latter figure is currently a key player in the British and European HEMA circuit, with his full-time fencing academy, the Sword Guy podcast and series of technical books that also include a self-help text on "The Windsor Method" (see the Guy Windsor Official Website and the Black Armoury Official Website). In his writings, Windsor, like Ido Portal, advocates the resting squat for better health and digestion. In such an attempt to live in a more natural way for human beings, he also promotes the use of minimal footwear, using medieval flat shoes when indoors. Moreover, he moves his attention to diet, shunning sugar from his intake – claiming that he is able to maintain very high levels of energy and vigour for sparring. Windsor has helped shape HEMA in Finland, where he lived for a number of years, and he now spreads his message through open-access books, PDFs and weekly emails with tips for his followers. The martial artist has become an author, entrepreneur, influencer and perhaps even a self-help guru for those operating within this specific sub-field of the martial arts. This shows the creativity possible from such innovators, who engage with the public through talks and interviews in order to garner a reputation and following. The same can be said of the creators of the newly created Mexican martial arts examined next.

Recovering a Hidden Mexico with Newly Created Martial Arts

Mexico is renowned for its success in professional boxing, and it has a rich heritage in that sport and also the vibrant cultural expression *Lucha Libre* (free wrestling) from the 1950s. In terms of its own Indigenous martial activities, Mexico's *Federación de Juegos Autoctonos y Deportes Tradicionales* (Federation for Autochtonous Games and Traditional Sports) has recognised the Lucha Zapoteca and Lucha Tarahumara among the Zapotec and Rarumari peoples, who have their own wrestling styes (https://www.juegosautoctonos.com/en/home/). The organisation explained the role of such games in Mexican society:

> "In Mexico, traditional games and sports play an essential role in the cultural identity of those who practice them, both as a community and as an individual. TSG [traditional sports and games] bond with cultures and societies in multiple ways: sometimes as a socializing tradition and sometimes they bond to religious rituals; in some cases that can be influenced by festivity calendar, productive activities, weather and seasons, ecosystems and the availability of local materials. They can also serve as a teaching method through oral tradition or simply as a recreational practice.
>
> In Mexican traditional games and sport universe, activities that have a link or have pre-Hispanic reminiscences and are still practiced by communities are particularly important, their millenary heritage strengthens Mexico's sport and cultural legacy." (https://www.juegosautoctonos.com/en/home/, my translation)

These ancient games still practised by native, minority ethnic peoples receive a degree of protection, while others have begun to ponder on the existence of a Mexican martial art. They connect with Indigenous languages and dress, are often practised in special places in the rural communities, and contain many rituals linking to a pre-Christian, Mesoamerican belief system. However, there is no official "martial art" registered by the Federation. This leads us to return to the social media, commentators and independent researchers. On YouTube, numerous videos circulate about independent researcher's investigations of such a system. If we take the working definition set out in the Introduction chapter, then all of these systems could be regarded as a martial art. Yet are they really Mexican and how might they connect with notions of heritage? I examine these in this short section.

One of the earliest of the new Mexican martial arts is Xilam, which is divided into seven levels emulating seven animals deemed sacred in Mesoamerica (snake, eagle, jaguar, monkey, deer, iguana and armadillo). Devised in the 1980s by veteran martial artists Marisela Ugalde and her ex-husband, it was registered by Ugalde in the early 1990s, who is still adding to the system through her research into pre-Hispanic Mexico and Mesoamerican civilisation (Jennings, 2015). Ugalde still leads the Xilam martial arts association in her late sixties, giving public talks and demonstrations while also teaching alongside her team of instructors. It is inspired by Mesoamerican warrior culture of the Aztecs (Mexica), Maya and Zapotec peoples and is shaped by the Mexica worldview (Jennings, 2016), a non-dualistic, process-based philosophy that related to many things, including gender and sexuality (Jennings, 2021a).

As I have shown in Jennings (2017), other Mexican martial arts include *Tae Lama* (a mixture of Korean Taekwondo and Polynesian Lima Lama) *Pok-at-Tok* (a self-defence oriented martial art inspired by pre-Hispanic imagery) and SUCEM, a mixed martial art that includes weapons inspired by the elite Mexica eagle and jaguar warriors (see Arte Marcial Mexicano Sucem, 2022). However, this art is less ceremonial and philosophical than Xilam, as in SUCEM, where the full-contact combatants use headdresses, shields and clubs that resemble the obsidian swords that the pre-Hispanic warriors would have wielded, while fighting in a ring or cage. This reflects the artistic nature of the martial arts, using the founders' imagination in terms of costume and dress. This martial art has expanded from its origins in the state of Veracruz, in the Gulf of Mexico to central Mexico, making connections with the government in order to be formally recognised.

Although these Mexican martial arts associations are united by their passion for the pre-Hispanic warriors, they tend not to collaborate in any way, and they are overt in their distinct claims of originality. For example, SUCEM proudly states that it was the first Mexican martial art converted for the combat sport arena (Jennings, 2017). The Xilam teachers, meanwhile, stress that the art was the first to be structured around Indigenous fighting arts and philosophy. Despite this creativity and elaborate design to deal with problems in combat and society, the Mexican martial arts have been criticised by members of the Mexican martial arts community – most notably online. Below many of the videos showcasing the arts and sharing newsreel from older recordings are many comments from detractors and trolls taking a sarcastic and cynical approach to Xilam. I have translated some of those comments from Spanish to English as: "It's something ridiculous. A terrible imitation of Silat. I would show how the art is worthless.", including a critique of the economic pursuit of the organisation as "The only thing they want to make with this invention is business.", and derogatory appraisal of the organisation's work as "I am creating a martial art in my neighbourhood, and to survive in the street. Inspired by great teachers like Yip Man, Darth Vader and Master Borja (Krav Maga) among others."

Other viewers have a more moderate response to these arts, showing a preference for other forms of combat alongside a willingness to accept the possibility of there being a truly Mexican martial art either in history or in the future:

> "I prefer the lucha libre and boxing. They aren't Mexican in their origin, but if they are trained, they appear to be born here."

> "Well whatever military (or warrior) society would have needed a structure of physical hand-to-hand training technique for their trips. In this sense, the pre-Hispanic cultures would have had a type of martial art. But, I do not believe that today there any surviving codices that describe those said training techniques (or sufficiently) to form a martial discipline to the level of combat. Mexico must have had martial arts, well structured, but like various ones around the world, they have been lost over time."

> "Nowadays there are recreators of pre-Hispanic weapons that, with serious investigation and experimentation, are seeking to recreate the arms, uniforms (based on sources) and tactics, without influence of the oriental martial arts."

The critique is not without any retort, as one of the Xilam practitioners with their own YouTube account decided to defend the organisation:

> "In Xilam, we reunite the main part of systems or format of combat that our ancestors have (note; they were not martial arts, but forms of fighting) with the wish of making a Mexican martial based on that, it is to recuperate our warrior essence, just like trying to return the Mesoamerican ball game."

The Mesoamerican ball game is an ancient physical culture connected to pre-Hispanic world views. It has survived in some rural indigenous communities, albeit without the ritual sacrifice and the large stone structures used as an arena. The game also inspired the creation of Xilam, which connects to the notion of the pre-Hispanic culture and the different directions (Jennings, 2018). Some other viewers considered the creativity of Marisela Ugalde in relation to other founders of martial arts:

> "If someone is going to create a new martial art, well wouldn't the logical thing to do would be to find similarities and the same movements to those that already

exist? I am saying, all of the martial arts that come here originate from another country and from whatever era have their origins in Chinese Kung Fu, and because of that, they have similar movements and positions…even identical ones."

"This is how all the martial arts and combat forms were both. Just like this lady [Marisela Ugalde], you and all the rest [of the founders]. It is a simple as this, everything initiates in the mind of a lady or a gentleman, independently, until it is born."

"If Bruce Lee can create his own style, why not this lady [Marisela Ugalde]?"

I have deliberately avoided showing the exact video sources of these comments, to avoid revealing the identities of the commentators. However, it is worth considering some of these comments along with other ones I have encountered over the years. Other comments resonated with Joe Rogan's more brash approach to scrutinising "bullshido" – a term explicitly used in some of the written conversations around the same videos. For instance, some viewers also noted the uniforms akin to Eastern martial arts. The coloured belts (ranging from white to black) of some of the new Mexican martial arts (as in *Pak-at-Tok* and *Tae Lama*) do resemble the Asian martial arts, although the belt scheme is actually a 20th century invention. Another crucial aspect of this critique has been the resemblance between many of the techniques used in arts such as Xilam and those found in the East Asian styles, such as the low, wide stances (akin to the horse stance), twisting punch delivered from the hip and kneeling in class (Jennings, 2021b). Some of the founders (Adán Rocha of *Pat-at-Tok* and Marisela Ugalde of Xilam) claim that they never took any aspect from the Eastern martial arts, being careful to only emulate the images seen in pottery, murals and other sources such as oral tradition. Marisela Ugalde defended her techniques, arguing that a punch has no exact paternity as it is a natural human movement, just like a kick (Jennings, 2021b).

There is no branch of McDojo Life in Mexico, but one young Mexican martial artist, Yann Lara has taken it upon himself to carry that mantle. Just like Rob Ingram, Lara has created edited videos showing clips of various Mexican martial arts, critiquing them and mocking them while pausing the clips, often with a comical, exaggerated set of gestures. The video "XILAM OTRO ARTE MARCIAL MEXICANO?" (see Yann Lara, 2018) has over 102,000 views, generating over 1,500 comments, which, accompanied by numerous subscribers, would allow Lara to begin making a living as a YouTuber with his one fan page. The description in the video can be translated as follows:

A TRUE MARTIAL ART IS DEMONSTRATED IN COMBAT. Karate, Kung Fu, Aikido, Muay Boran, Muay Thai, Lima Lama, Judo, Jiu Jitsu and all those that are known are demonstrated in combat, just like Bruce Lee demonstrated his Jeet Kune Do. This is a true martial art that demonstrated its functionality. We cannot go about life creating illogical movements without demonstrating them in combat, a martial art to know oneself, to have its own philosophy, demonstrate its functionality as well as a thousand other factors, but above all, is to DEMONSTRATE WITH ACTION IN COMBAT, not with exhibitions and to be supposing that we will make such a much and always be supposing, NOOOOO…do you want to create a martial art? OK DEMONSTRATE IT IN COMBAT because that is what is going to defend yourself in life. WE CANNOT BE SUPPOSING THAT IT WILL WORK IF WE HAVE NOT REALLY FOUGHT…it is to say that the teacher Mrs Marisela Ugalde that they do not fight in tournaments because it [Xilam] is only to strengthen oneself and that is a total stupidity, sorry, a martial art should be FUNCTIONAL IN A FIGHT, if not, it is simply a sport to exercise PHYSICALLY…A MARTIAL ART SHOULD BE THIS AND MUCH MORE. (https://www.youtube.com/watch?v=UmFENlLjtVw, my translation, capitals in original emphasis).

Lara's conceptualisation of the martial art focuses on the problem-based aspect of martial arts as applied to combat, and it does not seem to stress the societal aspect of cultural expression or challenging issues in Mexico (besides the need for self-defence). Returning to the Federation of Autochthonous Games and Traditional Sports, it is unsurprising that the new Mexican martial arts cannot be aligned to such governing bodies, with the political divisions and social media uproar that they can cause. However, it can be argued that these martial arts, although recent and with living founders, may act as a gateway to (in)tangible cultural heritage (Jennings, 2020), which is considered next.

Martial Arts Heritage: International and Local Projects

The United Nations Educational, Scientific and Cultural Organization (UNESCO) is well known and highly regarded for its identification and chartering of monuments and sites that are treasures for all of humanity. These includes pyramids, ruins and castles (including the aforementioned town walls of Conwy), and are typically regarded as tangible forms of heritage due to their physical and durable nature. Besides this important listing, the international organisation aims to avoid the conflict that martial arts are design to resolve:

> Since wars begin in the minds of men and women, it is in the minds of men and women that peace must be built. UNESCO uses education, science and culture to inform, inspire and engage people everywhere to foster understanding and respect for each other and the planet. (https://www.unesco.org/en)

Many martial arts such as Xilam focus on the value of respect, and they also cross the threshold between the tangible and the intangible. In recent years, UNESCO has begun to regard the martial arts as forms of intangible cultural heritage. Since 2016, in Chungju, South Korea, the International Center of Martial Arts for Youth Development under the Auspices of UNESCO (or ICM UNESCO for short) has been operating in an ambitious manner and at an accelerated rate. Now, with its devoted headquarters enabling full-time, permanent operations, the ICM UNESCO are expanding their activities to include webinars and short courses for instructors wishing to make their classes more inclusive for different populations (particularly young people, women and those people with disabilities) and a wide series of publications educating people about martial arts heritage and lesser-known martial arts movements.

Although it is not an academic organisation, like with many charities and governmental bodies, ICM UNESCO has an international advisory board that is composed of both practitioner-instructors and leaders of the martial arts organisations and scholar-practitioners working in distinct academic disciplines. One emerging project is the *World Martial Arts* (ICM UNESCO, 2021) book, an open portal that is expanding to account for the various martial arts from different countries and regions of the world. With it being a bilingual (English and Korean) online platform, images and later videos can be added to provide multimedia experience for the inquisitive reader and listener. It began with a list of 200 martial arts, and is likely to expand over many years as more martial arts are discovered by researchers and writers.

In 2020, ICM UNESCO devoted an edited set of chapters to the topic of *Traditional martial arts as intangible cultural heritage*. In the editorial, ICM executives explained the relationship between Intangible Cultural Heritage (ICH), crisis and the survival of martial arts:

> Martial arts are traditional sports and previous cultural heritage that embody the history, culture, religion, and philosophy of each country. However, most martial arts have for a long time not been able to gain the same traction as modern sports,

and thus have not been transmitted and developed systematically. (Lee, in ICM UNESCO, 2020, p. 5)

The preservation of martial arts as Cultural Heritage requires of researchers' efforts to conduct transdisciplinary studies that consider the historical evidence as well as the continuing development and reinvention of the martial arts from the perspectives of life histories and (auto)biographies of practitioners and teachers and in relation to different sociocultural contexts, and accounting the economic and politics landscapes over the time:

> Martial arts are intimately linked with the history of humankind, serving in prehistoric times as a means of hunting, for people to protect themselves and their families, enjoy games and festivals, and fight in war, and in more modern times as a way to train the body and spirit. Considering that martial arts have evolved and developed in various systems in every corner of the world, I believe this imbues them with an invaluable cultural heritage that has been enriched by human wisdom and philosophy. (Park, in ICM UNESCO, 2020, p. 7).

> Martial arts comprise a kind of ICH [Intangible Cultural Heritage] element that is transmitted and developed in close linkage with the history and identity of each individual and community, allowing practitioners to refine themselves and overcome their limitations through physical fitness training and mental discipline, while learning to care for others. As such, the philosophies and values of martial arts have permeated lives within each community through the repetition of transmission, transition, and recreation over generations, thereby contributing to the establishment of healthy societies. (Keum, in ICM UNESCO, 2020, pp. 9–10).

Finally, with sustainability in mind, ICM UNESCO concentrates much of its efforts on children and adolescents who are of course the future of the martial arts. Its *ICM Insight* is a yearly publication written in an accessible format that allows for non-specialists to grasp academic ideas on the martial arts – for instance, around the theme of quality martial arts education (ICM UNESCO, 2022).

So how might one set about studying martial arts heritage or martial heritage more broadly or to be more precise, in a local context? I consider such a future possibility with the case of Wales, a small corner of the United Kingdom with only 3.4 million people. Yet is an interesting case in point for what might be described as martial heritage – the broad connections between the past and the present through martial activities including archery, boxing, historical fencing and jousting as well as heritage sites such as battlefields, hill forts and castles (both ruined and intact). However, there has been very little academic attention paid to martial arts and combat sports in the Welsh context. This is rather surprising given that physically-demanding, competitive sport such as in rugby union and association football (soccer) is seen as an integral instrument in the development of a popular sense of Welshness (Johnes, 2000). With its tight-knit working class Welsh and immigrant communities producing many men's boxing champions and heroes over many decades, including the undefeated Joe Calzaghe (Harris, 2009; Jones, 2014; Stead & Williams, 2008), Wales is well-respected in combat sports, as seen in its vibrant Mixed Martial Arts (MMA) scene and wrestling spectacles. This reputation has been enhanced by Welsh women's recent exploits in the Olympic and Commonwealth Games with the likes of Jade Jones in Taekwondo and Lauren Price and Rosie Eccles in boxing.

Wales has more castles per square mile than any other country on the planet. Beyond the modern combat sports such as boxing, wrestling spectacles and MMA, Wales can boast of many reenactment groups operating in and around its plethora of medieval castles safeguarded by organisations such as *Cadw* (https://cadw.gov.wales/ literally "to keep" in the Welsh language). Elsewhere, lion and dragon dance performers during Chinese New Year connect Wales to international cultural heritage.

Moreover, in the burgeoning field of martial arts studies, South Wales is a world-leading a strong hub of scholarship (see for instance Bowman, 2019; Delamont, Stephens, & Campos, 2017; Jennings, Dodd, & Brown, 2020), with the flagship journal *Martial Arts Studies* hosted by Cardiff University. However, to date, there has been very little research on Welsh martial arts and combat sports and their relationships with Welsh identities, heritage and sense of Welshness. Britain as a whole has had a significant contribution to the popular imagination of the martial arts through advertising, comedy and television series, which includes the 1973 Monty Python sketch on Llap Goch, a supposed ancient Welsh martial art (Bowman, 2021). A study on real-life martial activities and combat sports (MACS – see Channon & Jennings, 2014) such as archery, boxing, sport and historical fencing, non-European martial arts and wrestling would add to our understanding of a diverse and inclusive sense of Welshness, Welsh identity and heritage in the 21st century.

Such a study would uncover the role of the media in developing a sense of Welshness through its coverage and portrayal of a broad spectrum of martial arts and combat sports (MACS). As an interdisciplinary project, the research would seek to: Understand the role of different forms of traditional and emerging media in constructing a sense of place / belonging and notion of Welshness in MACS; examine case studies from a range of MACS from diverse cultural origins as practised and taught in different regions of Wales; paint a portrait of contemporary Welsh heritage and living history through its people's long-term engagement in MACS. Due to the exploratory nature of the topic, I would anticipate the study as being a chiefly qualitative study making use of documentary and media analysis approaches alongside life history interviews with veteran martial arts practitioners. Data could be gathered from national media archives, university and specialist libraries as well as online searches and sampling recommendations from local networks. Some content analysis and record keeping / mapping might also be useful when dealing with the frequency of MACS featured in different forms of media, at specific time periods and in particular regions. Thematic, discourse and narrative analysis techniques could be used to examine the kinds of depictions and stories told about MACS in relation to Welshness, *Cynefin* (a sense of local belonging), Welsh national identity and cultural heritage. Theories can be drawn from cultural studies, ethics, media studies, sociology, sport studies and Wales studies in order to contribute to knowledge on sport media.

Beyond academia, the creation of a documentary film on Welsh martial arts heritage and Welshness could be premiered around the country. The documentary and publications could also help drive policies around martial heritage in Wales in conjunction with *Cadw*, the National Trust and other organisations concerned with safeguarding heritage. I hope to develop strong relationships with organisations such as the Learned Society of Wales (LSW), which has a vested interest in funding research on Wales and Wales studies. Funds could be utilised to examine the unique styles taught in the region that are relatively unknown in China (e.g., Lee, Feng Shou and Dragon styles Kung Fu).

Overall, for a country of only 3.4 million people, Wales does seem to offer many things for a martial arts scholar to explore. In the next section of the book, "Living and Breathing the Martial Arts", I use Chapters 8 and 9 to examine the life histories of martial arts instructors and long-term practitioners living in Wales who reflect the diversity, commitment and heritage touched upon in this final section.

Summary

This chapter has introduced a period that might be described as a "renaissance" (rebirth) of certain martial arts lost to time which are now being restored and reimagined by researchers, practitioners and pioneers of the martial arts. I began with Historical European Martial Arts (HEMA) in conjunction with historical tourism and the emerging industry of replica medieval arms production to show how HEMA exists alongside other industries that support and rely on it. This was followed by a section on the newly created Mexican martial arts from the late 20th and early 21st centuries that are inspired by the pre-Hispanic Mesoamerican warriors of the Aztecs (Mexica) and Maya. These arts have made use of artistic creations in the form of shields, weapons, face paint as well the philosophy to structure and drive specific martial arts for a new generation of Mexicans to be proud of their Indigenous heritage. Some of these arts are now being recognised by ICM UNESCO, who have noted of Xilam in their *World Martial Arts* collection. However, this is partly due to the writing on that particular style.

More research is needed on the Mexican martial arts and native forms of wrestling and martial dances and rituals in order to help identify and preserve these art forms in a more sustainable fashion. This links my previous study of those arts with future projects in my new country of residence, Wales. I then finished the chapter by turning to an emerging research project that I have planned to examine the martial heritage of Wales, which enables the field of martial arts studies to meet Wales studies. We next turn to the stories of four martial artists based in Wales, beginning with Billy Marshall, a HEMA instructor fascinated by castles, battles, swords and medieval heritage.

References

Arte Marcial Méxicano Sucem. SUCEM official YouTube channel. Available at: https://www.youtube.com/playlist?list=UU6szc-pltKg8phCOE7dTzvg. Last accessed 31 May 2022.

Black Armoury. Guy Windsor. Available at: https://www.blackarmoury.com/en/brand/47_guy-windsor. Last accessed 31 May 2022.

Bowman, P. (2021). *The invention of martial arts: Popular culture between Asia and America*. Oxford: Oxford University Press.

Bowman, P. (2019). *Deconstructing martial arts*. Cardiff: Cardiff University Press.

Cadw official website. Available at: https://cadw.gov.wales/. Last accessed 31 May 2022.

Channon, A., & Jennings, G. (2014). Exploring embodiment in martial arts and combat sports: A review of empirical research. *Sport in Society, 17*(6), 773–789.

Crudelli, C. (2008). *The way of the warrior: Martial arts and fighting systems from around the world*. London: Dorling Kindersley.

Delamont, S., Stephens, N., & Campos, C. (2017). *Embodying Brazil: An ethnography of diasporic Capoeira*. London: Routledge.

Domaneschi, L. (2019). Dress to fight: A comparative ethnography of material culture in two Eastern traditional fighting practices. *Etnografia e Ricerca Qualitativa, 3*, 385–406.

Domaneschi, L. (2018). Conditioning weapons: Ethnography of the practice of martial arts training. *Societies, 8*(3), 80.

Dragicevich, P., & McNaughtan, H. (2017). *Lonely planet: Wales.* London: Lonely Planet Global International.

Federación Mexicana de Juegos y Deportes Autoctonos y Tradicionales A.C. official website. Available at: https://www.juegosautoctonos.com/en/home/. Last accessed 31 May 2022.

Guy Windsor Official Website. Available at: https://guywindsor.net/. Last accessed 27 February 2022.

Harris, J. (2009). Boxing, national identities and the symbolic importance of place: The 'othering' of Joe Calzaghe. *National Identities, 13*(2), 177–188.

International Center of Martial Arts for Youth Development and Engagement (ICM) under the Auspices of UNESCO (2022). *ICM insight.* Volume 5: Quality Martial Arts Education.

International Center of Martial Arts for Youth Development and Engagement (ICM) under the Auspices of UNESCO (2021). *World martial arts.* Jeonju: ICHCAP.

International Center of Martial Arts for Youth Development and Engagement (ICM) under the Auspices of UNESCO (2020). *Traditional martial arts as intangible cultural heritage.* Jeonju: ICHCAP.

Jaquet, D., Sørensen, C. F., & Cognot, F. (2015). Historical European martial art: A crossroad between academic research, martial heritage re-creation and martial sport practices. *Acta Periodica Duellatorum, 3*(1), online access: https://bop.unibe.ch/apd/article/view/6977

Jennings, G. (2021a). Conceptualising sexuality through the Mexican martial art of Xilam. In J. Piedra & E. Anderson (Eds.), *Lesbian, gay and transgender athletes in Latin America* (pp. 75–97). Basingstoke: Palgrave Macmillan.

Jennings, G. (2021b). "A punch has no paternity!": Technique, belonging and the Mexicanidad of Xilam. *Ethnography* (open access online).

Jennings, G. (2020). Mexican Xilam as a gateway to (in)tangible pre-Hispanic cultural heritage. In S.-Y. Park & S.-Y. Ryu (Eds.), *Traditional martial arts as intangible cultural heritage* (pp. 132–143). Chungcheongbuk-do, South Korea: ICM.

Jennings, G. (2018). From the calendar to the flesh: Movement, space and identity in a Mexican body culture. *Societies, 8*(3), 66.

Jennings, G. (2017). Seeking identity through the martial arts: The case of Mexicanidad. In chinesemartialstudies (Kung Fu Tea), https://chinesemartialstudies.com/2017/08/14/seeking-identity-through-the-martial-arts-the-case-of-mexicanidad/

Jennings, G. (2016). Ancient wisdom, modern warriors: The (re)invention of a warrior tradition in Xilam. *Martial Arts Studies, 2,* 59–70.

Jennings, G., Dodd, S., & Brown, D. (2020). Cultivation through Asian form-based martial arts pedagogy. In D. Lewin & K. Kenklies (Eds.), *East Asian pedagogies: Education and formation and transformation across cultures and borders* (pp. 63–77). New York: Springer.

Jennings, G. (2015). Mexican female warriors: The case of maestra Marisela Ugalde, founder of Xilam. In A. Channon & C. Matthews (Eds.), *Women warriors: International perspectives on women in combat sports* (pp. 119–134). Basingstoke: Palgrave MacMillan.

Johnes, M. (2000). Eight minute patriots? National identity and sport in modern Wales. *International Journal of the History of Sport, 17*(4), 93–110.

Johnes, M. (2019). *Wales: England's colony?* Cardigan: Parthian.

Jones, G. (2014). *Dragons vs. eagles: Wales vs. America in the boxing ring.* Cardiff: Welsh Academic Press.

Keith Farrell Official Website. Available at: https://www.keithfarrell.net/hema/. Last accessed 27 February 2022.

Stead, P., & Williams, G. (2008). *Wales and its boxers: The fighting tradition.* Cardiff: University of Wales Press.

The Bartitsu Club official website. Available at: https://bartitsu.club/. Last accessed 31 May 2022.

The Knight Shop Official Website. Available at: www.theknightshop.com. Last accessed 27 February 2022.

UNESCO Official Website. Available at: https://www.unesco.org/en. Last accessed 31 May 2022.

Yann Lara. (2018). XILAM. OTRO ARTE MARCIAL MEXICANO? Available at https://www.youtube.com/watch?v=UmFENlLjtVw. Last accessed 31 May 2022.

Part III
Living and Breathing the Martial Arts

8

Teachers, Networks and Relationships in the Martial Arts

Today's increasingly mobile and diverse Western society boasts a far greater variety of fighting and human development systems than in the 1970s and 1980s heyday of the Kung Fu and Bruce Lee craze, where Judo, Karate and some Kung Fu schools would be on offer in the larger cities with a notable East Asian population, such as London, Glasgow, Birmingham, Manchester and Liverpool in the UK. With the next generation of students, branch schools would open in smaller towns and even villages as schools turned into associations and even federations and governing bodies. Arts such as Wing Chun spread as far as the Cornish peninsula and West Wales, far from any cosmopolitan or ethnically diverse cities. Now, even in an average sized town, a newcomer to the martial arts is welcome to try their hand in Capoeira, give Kendo a go and engage in grappling arts such as BJJ or even rarer systems such as Systema and new hybrid arts created by Westerners. Although sporting martial arts careers (as in boxing and MMA) can be relatively short, the martial arts journey can be over many decades, culminating in old age and death, when the person has fulfilled their potential, used the art to expand their understanding of human movement and healing as well as cultural heritage and creation: all themes of the previous chapters.

This final empirical section is composed of three chapters (8, 9 and 10). It provides case studies of people who touch upon the main themes of the book, showing how aspects of Asian martial arts have shaped the lives of Western exponents drawing on some of their philosophical, literary, strategic and practical solutions to combat and life itself. I also indicate several other themes from the analysis of their life stories, such as martial arts couples, fatherhood and mentoring, which run across these the four case studies shown in the next two chapters (8 and 9). More specifically, this chapter examines the stories of two committed martial artists who have engaged in numerous systems in their lifetime. These are male practitioners in Wales, Britain – Billy and David (both pseudonyms) – who have become my main informants in HEMA and Taijiquan and other internal martial arts and alternative healing systems over the last four years. Due to the biographical nature of this analysis, the writing is more heavily based on my field note observations of these two men along with life history interview and ethnographic interview data and reference to key videos and texts that they have advocated within our many discussions.

We begin with the younger of the two martial arts enthusiasts, Billy Marshall, who is currently enjoying expanding his HEMA academy while building his skills in MMA and BJJ. All names of their peers have also been changed in order to protect identities as far as possible, although, as with the rest of the book, dead, historical and more public-facing, celebrity figures in the martial arts are named in full. Due to the volume of data I have accumulated over the past four years of researching the fieldwork sites in which these men operate, many of the tales are summarised in my own words, leaving space for future publications and collaborations with these informants having more agency over their own narratives.

Billy Marshall: The Marshal of the Blade Academy

Billy is 33 years old, and with this relatively young age, is able to train on a regular basis in numerous martial arts and physical conditioning systems. Originally from Wales, he identifies as being mixed race as he is a quarter Malaysian (from his grandmother) and three quarters Welsh, giving him a swarthy appearance coupled with long dark locks that he sometimes ties back in a ponytail – otherwise leaving them to tangle above his shoulders. Despite his South East Asian heritage, Billy has taken to more Western, pragmatic approaches to the martial arts, although he is more interested in military and self-defence martial activities rather than sporting expressions of these. Billy's height of 6 foot 4 inches gives him an advantage in sword fighting, although he is also a keen grappler interesting in closing the gap and disarming his opponents. He almost always wears black – the colour of his Blade Academy's uniform – and normally bears a wolf medallion with a lock of his beloved wife's red hair within it. Indeed, when I meet Billy for a monthly coffee discussion about HEMA and other martial arts, he ordinarily dons his favoured black hoodie bearing the logo of his treasured academy – even wearing this over a smart shirt when he came to my university to speak at an industry event. This logo is also used for his WhatsApp profile and the icon for his emerging podcast. Furthermore, the shield is emblazoned on Billy's left arm in the form of a tattoo he had inked one year after opening his treasured Academy.

As a boy, Billy learned the basis of Western martial arts through boxing and fencing. His initial immersion into the imaginative world of martial arts as a child were through the Hollywood films *Highlander* (1986) and *Conan the Barbarian* (1982). In terms of informal tutelage, Billy's father was an avid fencer in the Royal Air Force (RAF), and it was he who first taught Billy how to wield a sword using sharpened wooden sticks as a young boy, with "pain being the greatest teacher." Billy continued with conventional sporting fencing, leading him to become his school fencing captain while later competing as an adult.

When I first met Billy to join his academy as part of my ethnographic research, he explained his eventual dissatisfaction with the sporting version of the art: "I was in a sport fencing competition, and pierced my opponent in the heart, but they got a flick on my shoulder just before that happened, and they got the point. That's not a martial art!" Seeking the study of the cutting edge aspect of blades, he later selected Kendo, which struck him "as more of a martial art." Nevertheless, Billy found difficulty in Kendo with is relative uniformity and lack of experimentation. Indeed, Billy regards tradition as "a double-edged sword", warning that "the traditions should be related to the community and the benefit to the students, but the martial art itself shouldn't be rigid. They should allow students to express themselves." However, Billy is disgusted by the childish display of Star Wars and Ghostbusters logos on some other HEMA practitioner's uniforms, which we had witnessed in one local event. He is also not a great admirer of Ludosport (the hyper-real Lightsaber combat studied by Judkins, 2016) due to its narrow vision of fencing. "You'll never learn to deal with someone with a sword and shield. You'll never learn how to halfsword. There's not a lot of room for growth there." The creativity of battle reenactment (with its study of tactics and logistics) and HEMA (with the individual expression of fighting styles) beckoned him some years later.

Billy's position on fencing has been to treat it as a martial art, and his Blade Academy is therefore devoted to the pursuit of martial excellence over sporting achievements through the HEMA traditions of *Fiore de Liberi*. In one meeting, he explained that this emphasis was on "the martial-ality...we are trying to make it martial; we are trying to revive an art." In his characteristically articulate manner, Billy declared, "I don't want to be the ice *sculpture* – I want to be the ice *sculptor*." By this, he meant that the sculptor has a long career of many creations rather than being defined by one product (a performance in a tournament), as he and another like-minded HEMA instructor agreed that "tournaments are a dime a dozen."

Billy is against people using tournaments merely to legitimise themselves as instructors, and he prefers to focus on developing high-quality workshops. Billy summed this ethos up as: "We are seeking to be martial artists, not tournament chasers." These martial artists, according to Billy, differ from martial arts practitioners, as the martial artists look to put the safety mats away and check the room before and after the class. This is despite his own success in tournaments where he has won gold medal for the longsword, side sword and sword and buckler. However, his own teacher Angelo quickly gave him a pasting "just to give me a sense of proportion." Billy shies away from the label of being a self-defence instructor, as he regards what he does as "self-defence in the medieval context." However, he has taught knife defence within his classes, and often discusses the legal aspects of self-defence and the carrying of replica weapons. Once, police officers asked Billy to open his large bag, which was full of swords. Billy winced, saying, "I'll open my bag but first of all, let me show you my card...here's my card...now I'll open the bag."

In his youth, Billy had enjoyed learning from a local Lee style Kung Fu school, which taught a rare form of Kung Fu and Taijiquan relatively unheard-of outside Britain (accounted for in Ryan, 2008). Although Billy no longer practises these arts, he has taken some of the principles of human motion into his training, including the phrase from Taijiquan: "Slow is smooth, smooth is fast." Ted, his own academic mentor from his undergraduate degree in creative writing and narrative at a local university, is a senior practitioner of this Lee style system. Billy admires Ted as one of his role models growing up, as he distanced himself from his late father, who became an alcoholic. Ted has visited the Academy to provide instruction for breakfall training for the students learning to disarm and takedown opponents swinging a stick. Here, we used the wooden rattan sticks utilised in Filipino Escrima (better known as Arnis in its homeland) and soft crash mats from gymnastics to provide a safe space for learning to fall and roll in stages. Billy stills sees the merits of Taijiquan in terms of posture and holding the bind in fencing, when two swords are pressed against one another. Despite not continuing with these arts after finding HEMA, Billy does make use of some of the warm up exercises, such as the "holding a grain of rice" exercise used to prepare the shoulders. He enjoys watching beginners struggle with this exercise on their first night at the Academy, often making jokes about the exercises and his bad memory and poor Italian pronunciation for the core guards and techniques in this Italian fencing style. Nonetheless, during the COVID-19 lockdown, Billy did seek out my partner Barbara to provide mindfulness meditation sessions for members of the Academy, as he felt that many of them needed that mental soothing during such a stressful period.

Billy also has a strong background in medieval military and battle reenactment, which stems from his work with the Viking Society, a group devoted to educating people about the Vikings and their battles against the Saxons. In one event, he met his wife Issie after she spoke to him about sword fighting lessons, being impressed by his "sexy Viking" look. He began teaching her on a private basis, only for them to become partners for life. They married under a poignant oath involving each of them pointing a dagger to each other's hearts, sweating never to break each other's heart under pain of death. This medieval wedding reflects their love of history, with Issie being a master's graduate in ancient history and Billy planning on studying a master's degree in medieval military history at a local university. He has worked with his first student Callum in reenactment events such as the famous dynasty-changing Battle of Hastings of 1066 where Billy and his comrades actually fought on the side of the losing Saxons. Besides this, he has featured in events in North Wales, where he played the role of a "baddie" fighting against one of his best friends, a young woman who became one of his aspiring students and later helped the Academy with bespoke yoga classes during the lockdown.

In his youth, Billy admits that he "wasn't a nice person", as he recalled getting into trouble and fights, partly based on anger from his childhood. However, he met an influential friend, Anton, who brought him into reenactment, returning him to the martial path. Sadly, his best friend passed away in his early thirties, and Billy has created a medal in his honour for the student of the year award.

Billy's first student is Callum, a tall and powerful young man now in his mid-twenties. Callum first knew Billy as his sister's boyfriend, but after the two split up, Callum asked to keep on seeing Billy as his student and friend, to his sister's amusement. Clad in black protective gear, the two are often seen near the main river of the city fighting within a wooded area that they deem "sacred ground" – once fighting off another group of HEMA practitioners for the rights to the territory. Now Billy spars with many of his students for free, always trying to test himself against tall, short, broad and agile opponents. Interestingly, both Callum and Billy often called each other "brother" when speaking and writing to Anton. Although Billy and Callum were distant from their fathers, and had no older brothers to look up to, they had found positive role models in the martial arts through their peers, teachers and historic heroes. Twelve years since first meeting each other, they are still best friends. After likening Callum to the medieval knight William Marshal's right-hand man, Billy reflected on this triadic relationship:

> It's like William Marshal and his wife Isabella…they were a good team together… she [Isabella] held down the fort, literally, especially when King John was in power…I wouldn't be able to do a fraction of what I do without Issie. She is the power behind the throne. It's great to be able to work with my two best friends. And Issie is my best friend.

One of Billy's most influential role models is Angelo (also featured in the Preface), an Italian medievalist and HEMA instructor who he learned from when leaving and teaching English out in Italy for four years. This followed a brief stint in Kazakhstan, where Billy first learned the ropes as a budding English teacher while spending his time with solo cutting drills on the steppes. Billy initially received a strong beating from Angelo in his first sparring session, especially when Angelo learned that Billy was friends with a rival instructor on Facebook who was one of Angelo's disgraced former students. Looking back at this, Billy laughed at this "Mexican soap opera of betrayal", explaining: "The schools out in Italy are very different from the schools here in the UK. They're very much like medieval Italy, vying for control." Billy, Issie, Angelo and Angelo's girlfriend Monica developed a strong friendship, scaling mountains during the weekends and visiting a monastery at night, "having this back and forth discourse on the Dao of HEMA as it were." Billy is still in awe of his teacher, often telling students in class that "the guy has forgotten more about fencing than I have ever learned."

From tales shared within the Academy walls, Angelo is said to be an unforgiving, strict teacher who runs a successful chain of HEMA schools in his region, and I was fortunate to meet him in an invited class, where he put Billy through his paces during an exchange of moving through the bind (where two swords meet). Despite Angelo being several inches shorter, Billy struggled to defend his rapid thrusts enabled by his graceful footwork, and Angelo whispered to him, "thank you for letting me hit you", thinking Billy had consciously permitted the attack. Billy looked back at such exchanged, gushing: "the speed and the precision…he's something to behold." At the end of this special session on the German longsword, Angelo congratulated Billy for the excellent way he was running the Academy "in the right way." Although Billy had moved outside Angelo's formal organisation and banner, he still regards Angelo as his primary teacher, and often refers to tales of his times in the fabled Italian academy. Angelo did actually wish for Billy to set up a branch school of his association, although when Billy sat him down with the plans for the Blade Academy in the UK, Angelo nodded, confirming: "You should open your own school." Billy reflected that he is not one for conformity, and he found it difficult to fit into Italian culture of football and fashion as he did with the South Wales culture of rugby and drinking.

With his life focused on the Academy, Billy rarely goes to reenactment events today, although several of his students also have this background, such as Templar John (often simply known among the Academy members as "Templar"), a Knights Templar enthusiast who has even painted his garden shed (where he houses his armour) with a giant red cross. Many other students work with Billy in an escape reality centre in the city, and they often walk around town in the hoody, even if they are no longer active students. Within such a supportive and eclectic community, Billy does sometimes offer informal training in reenactment with his close students, including Sam (another ex-colleague), who remarked that he now had "a manly scar" after Billy accidentally brought back his sword into Sam's eyebrow. Bringing this experience of reenactment of large-scale battles and skirmishes into the Academy, Billy hones his students in unit combat, a specialty of the school and a relative rarity in the local HEMA community.

In some of the "mixer" events I have been involved in with other HEMA schools, the Academy has held its own and often triumphed against the combined forces of their neighbours – so much that one occasion, we were asked to split up teams with other schools so as not to have the advantage. This is one of the Unique Selling Points (or "USPs" as Billy puts it in business vernacular) of the Academy within the region, which also includes outdoor sparring events in the woodland.

Lining up shoulder to shoulder, the Academy pupils intertwine their large round shields and move in formations, working in long lines, double lines and even in pairs for different games and exercises. This has moved on from axes and arming swords to include spears and even poleaxes, as the curriculum of the Academy has expanded from semester to semester. Some students are more adept in archery, while others have studied weapons that Billy has never learned, stating that he is merely "further along the path". In fact, Billy advises his students to "find your own version of Fiore", with that being more mobile approaches for the agile, different angles for shorter students and strong and stable positions for those with core strength. This expansion is enabled by the growth in student numbers and the extended number of classes in different venues.

The Academy began just on two hours on a Wednesday evening, and has since flourished, extending to a Friday evening in the same venue and a year later, another town on Thursday night and then a Sunday evening class on the outskirts of Billy's hometown. He wants – and feels the burning need to – expand across Wales, even thinking of training someone in the north of the country to represent the Academy for him. In order to maintain his own swordsmanship, Billy trains incredibly hard, rarely taking a rest day. He develops his strength in a local "spit and sawdust gym…that is more spit than sawdust" where is now learning BJJ. This followed several years learning Krav Maga, which helped Billy with the grappling aspects of Fiore's system. In fact, Billy confessed that the said gym had a dead pigeon in the fans for numerous weeks, with some feathers floating down to where people were rolling on the floor!

Billy interest in grappling was stimulated by a clinching scenario while fighting one of his young but sturdy students outside, when Billy became concerned that he might hurt the youngster's back against a tree root. He then took up BJJ not to compete (although his teacher is very keen for him to enter competitions), but to learn more about takedowns and controls on the floor, which he sees as an integral part of the Fiore system of late medieval combat. More recently, Billy has extended his cross training to MMA, as he admitted "it's been a long time since I've done any striking." When I last saw him at my university when he joined me for a guest speaker's seminar at my university, he admitted "I've been hit in the head so many times in my life", while sporting a bruise just off his left temple.

A keen collector who proudly wrote on his Facebook profile that he "bloody loves" swords, Billy holds many different kinds of blades in his small home – a place where he often trains outside in the concrete yard clanging against his metal pel, drawing curious looks from his neighbours as he works on cutting drills with various weapons. Some of these weapons are regarded as props and are of course dull metal and synthetic blades for the purpose of sparring, although he does own real antique swords kept for display, research and educational purposes. His own collection includes a sharpened Kukri from the Gurkha military and regimental tradition as well as a prize possession of a Russian hassar sabre from the Crimean War of the 19th century. Billy has proud stories that connect to each of these weapons. For instance, he was sharpening his Kukri in his mother's house when a drunk man stumbled in. In a post-class gathering in a pub, Billy told his students how he darted into the kitchen to confront the intruder with the blade, and the man immediately sobered up, explaining that he used to live in the house, and had gone on autopilot back home. Billy's own grandfather, still active in his early nineties, is also a collector of swords, and Billy had to rescue the treasured antique Russian hassar sword from a pawn shop when his estranged father was going to sell it for cash for alcohol. Billy has avoided drinking, as he has experienced negative situations of drunkenness from his childhood, and dislikes the kind of person he becomes when he is under the influence.

Beyond the seemingly violent activity of sword fighting, he is curious about the symbolic meanings behind the design of different swords, from the shape of the blade to their cross blades, hilt and often elegant pommels. His main weapon of choice is the medieval two-handed longsword, which reflects his power and grace in fighting (and brutality according to his wife Issie!). For Billy, the Christian cross is directly depicted in the design of this weapon. He is increasingly interested in the anatomy of other kinds of swords such as the elegant Chinese Xian, which may have Daoist symbology within it. Billy continues his research into the medieval period, which includes fashion and climate. He explained this in an interview: "Why use a rondel? You need to consider the fashion of the time, which was influenced by the climate. Climate affects farming, and farms affect population, and population affects conflict."

For the future, Billy dreams to be the best fencer that he can possibly be, while envisaging the Academy growing to be the premier HEMA school in the country. To do this, Billy trains fanatically, working on his cardiovascular fitness through High Intensity Interval Training (HIIT), strength through weight training, sparring with many HEMA specialists, cross training in other martial arts and of course engaging with HEMA gatherings, events and workshops. He has also set up his own podcast, with invited guests from the HEMA, reenactment and martial arts world, including people who forge swords, lead HEMA academies and work in the film industry. However, through his training, he has inevitably picked up pain and injuries requiring him to seek out specialist therapists to heal his ailing body. He regularly goes to a sports massage therapist, John, who was recommended by Adam, one of Billy's top students who is also a martial arts journeyman, spreading his attention between HEMA, Ninjitsu and stunt work as he develops his career as a stuntman for popular streaming series on Amazon Prime and Netflix. John was himself a top Judo player who peaked at a young age, and has since treated many people putting their bodies on the line for their passions. Billy has also undergone chiropractor treatment, linking migraines to compressed neck vertebrae, although he is hesitant about the methods used in this therapy, due to there not being any preparation of the soft tissue. His own interest in meditation stems from the need to mentally prepare for combat, and his reading of strategy extends from his love of Miyamoto Musashi's *The Book of Five Rings*, a classic treatise on swordplay and combat (see, for example, Musashi, 2020 – the bestselling fencing book) that he is proud to say that he has owned an older edition for more than half his life.

I named Billy Marshall after his hero William Marshal, an early medieval Norman knight renowned for his skill in the mass melee, single combat and military and political strategy of the courts of five kings (see Chadwick, 2005; Ashbridge, 2015). Issie is named after Billy Marshall's loyal and intelligent wife, Isabella. This is appropriate given the couple's fascination with that era and their engagement with the Welsh heritage organisation *Cadw*, of which they are full members, often visiting castles and historic sites. Billy and Issie represent an interesting phenomenon in the martial arts: what I call "martial arts couples", those pairs of people who devote their lives to the martial arts, living a lifestyle around training, teaching, travelling and performance. Neither of them aspires to have children, as Billy once admitted: "Because I'm a very selfish person. I think a child would pick up on that…that I would resent them for not being able do what I wish to do." However, Billy is very generous with his time and energy for his students and friends, being supportive of them when life deals them a blow.

Billy and Issie run the Academy side-by-side, with Issie mainly playing the role of assistant – apart from women's events, where Billy acts as the demonstration partner. Issie explained this dynamic to me during one group social event, "if it's about the talent of wielding a sword, it's Billy; if it's about organisation and finance, it's me." Billy's lack of interest in finances enabled Issie and several of the core members of the Academy to set up a Messenger chat group entitled "Taxes" in 2019 (to mark the first-year anniversary of the Academy), while secretly planning a present for Billy to thank him for founding and leading the Academy with passion and integrity. The gift in question was a custom-made sword forged and posted from Russia, which meant we students had to organise the birthday surprise several weeks in advance. In addition to Billy's present, the students also contributed to a large black quilt with the Academy logo for Issie. On another occasion, Alun, a real-life cobbler and the Academy's own leathersmith, thoughtfully presented a handmade notebook with the Academy shield at the front. Billy recounted the receiving of the gifts, smiling: "I was speechless. Words aren't enough; they are significant for how much this means to me." Such gift bearing is reflective of the effort Billy has taken in painstakingly developing the syllabi for each weapon and exams for the students' gradings, not to mention the care he takes in each of the two-hour training sessions. Gift bearing and meeting one's partner through the martial arts are also seen in the story of David, a long-term Karate practitioner and instructor of Taijiquan and Chinese internal arts including Neigong and Daoist meditation.

David James: From Karate to Taijiquan and Back Again (From the Inside Out)

David James, a veteran Karate practitioner and Taijiquan instructor who has just turned 60, is a quietly spoken, gentle man who possesses an impressive physical ability, including flexibility, postural and bodily control and explosive speed. Like many Taijiquan teachers, he speaks slowly and softly, making his students feel at ease. His back is very straight, his shoulders broad and sloping, and his arms long and loose, which he advertises as elements of the Taijiquan body, once reflecting in class: "Over time, you'll get slightly taller, your neck with extend, your shoulders will drop and your arms with lengthen." Normally wearing one or two navy blue tracksuits, a white t-shirt and black sports pants in class, he has a closely trimmed white-grey beard and a light, pinkish complexion reflecting some of his Norwegian ancestry. When he does strip down to a white or black t-shirt in warmer months, his arms appear toned and defined, reflecting the lifetime of dedication to the martial arts. Like many of his students, he often wears shoes with thick soles so as to better connect with the floor and sink his mass into the feet, as he believes Taijiquan is all about "sinking the mass" and "finding the floor," just as a boxer's job is to learn to punch. David explained this guiding principle to one of his core students in a WhatsApp discussion on our members' group. This is sometimes through quote attributed to other teachers: "If you still have tension someplace, it will prevent the accumulation of internal strength. When you relax, your arms will sink and become heavy, otherwise they will float." Or in his own words:

> For much of the time, you're either in a state of tension or you're in a state of collapse. When you're neither, you're sinking. And sinking is not an action, it's a result of acquiring the correct qualities of mind and inner body interaction. It's a skill or *Gong*. A western concept of relax is the outer body; it's of little help other than for the beginner. That's why your internal alignments, not external, are based on your relationship to gravity. That's all I have to say about that.

Along with the command "Hang the flesh from the bones", "The inside must come alive" is becoming an increasingly choice platitude for David who is more concerned with a Daoist reading of anatomy than a Western medical one. David is a popular teacher who has retained a great following over the last four years I have learned from him. To mark the recent occasion of his 60th birthday, David's loyal students organised a series of surprise gifts for him through a private WhatsApp group separate from the usual chat forum (so that it would a secret from David). Alexsander, one of the two Polish students in the school suggested a Xian, because David is interested in the weapons forms. The students also rallied round to buy David a red and white Chinese Fu banner to bring him good luck and prosperity as well as positive energy, to keep with the Daoist belief system they all follow. David is keen to teach what he regards as the authentic approach to Taijiquan, as opposed to the simplified "Taiji for dummies." He is concerned about the standardisation of Taijiquan according to the Chartered Institute of the Management of Physical Activity (CIMSPA)'s position statement (2022) in the UK, which would not recognise the qualifications of his own teacher and some of his renowned associates. He also stays away from Taijiquan competitions, joking on the WhatsApp group: "I've heard it all now, next they will have a meditation contest."

David began life in his hometown where he has stayed all his life, being fortunate to find the mentor for his life project of Taijiquan and Neigong in the shape of a man two decades his junior, Malcolm Reeve. David holds Malcolm in high esteem, noting to his students that "he is very accomplished", being the holder of various lineages of Chinese martial arts and healing systems. David is grateful for Malcolm's generosity and discernment, advising that "you've got to find the right teacher, or you stumbled into one, as I did." Malcolm, 40, is a British teacher of Taijiquan and Chinese internal arts who, alongside his Swedish wife and another British assistant instructor, is now living an entrepreneurial expat life in the picturesque European seaside resort. They specialise in Taijiquan and Neigong, which David explains is "a Daoist process of change." Malcolm is the founder and head of the School of Internal Arts, an organisation with branches around Europe and North America. Despite this success, David explained that Malcolm is "a really lovely guy, really down to earth, no airs and graces. He was funny as well…it's brought me so much laughter and open heartedness."

Malcolm's relocation to another country has enabled David to continue teaching the class he was once a student at in his hometown. However, David reflected how many of the members of the local class were not satisfied with the situation of learning from a fellow student, although one of Malcolm's original pupils is still training under David, showing humility and loyalty highly prized in the traditionalist martial arts.

Interestingly, Malcolm first learned the martial arts as a child from his father Brian, 62, a Karate expert who is now Malcolm's student of Taijiquan and other internal arts including meditation and qigong. Malcolm represents a new generation of Taijiquan experts who have travelled to a more open China to learn from various teachers. This follows a period of dissemination from Chinese teachers, as in the case of British Wing Chun explored earlier in this book. Malcolm has written numerous books on the art and related practices such as Neigong (inner work) which follows his pursuit of a Daoist cosmology, medicine and life philosophy. Several of David's most dedicated students have travelled to train with Malcolm in his residential school as well as in other branches of his international organisation. One of these includes Andrew, a South African student who moved all the way to Wales to train with David because Malcolm was unavailable during that time. With his Irish passport (thanks to Irish immigrant grandparents), Andrew was later able to relocate to Europe "to learn from the source", as one classmate put it. After learning from Malcolm until his departure for China, David continues to stay in touch by attending instructor retreats with him in Europe.

David believes there two things that "sowed the seed" of his fascination for the martial arts. First, as a child, David witnessed his father practising Karate and its various Kata in their home, which was a rarity in 1960s Britain. Second, in his adolescence coincided with the Bruce Lee and Kung Fu craze of the 1970s and 1980s. Indeed, David admitted that the hit Bruce Lee movie *Enter the Dragon* (1973) "changed everything for everyone." Despite this period of enthusiasm for the martial arts, David's parents later divorced, which David admits hit his self-confidence levels. Around the age of eighteen, David decided to take measures to work on his confidence, although he felt he was a creative and sensitive person, he was "very Yin, introverted and quiet." He was not taken by team sports as a child, instead being interested in individual activities that were "about you and your development." After saying to himself "I need to do something", David found a Shotokan Karate teacher within a post-industrial area of the multicultural city's bay known for its influx of sailors and communities from around the globe. Training in the 1980s involved relatively little health and safety, with "no gloves, no gum shields, nothing", noting that the level of brutality often made David want to cry. However, he persevered as others dropped out of training, as he found himself toughening up.

Nonetheless, a serious injury meant David taking time out of training while he entered art college. Some years later, at the age of 30, he bumped into one of his old seniors in the Karate dojo who told him that he has taken on the leadership of the school. "He's been my friend and teacher for the last 30 years"

David reflected. He gained his Shodan (1st degree black belt) in 1996 after being a brown belt for many years. Training continued to be tough, including the full-contact Dojo Kumite accounted for in Goran Powell's (2006) respected memoir *Waking Dragons*. This developed a strong willpower, but a stiff body, which is "a double-edged sword" according to David with the hindsight of his internal martial arts training.

Another form of arduous training came in the travelling to various courses led by respected Japanese Sensei who "were notorious for being brutal" (as in his midnight journey up to Aberdeen, Scotland) and the countless repetition of techniques "in the baking hot sun", which David admitted was to develop a sense of spirit rather than refined technique. This has parallels with the notion of Japanese spirit that Twigger (1997) writes of in the famous *Angry White Pyjamas*. David now sees much of this as necessary for young people with all their energy, although the "very scathing" comments in the texts that his Taijiquan organisation refer to consider such use of physical energy and muscle (Li) as dull or "stupid" force. David began to notice the internal potential of such softer arts through his exposure to Aikido from an acquaintance, noting: "That was really useful, that bridge to the softer arts."

In his Karate class, David met his wife, who continued to train alongside him until she became pregnant with the first of his two boys, now young men in their twenties. David did continue training during his children's infancy, which he looked back at being "quite selfish." Although he has since moved across to the Chinese internal martial arts of Taijiquan and Baguazhang, David still trains and teaches Karate in the local community. When I met him for a life history interview in one of his favourite local cafés known for its work for the homeless, David was reading a Karate magazine in which his friend – Malcolm's father Barry, another respected Karate and Taijiquan practitioner – appeared on the front cover. David's own students do tend to be white Europeans, mainly British (both English and Welsh) and Polish, along with one Romanian, one Indian man and lately, one Black British man. Taijiquan does tend to attract more white people in Britain, which is a theme for a future research project devoted to examining demographics in the martial arts. There are a few women in his classes, although only three female students are longstanding.

In recent years, David has gained international students, with one American woman living in the UK and another of her compatriots joining the Saturday morning Taijiquan class on Zoom at her 5 a.m. in the Eastern seaboard! There is also one trans Spanish woman living in Barcelona who has joined some of the

Zoom classes for meditation, qigong and Taijiquan, which adds to the increasing diversity of students.

David offers a free meditation class at 7 a.m. on Thursdays, regarding this as "sitting practice" for the foundation of meditation. Some of his students are early risers, with the energetic Tom, a smartly dressed and confident man in his 50s, joking that "you seize the day before the day seizes you!" According to David, this kind of light-hearted humour is important for the Daoist approach to self-cultivation, and he is pleased that his students have this good-natured approach to laughter. For instance, in the hall where he directs his evening classes, there have been several large camels left from a nativity play, which are often the butt of light jokes. When one student told David that camels do not age as humans do in the external sense, he replied: "That's the way to go, isn't it – look young until you keel over." Later, on the final evening for the camels in the hall, David was sure to take some selfies with his students and the camels, sharing the funny images on WhatsApp. Despite such jokes, David is far more concerned with the invisible, inner body of organs and connective tissue than the visible, outer body of bones and muscles. David focuses on his student's self-cultivation, which is "trying to be a better person…through training, these things will happen. We don't need to say 'I must be a better person, I must be less envious'" as according to him, those kinds of characteristics and behaviours will manifest as a consequence of the training.

Previously, David split his class into one longer session on Taijiquan and one shorter class on Qigong, although he ceased the Qigong / Neigong training during the COVID-19 lockdowns and restrictions to his fear of accidents with the latter set of activities. David has since modified the structure so he runs two classes in the evenings: A 90-minute beginner's class and a 2-hour intermediate class for those students beyond the "cross hands" posture of the Short Form. Whereas the shorter beginner's class is heavily focused on teaching the art of Taijiquan, the second intermediate class often gives students the agency to select their preferred aspects to practise.

In a recent session, David remarked to my fellow intermediate learners: "You know, this doesn't feel like a class…it feels like I'm with a group of friends and we're practising together." These classes try to teach students to use *Yi* (intent) rather than *Li* ("dull force"). David explained that even in his Karate, which is now much softer, he is still straightening the elbow with dull force, "as you're not using Qi." This *Qi* is often regarded as "the engine" of internal martial arts, unlike the muscle and bone of external ones. Both of David's classes are concerned with the principles behind Taijiquan – namely Song and Ting, "letting go and listening." David explains their symbiotic relationship as follows: "The more you listen, the more you can let go, and the more you let go, the more you can listen. Song and Ting…simple but elusive." The combined training of Taijiquan and Neigong is supposed to develop "a soft, relaxed, strong body" rather than a soft, relaxed and weak body.

Overall, David regards his role as being "a gateway to the School of Internal Arts, really." Many of his more dedicated students have journeyed to train with Malcolm and become qualified instructors in Taijiquan and Neigong – even learning aspects of Chinese medicine and astrology. David primarily teaches in two venues: a refugee support centre on one evening and in a multicultural primary school on another evening, which reflect his humble roots and connection to working-class communities. Although the venues are often difficult to secure in the long-term, especially with dwindling student numbers, David is keen to stay in the places his students are fond of. On occasions, he rents a hall in a local rugby club where he offers day courses in the form, conditioning exercises and pushing hands training. This variety and intensity of training has attracted many people with extensive martial arts experience, as David once remarked, looking around the hall: "I just realised that everyone here has a martial arts background." Many students have practised arts such as Aikido and various forms of Kung Fu, and Aidan, explored in the next chapter, is one such example of someone who has made a successful transition from a more contact-based martial art to Taijiquan, which he regards as switching vehicles. The car metaphors are common for David as well, as he used analogies of engines and motors: "Imagine you have a beautiful new Ferrari, but it has no engine. Is it still a car? Is it still Taiji without the internal engine?" David regards much of Taijiquan today as being mixed with New Age ideas and visualisation, seeing these influences exported to the East and re-exported to the West." He also laments the Westernisation of Traditional Chinese Medicine (TCM), stating with a sigh: "It's all been watered down too much."

Summary

Both Billy and David are extremely passionate teachers who are now striving to make a living from their beloved HEMA and Taijiquan. After sadly being made redundant from a graphic design company, David supplements his more intense classes with more relaxed sessions with a cancer support group, while Billy, also temporarily laid off during the pandemic, now teaches numerous private classes to students. These instructors position themselves in contrast to approaches to the arts that they would like to distance themselves from. At the same time, they draw close to a circle of trusted friends, students, training partners and loved ones to develop a community of practice and support that enables their schools to flourish.

Both men met their life partners through the martial arts, and he retain a sense of brotherhood with peers of a similar skill level. They also identify with and against different people, such as a grandfather, father and hypothetical children. Their martial arts journeys are intended to be lifelong ones until old age and eventual death, and it is likely that they will meet many more important characters along this path. A relational sociological approach like that advocated by Crossley (2010) could help make sense of the dynamic and evolving networks of people that constitute our society. The networks might include alliances between local martial arts schools, branches of an international association and connections between people in a martial arts body lineage. Two people who speak to such themes are George and Aidan, examined next in light of the investment and return of their capital to forge their minds and bodies through martial arts and related practices.

References

Ashbridge, T. (2015). *The greatest knight: The remarkable life of William Marshal, the power behind five English thrones*. London: Simon & Schuster.

Chadwick, E. (2005). *Greatest knight: A gripping novel about William Marshal – One of England's forgotten heroes*. London: Sphere.

Chartered Institute for the Management of Sport and Physical Activity. (2022). A position statement from the Chartered Institute for the Management of Sport and Physical Activity, the Tai Chi & Qigong Union for Great Britain (TCUGB) and the British Council for Chinese Martial Arts (BCCMA) March 2022. Available at: https://www.cimspa.co.uk/standards-home/professional-standards-and-consultation-guidance/position-statement-for-tai-chi-and-qigong. Last accessed 28 May 2022.

Crossley, N. (2010). *Towards relational sociology*. London: Routledge.

Judkins, B. (2016). The seven forms of lightsaber combat: Hyper-reality and the invention of the martial arts. *Martial Arts Studies, 2*, 6–22.

Musashi, M. (2020). *The book of five rings: Deluxe classic edition*. Independently published with Amazon.

Powell, G. (2006). *Waking dragons: A martial artist faced his ultimate test*. Chichester: Summersdale Publishers Ltd.

Ryan, A. (2008). Globalisation and the 'internal alchemy' in Chinese martial arts: The transmission of Taijiquan to Britain. *East Asian Science, Technology and Society: An International Journal, 2*, 525–543.

Twigger, R. (1997). *Angry white pyjamas*. London: Weidenfeld & Nicolson.

9

Investing into the Martial Arts and Related Practices

The last chapter showcased the tales of two dedicated martial arts instructors, Billy and David, who also featured in the preface to this book due to my ongoing engagement with them as part of my ethnographic research started in 2018. Both Billy and David are everyday, non-celebrity practitioners who keep a relatively low profile as they concentrate on their own personal development and the steady expansion of their schools now that they are in a position to work as semi-professional and professional instructors. This chapter offers two example stories from another pair of devoted martial artists who have experimented with different training protocols and martial arts along their journey through life. These men have transitioned between martial arts schools and styles, and although they have operated as instructors at certain parts of the martial arts journeys, they prefer to remain as long-term students of the martial arts and related practices that that they use for their personal development and self-cultivation in conjunction with a trusted group of people around them. Both of these men are contrasting in some regards, as George (real name requested) follows Western training methods of lifting weights and sporting practices while Aidan (pseudonym) adopts a more spiritual, Eastern perspective on martial arts and life. However, George and Aidan both invest a great deal of time, energy and financial resources into their martial arts and supplementary personal development, as they gain new identities, cultural knowledge, transformed bodies and life skills that are a reinvestment back into their health and wellbeing.

We begin with George, a father of two who continues with his Wing Chun development along with his quest to learn more about the more esoteric aspects of the Southern Chinese martial arts. His story is followed by that of Aidan, a grandfather and retired fireman who held instructor ranks in Aikido and Chen Hsin before stepping off one martial arts vehicle to that of Taijiquan and the internal arts connecting to it.

George: Fighting Fit as a Martial Man

Like me, George (51) is another English "ex-pat" martial arts enthusiast living in Wales, and with the same Wing Chun Sifu John Bridge, we have struck up a strong bond. Of average height and build, George shaves his head while sometimes growing his greying beard thick in the winter. In recent months, he had slimmed down to a very lean 10 and a half stone, which he is now building up muscle after following a strict, calorie-controlled diet consisting of chicken burritos and other prescribed meals. George is a long-term partner of Chloe (pseudonym) and a father of their two children. He relocated to Wales from his home town in a rural pocket of the county of Devon two decades ago due to an exciting management position available in the international logistics company he has worked for the last two decades. This was initially in customer services, which George believes has served him well when negotiation with difficult characters in the martial arts world and political field of Wing Chun.

George still speaks with traces of a Devonshire accent, although as his parents were originally from Northamptonshire in the East Midlands, he reflected, "I'm not from Devon genetically…I'm not a farmer." Being from one of the heartlands of English rugby union, he played the game throughout secondary school and still follows rugby in another region passionate about the sport, South Wales. Respecting strength and athleticism of the players, George cross trains with a military-style boot camp in the weekends that is popular among his seaside community, and after its own politicised division causes by a breakaway group, the camps have extended to some beach rugby training with two former professionals from Samoa.

George's story is one of long-term commitment to a core martial art that is supplemented by many different experimental training regimes and diet programmes in a bid to live a long and healthy life while offsetting the natural loss of muscle mass from his 40s onwards. He and I have trained together and spent a great deal of time together over the past five and a half years, and this section is reflective of the martial arts and training stories that George has shared with me time and again while having our traditional pre-training coffee or when travelling to seminars and events.

George got into Wing Chun as a young man in his twenties, entering the school of Sifu John Bridge some years before I moved to the region. He first learned a slightly different style of the martial art as his teacher went out on his own, forming an independent research association before seeking out his current teacher, a renowned Sifu from Macao based in the U.S. In Bridge's Academy, a proudly displayed archive photo showing a 1999 seminar from Master Li include a youthful George lined up with many of the colourful characters of Li's former European Federation that dissipated shortly afterwards. George moved up the ranks to eventually be awarded his black sash in the art, even taking responsibility for one of the branch schools in a nearby town, at a time when Sifu Bridge's Wing Chun association was flourishing in the Westcountry through over a dozen different venues. However, leading the branch school was a difficult responsibility to maintain, especially when George's partner Chloe complained about him needing to go to the class to open the hall up on a night when she felt unwell – something that George reports that she often reminds him about. However, George remains a loyal follower of John's, respecting him as someone "who can actually use it [Wing Chun]…as opposed to just being a theoretical teacher." Indeed, John has a background as a tough man from the East End of London who had been involved in hooligan activities with the England and West Ham firms.

However, George has been tempted by other seminars from different teachers, although he is sensible to prioritise his domestic expenses over travelling to rather expensive events. He told me of one occasion when a Sifu of repute was organising a seminar in Southern England, which would cost a considerable amount. However, the very same weekend, George's washing machine broke down. "He didn't seem to be too pleased with that, saying, 'oh well, never mind George.' I did seem to annoy him with that, but it was a genuine situation." Recalled George, thinking of how many Sifus are very much money-driven, with Wing Chun being their sole income.

Meanwhile, he remains active as a social media follower (rather than creator of content), which includes videos posted by Sifu Jemima Ramsey, a senior Kung Fu sister to Sifu Bridge (featured in the Preface of this book), who showcases alternative ways to work with the wooden dummy as well as supportive strength training using Persian clubs. George's late father admitted to having some Indian clubs, and George has trialled methods such as kettlebells into this own routine. He isn't alone, as he follows other notable teachers such as Alan Orr and Mark Phillips (of London Wing Chun), the latter being one of the Wing Chun influencers with his own brand of "Fight Science" (https://www.youtube.com/c/londonwingchun) that George follows on social media. As a close relative of someone with a kidney disorder, George has used his athletic ability and willpower to good use by raising money for charities such as Kidney Wales through distance running, fun running and assault courses such as Tough Mother.

Upon arriving in Wales, George sought out other Wing Chun schools to learn from. However, he did not find the standards of skill among the different teachers, regarding it as "like learning off one of your brothers." Instead of learning from a local Sifu, he continued to travel down to the South West of England to continue with private lessons from John Bridge while also taking the opportunity to visit his elderly parents. They have sadly passed away in recent years, which gives George less of an impetus to make the long journey down to the old *Kwoon*. Like some of my older colleagues at work, he has also recently admitted to having less energy than before, and there is the issue of the cost-of-living crisis of 2022, with inflation in the UK rising to an average of 9%. The conflict in Ukraine has caused a massive rise in cereal and fuel prices for people around the world. Unfortunately, after a takeover from a large conglomerate, George's work has stopped the benefits of a company car and free fuel from the various depots around Britain, so he has had to buy a second-hand car from a work colleague. His 17-year-old daughter now has a car after George's careful check on a small vehicle for her birthday (the legal age for driving in the UK), and George remarked, "I didn't realise how expensive cars have become! It's been years since I bought one." This has increased his family's expenditures, while his income has remained the same, meaning the travel for the quarterly Wing Chun seminars is a bigger decision requiring careful planning. Meanwhile, Sifu Bridge's life has changed, with him needing to take on work as a delivery specialist for the National Health Service (NHS), with the fatigue from the long hours behind the wheel meaning the evening classes are finished earlier on. Sifu has decided to increase the price of the seminars from £40 to £60, which is a 50% price hike designed to make students take the seminars more seriously. With the five-hour round trip and greatly increased price and expenses, George is still mulling over his options, with understandable hope for the seminar costs to be reduced.

Through his contacts, George became acquainted with Jan, a Polish practitioner of Mok Gar Kung Fu, a style renowned for its kicking. This practitioner also studied Taijiquan, which he believed helped offset the damage done by the more explosive and combative Kung Fu art. The two men would meet up to train together in their homes, starting light sparring sessions by crossing arms (as in the iconic tournament in Bruce Lee's *Enter the Dragon*). Jan became accustomed to George's direct attacks to his centreline, so he was able to drop down and swoop at the back of George's knees using a clawing technique, knocking George off balance. George has demonstrated this technique on me in person, showing how the unexpected movement would be difficult to defend and counter. Although Wing Chun theory and maxims stipulates "use hands against hand and legs against leg", Jan was able to use his agility and mobility to challenge the thesis, opening George's eyes to other approaches in the Chinese martial arts.

The series of exchanges was short lived, however, as when Jan's British partner passed away, he relocated to another region of Wales that was too remote for George to continue training with him. His friend did admit that when he visited China in a village purported to be the home of Mok Gar, the villagers watched him demonstrate some of the techniques he had mastered, only to receive the comment: "What is that?! I don't know what that is, but that's not Mok Gar!" Apparently, as with Lao Gar, the Mok Gar that is practised around different pockets of the UK is far removed from the Mok Gar taught in the People's Republic of China. This might be due to the sportification process in which Kung Fu styles entered kickboxing-related tournaments or were not taught in their entirety, or were modified to suit Western students' interests in the more realistic hand-to-hand combat aspect of Kung Fu (as opposed to the weapons and Eastern healing systems). It also might be due to the Cultural Revolution of the 1960s and 1970s in Communist China impacting on the traditionalist martial arts regarded as feudal and even bourgeois. This mirrors comments from our Wing Chun Sifu reminiscing of his travels to Foshan, the home of Wing Chun in the Guangdong (Canton) Province, which he saw as not having evolved – in his words, "wooden." His own teacher, Master Li believes that students should look to the future instead of the past: "Don't look back fifty or a hundred years. Use your fifty years [of Wing Chun training] to add to the system and make it better for the next generation. Then they will add their fifty years, and so on."

However, George is fond of comparing these Southern Chinese martial arts, and he subscribes to popular "The Martial Man" YouTube Channel (see https://www.youtube.com/c/THEMARTIALMAN) led by a British martial artist who conducts his own technique-based research using crowd funding and subscribers to make a living. This now includes partnerships with notable instructors with their own online short courses to produce what The Martial Man claims as being "the best online platform for learning martial arts" (see https://themartialman.com/). On the YouTube channel, this investigative series of episodes features more esoteric systems such as the Five Ancestors Kung Fu, which purportedly contains a version of Wing Chun within its curriculum. The Martial Man even runs his own retreat based on a Thai beach resort, where students (almost exclusively young men) get to learn off a new generational of charismatic, influential and controversial teachers of traditionalist lineages and styles in their forties who can explain the art in the English language. The martial arts styles featured such as Pak Mei, Five Ancestors and Mindful Wing Chun tend to be towards the "softer" category of Chinese martial arts while also focusing on the internal aspects of relaxation and internal power development. George has shared numerous videos from The Martial Man to stimulate our rich discussions each Saturday, sometimes sharing the video links on Messenger and WhatsApp a few days in advance of our meet up in order for me to digest the material.

George was particularly fascinated by the video of the Five Ancestors Kung Fu, which had an intriguing sticking technique that one teacher demonstrated on the host, who seemed unable to escape from his touch. On other occasions, he shares content after our discussions over tea and coffee at the start of the training session. Indeed, our own exchanges reflect those seen in private lessons with our teacher, who used to make tea for his long-term students in the small kitchen in his martial arts centre. George is open minded about the internal aspects of the martial arts and notions of *qi*, and finds the critiques from the likes of Rob of McDojo Life (see Chapter 6) annoying. On one occasion, he lambasted the videos circulating around traditional martial artists being defeated by MMA fighters:

> "You don't see a man in his fifties fighting another man in his fifties, do you? You see a man in his fifties getting beaten up by a fit guy in his twenties. Also, you got to remember, a lot of people in Wing Chun don't train to be fighters; they train two hours a week, not as professional fighters."

It's like us [George and I] getting attacked by someone who is younger and fitter who trains all the time, whereas we just train once a week for two hours.

Once our Sifu had read of my move from Mexico to Cardiff Met in 2016, he wrote to me on Facebook Messenger to inform me of George's residence near Cardiff. The same week, George had contacted me after reading an article I co-authored with Anu Vaittinen on our collaborative project on the virtual pedagogical strategies of Wing Chun learners (Jennings & Vaittinen, 2016). He read this article with interest due to his subscription to Ben Judkins's popular *Chinese*

Martial Arts Studies (Kung Fu Tea) blog, which blends the typical shorter blogs, discussions of recent published work with original academic articles (see www.chinesemartialstudies.com). George often uses his mobile phone to scroll down to read the latest posts written by Ben Judkins and guest authors. These articles are free to read and are sometimes only 2,000 to 4,000 words in length, unlike traditional journal articles that are not open access to members of the public. Modern technology has enabled George to digest this material while waiting in the car for his partner and children while they are out shopping in town, although George admits that some of the articles are less relevant to him, as he is not an academic interested in the status of the field of martial arts studies in universities. Indeed, when I invited him along to a martial arts studies event in Cardiff, he was slightly doubtful of his ability to understand some of the disciplinary jargon in martial arts research. As an honest and sometimes direct man, George even admits that he did not care much for my research on Xilam, as "I only read about martial arts that I rate. You are more interested in the social aspects, whereas I'm interested in the historical topics." This fascination with the history of Chinese martial arts has led George to seek out many books on different Wing Chun lineages, as in *Mastering Kung Fu* (Gee, Meng, & Loewenhagen, 2004) available in his local library, although he found this too technical and difficult to finish: "You're [the authors] making it far more complicated than it is, talking about vectors and stuff like that." He also admires the book *Complete Wing Chun* (Chu, Ritchie, & Wu, 1998), which was one of the first texts to declare the existence of multiple Wing Chun lineages outside the Ip Man branch.

Closer to home, George also follows the activities of teachers of village styles of Wing Chun such as Gwaolo Wing Chun and hybrid approaches to the art, although he does tire to the online bickering about the "true" and "original" style. When I asked him if the martial arts had acted as a gateway to other forms of thinking, George did admit: "I doubt I would have read about Buddhism if it wasn't for martial arts. Also, the same goes for Daoism – I probably wouldn't have read anything about Daoism if it wasn't for Wing Chun." This wider reading stems from a more open mind, where Chinese views on the body and energy systems permit students to consider other paradigms and realities. This extends to George reading about alternative histories of the world, including theories on the origin of humans, alien contact, the creation of religions and even giants. He has borrowed books on these topics, including those stored in the mysterious basement level of the local library, which the librarian explained to him was "a section for books that not many people request."

Asides from Wing Chun, George has also tried his hand in Muay Thai kickboxing from a well-respected former champion. Being away from his regular teacher and frequent evening classes permitted him the time and physical energy to learn something new. George enjoyed the physical challenge stemming from sparring and hitting the bags, which differed from much of Wing Chun training attempting to economise on effort and movement. In fact, he was surprised at the relatively looseness of the technical training, with his instructor saying: "You know how to throw a hook, don't you? You know what a roundhouse kick is. So just throw a hook and a roundhouse kick." He has told me of a particularly memorable sparring session against another beginner who he believes must have had learning difficulties. George recalled stalking the man around the ring, as he did not put up much resistance. "It was quick good fun hunting him, although it must be a different story on the receiving end." He shrugged with a wry smile. However, the fun had to stop when George suffered two different injuries: one small chip to the elbow by hitting into a heavy bag and one Anterior Cruciate Ligament (ACL) tear. The elbow was actually remedied by taking the painkiller Ibuprofen upon the recommendation of George's doctor – something George initially thought to be ridiculous advice. To his surprise, the swelling went down and the pain reduced so he could return to action. However, the second injury required rehabilitation in hospital. After learning a jumping kick, George began to train it in the air, until he heard a popping sound. His coach came to his side, believing it to be an ACL tear. "Oh, we only really use that technique for showboating; you wouldn't use it in a fight." The instructor said nonchalantly, as George felt a sense of resentment for being injured for a technique that would not serve him in a real fight (or a competitive one). The long recovery for an injury sustained in his first six months of Thai boxing contrasted with the ten years of practising Wing Chun without any serious injury.

Among the martial art communities in South Wales, the Chow Gar Praying Mantis has an excellent reputation for its quality and unique characteristics. Indeed, in the Wing Chun seminar led by Sifus Karl and Jemima (described in the Preface), another teacher from Wales spoke highly of the school as we walked up the hill from our lunch break. This niche martial art was taught by a Chinese Sifu from Hong Kong who managed a Chinese restaurant in the local town. When the Sifu had heard that George had learned Wing Chun, he paid him a lot of special attention, and George quickly picked up the fundamentals of the art. However, after some months, he found himself repeating the same partner drills – most notably the "grinding" exercises in which partners would stick to each other's wrists, taking turns to attack with a phoenix eye attack [using the middle knuckle of the forefinger] while the other defended. The Sifu explained that this drill helped the students to condition their forearms (with George recalling the teacher having "huge forearms") while also learning how to power through other people's guards, even switching angles from the square-on position shoulder to shoulders facing to a side-on fighting stance.

Sifu Bridge was eager to know more about the Chow Gar style of Kung Fu, although when George expressed this potential exchange of knowledge, the Chinese Sifu became suspicious and protective, closing the opportunity. George then continued with Wing Chun with Sifu Bridge, who he had formed a warm relationship based on openness and a family-like ethos of talk, training and confessions around family and health issues.

George and one of his brothers have always been interested in strength training, and he recalled how they wanted to try to lift the stones in Scotland that feature in the Netflix documentary *Stronglands*. These days, George is a keen collector of antique books on subjects such as weight training, as in old texts from the 1920s to 1950s on physical culture. As his son his entering his teens, George is pleased that his friends are showing an interest in George's own resistance training. "I saw some weights in your shed. Does you dad lift weights?" Asked the adolescent boy, intrigued. George hopes the boys will be inspired to lift weights themselves, and he maintains his own motivation by reading about the methods of figures such as Arnold Schwarzenegger. Like many people, he watches various sports documentaries on Netflix, looking into different diets such as the vegan lifestyle advocated in *Gamechangers*. However, he finds some of their arguments dubious, while reading into the debates around the scientific experiments conducted on the programme. Although George does not often follow MMA, he enjoyed watching the biographical documentary on Ronda Rousey, shocked at how despite her success in Olympic Judo, she felt the need to sleep in her car before morning training sessions. He admired her coach, the renowned grappler Gene LeBell while lamenting Rousey's eventual losses due to her attempt to play out a stand-up fighting strategy against the taller kickboxer Holly Holm.

Pierre Bourdieu's (1990) framework has been utilised to a great extent in martial arts scholarship since the time of Wacquant's (2004) ethnographic study of boxing, bodily labour and bodily capital (e.g. Sánchez García & Spencer, 2013), and it serves as a helpful analytic lens for understanding this tale. George's story is one of ongoing dedication to his main martial art of Wing Chun that has involved a significant investment of physical / bodily capital (time and energy), economic capital (fees for private lessons and now fuel), travel (a combination of both physical and economic capital) and cultural capital (reading into the

Chinese martial arts and other forms of Wing Chun). He is aware that Wing Chun, with its focus on the economy of motion and effort, does not work the body as more athletic endeavours do, so he maximises his opportunity to go running, take part in charity fundraising events and engage with other people in dynamic boot camps and adapted sporting activities. The martial arts have also opened a gateway to new way of thinking about Eastern philosophy and concepts such as *qi*, which George remains open to.

Another person who has invested a great deal of capital into his martial arts and personal development is Aidan, who has adopted a more Eastern and esoteric viewpoint on the body, health, consciousness and relationships.

Aidan Evans: Changing Vehicles from Cheng Hsin to Taijiquan and Neigong

Aidan began training in martial arts at the age of 28. He is a charismatic and talkative man keen to pass on wisdom to the next generation, noting "you want it for your children and you want it for your grandchildren. What could I have been like if I had started it [training] young?" He is a retired firefighter and grandfather with decades of martial arts experience who is proud to have the free time to explore many pursuits and passions in his remaining years, sometimes telling me that Taijiquan "keeps an old man alive." Tanned and well-built, with a goatee beard and greying hair, he is still strong and powerful at a time where many men are inactive and unwell.

At 64, Aidan is still immersed in the martial arts through his regular practise of Taijiquan as well as Neigong under David's tutelage and an online course with Malcolm, for which he holds an annual subscription. In this relaxed environment where uniforms are not expected, Aidan tends to wear the colours white or green, sometimes opting for a green mandarin suit during the colder months. Like many of my other informants, Aidan is also from South Wales, and he received a Roman Catholic upbringing in a working-class community. He has stayed in his hometown, where he has raised his family (two daughters and two small grandchildren and a wife of many years) and upgraded his house to become a spacious home in a peaceful suburban area. Like some of his friends, Aidan has moved away from his original religion, seeing it as overly negative and concerned with confession, and he has been interested in alternative spiritualities and Eastern philosophies for numerous years. He is a very interesting case study of a martial artist engaging with a hybrid mix of Eastern and Western practices available to him, including meditation, martial arts, musical instruments, shiatsu massage and singing.

Although Aidan was exposed to the martial arts through popular culture as a child in the 1960s (as in the *Kung Fu* television series starring David Carradine), so admits that he started "late" to training. In his young manhood, Aidan admits to having been "a drunken womaniser", and this was reinforced by the macho culture of firefighting in the 1970s and 1980s which was concerned with "how hard you were and how much you could drink." However, deep down, Aidan admits that he is a Highly Sensitive Person (HSP) like the estimated 20% of the human population that Dr. Elaine Aron researches (see https://hsperson.com/). On several occasions, Aidan explained how he first got into the martial arts after reading of several violent intruders who came into a family home elsewhere in the UK. At the age of 28, Aidan was shocked by the brutal rape of the family man's two daughters while the father was restrained and bound. As a new father of two little girls at the time, Aidan was adamant that he would do everything he could in his power to defend his beloved girls so that such an event could not befall his family, and he turned to the martial arts in his local area. It was at this stage of his life as a young adult that he "learned how to learn", unlike in school, which did not seem to suit Aidan. Aikido was popular for self-defence and spiritual development in the 1990s, so he approached the art with great seriousness for 20 years, learning from all the Senseis in his hometown and the surrounding area, eventually settling on the Iwama style. After finding some teachers to be too political and narrowminded, he moved to other instructors who he felt could push him to the next levels of understanding. One such teacher was near the border with England, where Aidan travelled to his dojo, wearing his full Aikido uniform and proudly bearing his first dan black belt. Aidan recounted this incident, in which the Sensei asked Aidan to grab him hard by the arm, Aidan complied, only to be thrown across the room. "I've never felt anything like it!" Exclaimed Aidan, remembering that he told the Sensei that he would not continue to wear the black belt. "You don't have to, but I'd appreciate it if you could." Replied the Sensei. This tale reflects the great differences between dojos and teachers of the traditionalist Asian martial arts – partly due to the artistic interpretation of technique and stylistics, but also the deeper meaning teachers hold of what the art exists for in the first place. However, all of these teachers are united in their respect for the founder Morihei Ueshiba, who Aidan quotes as having said, "when you cut a sword, you are trying to purify yourself. Every time you polish the stone."

After gaining his black belt in Aikido and visiting some renowned instructors, Aidan came across the name of Peter Ralston, a Californian figure in the alternative consciousness movement who had founded his own hybrid martial art in the 1970s: Cheng Hsin, "the art of effortless power" or quite literally, "honest heart" (see www.chenghsin.com). During and after our Taijiquan training, Aidan is fond of beginning sentences with "Peter Ralston said...", which is inevitably followed by words of wisdom from the American martial arts figure who Aidan reveres, regarding him as a genius and a formidable figure who he found difficult to approach in person due to his brooding intensity. Aidan has trained directly with Peter within one of his intensive retreats. When I met Aidan for an interview on his experiences, he reflected on how Peter came from a rich family, which enabled him to devote his time to training the martial arts. According to Aidan, during the 1970s, Ralston allegedly took part in full-contact martial arts tournaments, entering and winning as a "one-man American team" in his weight category. Aidan recounted a tale of how Ralston defeated a powerful Mongolian fighter in Taiwan by using the man's brute strength against him to power up his own punches.

Peter Ralston began his martial arts training in Judo before moving onto the Chinese martial arts. Learning from the Chinese-American Sifu Wong Jack Man (the rival of Bruce Lee in the San Francisco Bay area), who, according to Aidan's interpretation of Cheng Hsin lore, actually beat Bruce Lee in that pivotal fight. He explained how Peter developed an impressive ability to read people's intentions and movements through a heightened sense of awareness. Peter cross trained by learning Western boxing, and eventually mentored a professional African American boxer, telling him, "I'll teach you how to dodge." Aidan explained to me that the boxer was initially sceptical about Peter, as he had witnessed a training session in which Peter and his students performed the "wet noodle" exercises used to develop a relaxed, explosive force. Aidan noted that Ralston also mentored high-level Aikido practitioners. In one conference, he told another Taijiquan practitioner that there was only one other martial artist who could match his awareness and positioning to cancel out one another's attacks: William Chen, noted student of Taijiquan master Zheng Manqing, known as "the soft boxer" (see Smith, 1974). Such softness and relaxation are important in Cheng Hsin, as evidenced in the "outreaching" exercise that Aidan demonstrated to me, gently touching my shoulder:

> Aidan placed his right hand on my right shoulder. "What's the immediate thing that I feel? There's some kind of sweater. Now what's beneath the sweater? Can you feel the mass of a shoulder? But it's not just a lump of meat, otherwise it would fall to the floor. There's something attached to the shoulder, as in bones..."

Similarly, Ralston regarded a combative situation as "being in relationship with someone", with Aidan explaining this concept as "if you label something as a fight, you've already added a level of tension." Aidan demonstrated this principle of a relaxed relationship when I grabbed his wrist. Instead of struggling with muscular force, Aidan simply turned away in a relaxed manner, walking away. He asked me to do the same, but I was using too much force, which causes a similar degree of tension in my mind, leading me to struggle even more. I was treating the exercise as a fighting scenario with winners and losers rather than just another situation of human relationships. On two occasions, Aidan had shared an insight from Ralston with me. Making a tense fist, he asked me: "Is this a hand?" to which I replied, "Yes." Aidan then responded, "No…a hand is free", wiggling his fingers in a relaxed manner, adding, "that's the metaphor for how you want to live your life."

Aidan eventually moved away from Aikido, working up to the level of being an instructor in Cheng Hsin and representative for his local area. Using his clearly effective teaching skills, he likened the wet noodle principle to having a plate of spaghetti thrown at you, which would be both a shock and difficult to defend against. Using sound effects and visual expressions in his kitchen, Aidan demonstrated the "wet noodle" movement, which were akin to the loosening exercises seen in Taijiquan. Although the notion of wet noodle is actually derogatory in Taijiquan, it is a core practice for developing a relaxed, interconnected Cheng Hsin body.

Another exercise is "the corner game" or "corner dodging", which aims to maximise the space available and get out of "victim mode" while receiving blows from 12-ounce gloves. The idea behind this is to attune to "the honesty of this moment…not on the past moment when you were just hit." Aidan recalls students curling up and crying, which Ralston aimed to overcome, as it was seen as the child stage or "the perpetual juvenile" in his system. David (featured in the Preface and Chapter 8) also regards this child stage when the student is only focused on the fighting aspect of martial arts. Similarly, there are parallels between Ralston's system and Taijiquan through their discourse on "standing back" to become an observer of one's own movement. Aidan noted this: "It's not intention; it's attention that we want." However, Aidan did admit that Peter Ralston did take many aspects of Taijiquan for his system. He also believes German Karate blogger and influencer Jesse Enkamp's theory that Mike Tyson's coach Cus D'Amato was inspired by a combination of Karate and Taiji for the flowing movements enabling Tyson to "cock the gun while finding the floor." Aidan demonstrated this in his kitchen, sinking into one leg to draw up a punch from the floor. He also reflected on how Ralston found boxers to be the most laid-back of all martial artists, due to their actual fighting of others, unlike the other stylists such as in Aikido, who were creating a fantasy.

After classes, when Aidan kindly dropped me near my old home, he would sometimes demonstrate the partner exercises that Peter developed. One such exercises, "trap the fly", included sticking to the opponent's skin, moving as they move as if you are trapping a mosquito against the flesh: not pressing to hard so as to kill the fly but not releasing the pressure so that if could escape. In terms of attack, Aidan explained to me how Cheng Hsin develops explosive force as well as yielding energies. Using the metaphor of a wave, Aidan claimed that the punch can be turned into a tsunami. Paraphrasing Rolston, Aidan stated: "The spray is disparate from the wave. The spray gets you wet, but the wave knocks you down."

Aidan remains in awe of Peter's creativity and vision, and he often shares copies of his many books with friends and neighbours, as in the deep and meaningful *Zen Body Being* (Ralston & Ralston, 2006), "written for anyone who has a body" and the more martial *Principles of Effortless Power* (Ralston, 1989). Like Peter, he regards many martial arts as ineffective for real-life combat, although he stressed that these arts are highly valuable in and of themselves as lifestyle activities where "you never know enough." Taking the history of Aikido into account, Aidan regards it as a belief, "as its original inception was as a spiritual practice. It is a fantasy, an image you have created." He also highlighted how the techniques in Aikido are highly controlled and responsive to specific attacks that need to be delivered in a specific plane of motion. Nonetheless, in a recent interview, Aidan admitted that "I'm glad that I've jumped onto Malcolm's vehicle and off Peter's vehicle." By "vehicle" he is referring to the philosophy, system and pedagogy of each of these influential martial artists and teachers. Whereas Peter's system leads the practitioner to many partner training exercises to understand other people's intent while being completely present in the moment, Malcolm's is very much about self-understanding and self-exploration through solo training, qigong and forms, which seem perfect for this stage of Aidan's life.

However, on occasions after heavy training using solo exercises and standing postures, Aidan has admitted to me that "I do miss working with another body." This was even more apparent during the COVID-19 lockdown in which we were all unable to touch and push hands together. In a recent post-pandemic training session, Aidan was praising of my development since before the lockdown, remarking to David, "you've completely changed his body!" Responding to Aidan's comments, David performed a technique on me, noting that he could "feel the lines." The next morning, Aidan wrote me a WhatsApp message simply stating, "well done mate." This was very helpful feedback aided by the partner training, which Aidan regards as being crucial in Cheng Hsin. Aidan commented that "you have to create the Taiji body; you can't do it without the vessel." This might take many years for people with very different bodies considered with tension, such as labourers on the building site, aggressive people and bodybuilders. Tension blocks power, and Aidan used the analogy of a garden hose: "I want my water – my jet – to travel." In order to develop such power, Aidan told me by answering his own question "how am I going to get the force in upper body?" with the response "the first thing I want to feel in the ground." Ralston also taught Aidan to punch more effectively by imagining "reaching for a peach…you want to take it gently and activate your hip to not squash it."

Aidan believes in the Chinese and Japanese approach to the martial arts as combining with other art forms, reflecting:

> "In order to be a true martial artist, they need to have an art. It could be tea ceremony or calligraphy, but something to balance the left and right sides of the brain…or as my friend Juan says, the eagle and the condor [according to South American shamanistic traditions]."

These arts are all for self-cultivation to forge oneself like a Japanese Katana, as Aidan admits that he will not "make a penny from it…I spend a fortune on it, but to what end? What comes out of it? I'm going to be a better father, a better grandfather, a better friend." That end is health, wellbeing, learning and human connection – something Aidan sees as missing in contemporary society, noting that mental health issues have become "a bit of an epidemic since lockdown." He compared this to the Welsh Valley mining communities in which Saturdays would be devoted to rugby and beer, Sunday chapel and another evening in the week for choir, which was a spiritual practice benefiting the men's mental health. Outside his own martial arts learning, Aidan works with fellow Taijiquan enthusiast and former Lau Gar Kung Fu practitioner Tony as part of a band. Although Tony is Aidan's senior in Taijiquan in which David often prescribes him separate sections of the form and Qigong sets, there is more horizontal relationship in their musical relationship. The two men work with a budding singer in their own small band, practising for hours in Aidan's garage until they feel ready to perform in public.

Besides his instrumental work on the guitar, Aidan regards the human voice "as the best instrument" and he learns from an opera singer, who teaches him to sing passionate ballads "from the twins" (testicles) rather than the throat, diaphragm or stomach. Such songs include the moving track "Bring them home" from the long-running West End production *Les Miserables*, which Aidan felt he was not ready for. Indeed, despite his confident exterior, Aidan admitted to me that he suffers from doubtfulness in his life. The singing was a cathartic release for his, leading him to weep after achieving a strong performance of this daunting challenge. I was fortunate enough to bear witness to Aidan singing in his kitchen, showing great power and poise, his skin colour darkening and his eyes glistening as he shocked me with the volume and control issuing from his body. It was almost frightening, and it reinforced Aidan's quote from Pavarotti: "Singing is controlled shouting." As with the Taijiquan training, Aidan has benefited from ongoing instruction over Zoom, working on his body and breath at a time where the two aspects of humans are increasingly vulnerable to the highly infectious airborne virus. This includes work on his posture, which is excellent for his age (just like his teacher David's straight gait). He says that as in the martial arts, one must bend the knees in singing, as straight legs cause tension. Singing is also about creating space within the body, as in Taijiquan. Aidan recalled an episode of the British television programme *Anyone Can Sing* in which an elderly man commented, "my posture was making me old." Aidan reflected how "we are all going through some level of incorrectness."

In addition to his direct tutelage under these two formal teachers, Aidan subscribes to Malcom Reeve's online academy page, which enables him to access the many videos and readings to stimulate his learning of the internal arts. He wholeheartedly recommended paying the annual prescription for these online resources from "such an incredible individual" who he deems "the real deal." Beyond Malcolm's skills and knowledge, Aidan admires the man's attitude, recalling him commenting: "I have no right to call people my students", as this would imply a sense of possession of autonomous human beings free to go about their own martial arts journeys. This differed from the possessiveness he encountered from Aikido instructors who felt threatened by Aidan's interest in learning from a visiting instructor offering a seminar. Instead, Aidan regards all the martial arts as different vehicles for continuing the journey through life, changing vehicles to suit his needs to move up the mountain. He also uses Malcolm's understanding of Kung Fu / Gong Fu as being "married to your skill." Advising a neighbour with a depressed 38-year-old son, Aidan suggested the man to find something he loves and devote himself to it. Following a Daoist medical model, Aidan thinks that all people are actually ill, unless they are enlightened. And he believes Peter Ralston is one of the few enlightened beings he has met in his lifetime.

Finally, beyond the martial and musical activities, Aidan is a qualified Shiatsu and Seiki therapist, regarding the latter, lesser-known approach to massage as being far more sophisticated. As with other martial artists seen earlier in this book, Aidan sees a direct connection between Eastern martial and healing arts, adding, "there is something very nourishing about touch – good quality touch." In class, he has bemoaned the sad state of affairs for many people who had suffered abusive forms of touch, as in sexual relationships. A ladies' man in his day who is proud of his poetic capabilities, Aidan likens touch to "when you have sex…with a woman. Some women have only experienced harsh touch rather than soft touch." He later added, "not everyone likes to touch other people and not everyone likes to be touched."

In a Western country where the life expectancy for men is increasing, yet quality of life is relatively poor for the elderly, Aidan is keen to live a long and rich life full of learning. He is settled in his hometown, despite having aspirations to retire on his own ranch in Catalonia, Spain, which he has since sold due to his wife not wanting to live there. He is of course not in control of all aspects of his life, as he has recently lost both of his parents, but he is determined not to leave his daughters or grandchildren responsible for his care, wishing to remain active and mobile for as long as possible. This contrasts to his own father who was in a bad state of health in his final years. "It keeps me alive" or "it keeps an old man alive" is a phrase Aidan has used on several occasions, with "it" being Taijiquan and Neigong. He particularly enjoys lifelong pursuits, noting "I don't want to learn something that you can learn in a year," later summarising this as: "it's the learning that matters." He mentioned how a student can be told something 1,000 times only to have a eureka moment that was deeply revealing for them.

Aidan rarely drinks alcohol and avoids caffeine, instead opting for herbal teas such as the peppermint and liquorice tea he offered me at his home, which Aidan was recommended by Sandra (a Taijiquan classmate) for its qi-stimulating properties. Learning to sing like an opera singer is also a lifelong quest, as Aidan told me that "it takes longer to be an opera singer than it does to become a doctor." So far, he and I have been training Taijiquan for around four years, but we have yet to complete the Short Form, let along begin the Long Form and the weapons. Perhaps becoming a proficient practitioner of this style of Taijiquan could take much longer than one or several medical degrees.

Summary

Like Billy and David, George and Aidan represent two different approaches to engaging with the martial arts, with one being more connected to Western training methods and combat sports and the other more related to theories of consciousness, Daoism and self-cultivation. Yet, their stories are united by the near-universal metaphor of life-as-a-journey (see Lakoff & Johnson, 1980) in which the martial arts are deemed to be vehicles for exploration. Other practices such as weight training, yoga, meditation and qigong are used as supplementary tools to train the vessel that is the body. These martial artists have used specific martial arts styles during certain moments of their lives only to move onto another school and teacher that suited them at that time. They have invested much physical, economic, cultural and social capital into the development of their martial habitus, which has some economic returns for the instructors Billy and David now trying to work as professionals in this highly competitive industry lacking government support. George and Aidan have worked on their bodies to try to live long, healthy lives as fathers and family men, wanting to avoid an inactive old age that many people live in today's Western societies.

Overall, these men live and breathe the martial arts through what they read, watch in the form of documentaries, talk about with their friends and take up as new hobbies. Their dispositions (their habitus) reflect this in their manner of standing straight, walking with intent and making intense yet friendly eye contact with a firm handshake. With these stories as illustrations of the investment given to the martial arts by people who live and breathe them, I shall now share my own story through autoethnographic vignettes before coming to some conclusions around how martial arts are being reinvented for different purposes in the 21st century Western society. This will allow the reader to understand my own position on the martial arts as a white, British, male social scientist with a background in exercise and sport sciences and more traditionalist schools of the fighting arts.

References

Bourdieu, P. (1990). *The logic of practice*. Cambridge: Polity Press.
Cheng Hsin Official Website. Available at: https://chenghsin.com/who-is-peter-ralston/. Last accessed 8 May 2022.

Chu, R., Ritchie, R., & Wu, Y. (1998). *Complete Wing Chun: The definitive guide to Wing Chun's history and traditions*. North Clarendon, VT: Tuttle.
Chinese Martial Arts Studies (Kung Fu Tea) Blog. Available at: https://chinesemartialstudies.com/. Last accessed 20 May 2022.
Fight SCIENCE Official YouTube Channel. Available at: https://www.youtube.com/c/londonwingchun. Last accessed 28 May 2022.
Gee, G., Meng, B., & Loewenhagen, R. (2004). *Mastering Kung Fu: Featuring Shaolin Wing Chun*. Champaign, IL: Human Kinetics.
Jennings, G., & Vaittinen, A. (2016). Multimedia Wing Chun: Learning and practice in the age of YouTube. Available at: https://chinesemartialstudies.com/2016/09/08/multimedia-wing-chun-learning-and-practice-in-the-age-of-youtube/. Last accessed 20 May 2022.
Lakoff, G., & Johnson, M. (1980). *Metaphors we live by*. Chicago: Chicago University Press.
Ralston, P., & Ralston, L. (2006). *Zen body-being*. Berkeley, CA: Frog Books.
Ralston, P. (1989). *Cheng Hsin: The principles of effortless power*. Berkeley, CA: North Atlantic Books.
Sánchez García, R., & Spencer, D. C. (Eds.). (2013). *Fighting scholars: Habitus and ethnographies of martial arts and combat sports*. London: Anthem Press.
Smith, R. W. (1974). *Chinese boxing: Masters and methods*. Berkeley, CA: North Atlantic Books.
The Highly Sensitive Person Official Website. Available at: https://hsperson.com/. Last accessed 28 May 2022.
The Martial Man Official Website. Available at: https://themartialman.com/. Last accessed 27 May 2022.
The Martial Man YouTube Channel. Available at: https://www.youtube.com/c/THEMARTIALMAN. Last accessed 20 May 2022.
Wacquant, L. J. D. (2004). *Body and soul: Notebooks of an apprentice boxer*. Oxford: Oxford University Press.

10
My Martial Arts Journey: An Autoethnography

This final chapter shares my own martial arts story from my early childhood exposure to the meditated martial arts to my merging of academic research and martial arts practice, leading to accounts of recent encounters and potential new research projects. It is written as an autoethnography (see Sparkes, 2002) – and an evocative ethnography at that – a genre of writing designed to invite the reader in the social and personal world of the scholar-practitioner. The chapter is divided into vignettes written in chronological order, with some reference to cultural texts from media, popular culture and martial arts literature along with some influential academic references that have shaped the way I view the martial arts and combat sports, and therefore, how I have gone about developing this book, which reflects my research interests, training experiences and the social issues I have encountered.

Turtles, Tim and Taekwondo: Getting to Know the Martial Arts

None of my family have ever practised the martial arts before, and I have no Asian heritage that I know of, so I had a relatively open blueprint with which to work from when I was born in the average-sized English town of Cheltenham, Gloucestershire (South West England) in 1984. I am the eldest of three brothers, and although my family might consider themselves as middle-class due to our relatively well-off grandparents and ancestors (from farming and banking backgrounds), my mother became a single parent on a low income and government benefits when my father left us when I was aged five. This led my early years to have little male influence other than my grandfather and from what I saw on television. As a child of the 1980s and 1990s, I was exposed to popular discourse on the martial arts from an early age through the *Teenage Mutant Hero Turtles* cartoon series, which was by far my favourite form of entertainment as a small boy. I had several of the action figures, which seemed to impress other boys visiting my home, and have fond memories of going to watch the first *Teenage Mutant Ninja Turtles* in the cinema as well as the *Batman* film with Michael Keaton. I immediately recognised the references to the martial arts in these films, as in the rooftop battle when Batman defends against a flipping, wild assailant. Even at the age of five and six, I was able to read such cultural texts and detect what the martial arts were, even though I might have been thinking of "Karate", "Ninja" and "black belt" rather than "martial arts." The black belt seemed to carry a mythical status, and speaking to adults who had practised Judo, it appeared to have honourable and respectful connotations.

Some years later, in year six (aged ten), a new boy arrived at my primary school: Tim, a boy of Chinese and Malaysian descent who had come from Warrington, in the north of the country which gave him a distinctive accent. He struck me as a confident, lively and outgoing youngster who had qualities that I lacked back then, being a relatively shy child interested in books and history and the company of a few close friends. I spent a lot of time looking through the school library to learn about different parts of the world and the people that lived in them. Despite our differences, we quickly formed a close friendship that has lasted to this day. Tim had practised Karate for a while, but he had moved to Taekwondo, which he showed great talent in, eventually competing for England for numerous years as an adult. It was at the age of ten that I heard about the martial arts icon Bruce Lee, and for some reason, I could already conjure an image of him in my head, with thick hair, a lean, muscular physique, and black trousers. Perhaps I had been exposed to some image of him that stuck to my subconscious, but this name would be crucial for my development during my teens.

Tim and I attended the same secondary school for the first two years, until I managed to gain a scholarship to a private school based on my academic ability. This enabled me to flourish in a safer environment in which I felt more comfortable. After our usual casual game of basketball in Tim's local recreation centre, I asked Tim more about Taekwondo. His art was a mysterious thing to me, and it seemed to help him with other sports such as basketball and football in terms of athleticism, while giving him a different identity. I did not follow any sports at the time – just playing football with friends and following the conventional physical education curriculum of Western competitive sports, which followed a more holistic, mixed-sex approach including dance and gymnastics. Rugby is very embedded in the culture of Gloucestershire although I had not taken to the game. I had some poor-quality physical education experiences from rather militant teachers who would occasionally manhandle and invariably shout at certain pupils, ordering them with "you…running!" to go jogging laps if they did something wrong. I was ordered to run after an incorrect rugby tackle to a shield, even though I never learned what was wrong with the technique. Unlike the more academic subjects such as English and maths, in which I had progressed to the top set in the state school, physical education seemed to be my weakest subject. It became easier when I moved schools in an environment where the teachers were less aggressive and where there was no physical bullying in the changing rooms from the less academic and resentful pupils who disliked me for my studiousness, straight-laced nature and well-spoken manner that they associated with being rich.

In search for a focus on my life, I entered the beginner's course in Taekwondo at the age of 14, in 1998. This was initially a dauting prospect, since the training was in my old secondary school. Yet, it was an evening class where some of my old classmates and tormentors would not see me. The first class involved breaking down the martial arts to the very basics, including how to hold a punch. Lining up in a row, we beginners held out what we thought to be a correct fist, only to be corrected by gentle physical manipulation, with our teacher adjusting the hand so that the fist was places around the first two fingers. I was one of those without experience of fighting whose thumb was adjusted – a lesson I never forgot. The Taekwondo classes continued to be rewarding, as I gained a high level of physical fitness and an aptitude for exercise and new ways of challenging my body. Although Tim was in the more advanced class, we kept in touch while I also experimented with some other martial arts systems with my school mates, including kickboxing and Kendo. We also enjoyed Kendo in the local YMCA class, as it offered a very different outlet for our youthful energies. One of their students was a familiar face from the local Kung Fu and kickboxing class, a kindly, mature Irishman known for getting very sweaty. That Kung Fu class seemed to focus on the forms of the Lao Gar system, while the chief instructor had created his own martial art named after his surname. This was a cross between Kung Fu, Karate and kickboxing, and his white English family were involved in the competitions and instruction. In one seminar over the weekend, I was struck by the speed and skill of his ten-year-old son who could execute fifty consecutive spinning back kicks on the spot. Yet immediately after this, the boy wobbled around the floor in disorientation, leading two of the older women in the group to whisper, "that poor kid." This was despite the head instructor's tale of his own wife's coach who "put her on a five mile run the day she was due to compete. She was never the same again, my lady wife." Although attending the seminar on kickboxing and the hybrid fighting system allowed me to know more about the mixture of techniques and lineages available, it did not quite satisfy me in terms of what I was seeking out from a martial art. I wanted something firmly grounded in efficiency and directness, and Wing Chun was just what I was looking for.

"Kung Fu crazy"

I wanted to learn a more practical martial art in which I felt I was progressing that was less concerned with competition (as in Taekwondo and kickboxing) or ritual (as in Kendo). For a Christmas present, my mum thoughtfully bought me a copy of a Bruce Lee biography, *Fighting Spirit* (Thomas, 1994), which changed my orientation to the Chinese art of Wing Chun Kung Fu that Lee had studied in his youth. I eagerly devoured the book, looking back at various sections with interest. The chapter "Kung Fu crazy" resonated with me, as like Lee, I had become obsessed with the martial arts. Later, in school, my other friends who had trained kickboxing and Kendo with me started to circulate copies of Bruce Lee's 1970s movies, and we borrowed each other's copies, as no one had the full collection. When *Enter the Dragon* was on television, I was sure to tape it on VHS, which was still common in the late 1990s. Later, I was sure to buy all of the films for my own DVD collection, which later extended to some of the Hong Kong Legends series such as Jackie Chan's *Drunken Master* and the *Magnificent Butcher* starring Sammo Hung, as I moved towards the Kung Fu comedy genre of the late 1970s and early 1980s.

My mum started to work as a clerk for several of the parish councils in the areas – a role she holds to this day. One day, in a library near my mum's workplace, I searched for "martial arts" in the computer. To my great surprise and satisfaction, there was a Wing Chun Kung Fu school in the area. I had heard about the classes from two younger boys who had taken a trial lesson, showing me some of the principles they had learned. The same tricks were used on me as I kept a punch out, first resisting the force of an entire hand only to be manipulated by a little finger. This trick showed the beginner how our bodies can read and resist direct, brute force, unlike more subtle, instantaneous force that is difficult to register. The boys also showed me how Wing Chun practitioners avoid getting punched by turning on their heels, transferring weight onto one leg while pivoting. I was surprised at how these complete neophytes avoided my straight punch with ease, so when I was able to join the local club on Saturday mornings at the age of 15, I grabbed the opportunity.

The Wing Chun school consisted of a more mature cohort in their mid-twenties to late forties, which seemed quite old to me at the time. This is quite typical of the art that focusses on economy of motion and effort, sometimes dubbed "Kung Fu for lazy people." Unlike in the intergenerational Taekwondo class, there were no children in the cohort, and I was significantly younger that my fellow students, although they accepted me with open arms, with one of the men giving me a supportive thumbs up when I left my first session. They only wore the t-shirt of the association over tracksuit bottoms of varying shades and designs, with trainers on. This gave the school a sense of realism and practicality, as Wing Chun did not require a loose uniform or an extensive warm up to perform any of the techniques. To compensate for the lack of physical training in the classes, I kept up my own routine of jogging and later going to the school gym when it was open to me at the age of 16. Inspired by the edited collection of Bruce Lee's training regimes of the 1960s and 1970s in *The Art of Expressing the Human Body* (Little, 1998) alongside some of his other writings on the Chinese martial arts (Lee, 1963; Little, 1997), I followed many of the weight training routines, using three sets of ten repetitions for speed, power and definition. My physique was recognised by some guest trainers, who asked if I was a gymnast or a swimmer, and I struck up a good relationship with a personal trainer who came to manage the gym during physical education lessons in my Sixth Form years. He had studied Bushido, a hybrid martial art inspired by the Samurai philosophy. Although in my youthful naivety, I believed this to be a genuine martial art, my other class mate put it matter-of-factly, "it's completely made up", noting that the boys, who suddenly felt very powerful thanks for those bespoke group training, were "amateurs." By then, I was keen to study a sport science or exercise science degree in pursuit of a career in physiotherapy and personal training – all due to Bruce Lee and the martial arts. Without that inspiration from my long-dead role model, I doubt I would have selected that subject for university, as I actually excelled in geography, with an interest in human geography.

I trained hard at home, often irritating my mother by steaming up the mirrors and windows with my sweat built up from training inside. On the Saturday mornings, I sometimes spent extra time with Ben, a fellow student who was also single and able to commit his weekends to his training, mixing Wing Chun with jogging with friends. He would sometimes come to my grandmother's house, as she had a flat garden with a patio that would train on.

Martial Arts as an Object of Academic Study

During my A Level Physical Education studies, students had to select a sport to study over a period of time. There was only one martial art available on the curriculum at the time – Judo – so I took this up at the same YMCA where I had learned Kendo. "Judo is different…it's about speed" warned one classmate. And I did find profound differences between Judo and Wing Chun, as I found it difficult to throw my larger, more muscular opponents down. When training with one veteran Judoka with a red belt who has "been there in the beginning… in Japan!", I couldn't offset his balance at all. Years later, reading the classic sports book *The Pyjama Game* (Law, 2007), I could read this situation as a common one, with advanced Judo players merely holding beginners with minimal effort. Some of my training partners were more daunting figures, including a tough bouncer in a local nightclub, who was rebuked for being too rough on me. "He's doing it to himself!" He retorted to our Sensei. Although I found the throwing aspect of the sport difficult, I seemed to fare much better in the groundwork game, and this served me well in later Brazilian Jiujitsu (BJJ) training with my university workmates – when I even managed to tap out a black belt in Judo.

Even selecting universities was partly determined by access to a good Wing Chun school. "You're choosing that city just because of the martial arts?!" Exclaimed one fellow sixth former, who was also shocked that one of our more rebellious female classmates was keen to join a university in London because of the nightclubs. Having settled on the sleepy town of Exeter due to the small and friendly campus environment (as advised by my mum concerned for my other option of the far larger city of Birmingham), I immediately sought out a Wing Chun school after scouring the advertisement pages of *Combat* magazine, a British monthly circulation devoted to the traditional martial arts. I had subscribed to this magazine for several years, especially as it was advocated by some of my fellow Wing Chun students. Some of my Sixth Form peers laughed at this publication due to the fanciful characters that featured in it. "It is laugh a minute" said one jovial pupil, noting a year later that "I see it still isn't made of proper paper." Another student, a former Karateka, remarked: "I'm sorry, George, but you've got to admit, the people who do martial arts are pretty weird." Some of the more immature boys laughed at how the male martial artists looked, with fanciful moustaches and intense demeanours. It was common for Wing Chun teachers to feature on the front page of this magazine, and many of my classmates had recommended it, often bringing copies to class. We students used to borrow each other's books on Wing Chun, and my teacher started to note my curiosity, joking "another one for the library!" I also started to subscribe to the American magazine *Inside Kung Fu*, ordering it from my local newsagent. My *Sigung* (teacher's teacher) had been on the front cover of that outlet, and some of the articles provided interesting tips for teaching and training in the martial arts, including the often neglected cool downs which are overshadowed by extensive warm-ups.

I called Sifu John Bridge to find out about his association, and he put me in touch with one of his senior students, Steve, who became a close friend and mentor to me. We caught a lift with a fellow student whose routine involved the offering of chewing gum while listening to the *Top Gun* soundtrack. The second Wing Chun school, Bridge's Academy, was a marked contrast to my first school. Whereas my hometown kwoon was run by two "Kung Fu brothers" who worked as an engineer and a physiotherapist, Bridge's Academy was a full-time centre for the Chinese martial arts including weapons from Choy Lay Fut, San Sau kickboxing, lion and dragon dancing, and Sifu Bridge's main martial art, Wing Chun. Sifu Bridge was originally from the East End of London, and retained a cockney accent and set of mannerisms, while some of his senior students and assistant instructors were from Liverpool and Derby. In a seaside town in the South West of England, landlords trained side by side with car mechanics and dentists threw punches at carpenters. The eclectic mix of people from different regions and backgrounds led me to investigate the subculture of the kwoon, focusing on the development of identity (from Goffman's dramaturgical perspective) and social class (using Bourdieu's framework). Over the years, the gym became more diverse in terms of nationality, ethnicity and gender, reflecting a changing British society and demographics in the martial arts. Today, the school has far fewer numbers, while Sifu's focus has reduced to teaching Wing Chun to small groups and in private lessons.

After moving away from these magazines, I became interested in *Men's Health*, following the routines and lifestyle tips in a bid for continued personal development and wellbeing. However, some of my housemates taking the sociology module pointed out the discourses of health around physical health, which overlooked mental and social wellbeing. Despite their banter around my obsession with nutrition (as in adding olive oil to tomatoes, which was supposed to reduce the risk of cancer), I did start to open my eyes to the commercial and addictive nature of these magazines, which were not journals. One classmate had taken sociology in his second year and remembered the lecturer telling the students about his friend who was obsessed with weight training and his body, but was still alone, with no partner. "They write about physical health, but not mental health, which is just as important, if not more." Then one day, my life changed direction, as it was time to select a dissertation topic for the final year. Normally I was very attentive in class, but with coursework looming, I had skipped the dissertation ideas session.

"David Brown is interested in martial arts, George." One classmate told me. Having cleared this option with the dissertation coordinator, I knocked on David's door. By then, it was a sunny spring period, and David spotted a bruise on my forearm from my Wing Chun training. "Wing Chun! That's what I do... or did." He said, as we struck up a positive working relationship. As I left his doorway, he told me: "That bruise on your arm...it tells a story", adding: Don't do it because it's Wing Chun...do it because it's sociology." I nodded, going home to compose a list of research themes and questions. Returning for my first formal tutorial, David listened to my research questions listed in my notepad. Sitting back in a relaxed manner, he answered, "all of those questions can be addressed within one approach: an ethnography." From then on, I immersed myself into the world of ethnography, reading classic texts kindly loaned to me by David as well as specialist books in the various libraries of the university. One such book was another key reading for me: *When the Body Becomes All Eyes* by the late drama professor Phillip Zarrilli (1998), which was a pioneering ethnography of the South Indian martial art of Kalarippayattu. The depth of Zarrilli's study was impressive, and I was equally inspired by sociologist Löic Wacquant's (2004) study of boxing in *Body and Soul* and his earlier publications. Both of these authors had captured the settings in which they immersed themselves while also accounting for rich characters, especially the Kalarippayattu *gurukkals* (literally, teachers who are part of a line of teachers) and boxing coaches. Wacquant was particularly good at representing how the working-class boxers he interviewed and observed actually spoke, and this stimulated my interest in conducting an ethnography of my own Wing Chun school in terms of social class and subculture (Jennings, 2005). I was very fortunate to watch Phillip's students in action in their regular training sessions of a mixture of Taijiquan, yoga and Kalarippayattu (taught in three distinct parts), as they were based at the same university, and I am pleased to have interviewed the man himself when I relocated to Wales and started working with a local media company. However, both of these men had become practitioners of their studied bodily arts, while I became an ethnographer and qualitative researcher after several formative years in the martial arts.

Chinese Philosophy in the Flesh

At the end of my bachelor's degree, I came across a poster advertising Chen style Taijiquan in my hometown. Although I had read several articles and books on Tai Chi (as it is often written), which seemed very appealing to me, I had never practised it myself. I invited my grandmother to come along with me, as she was then in her seventies and not as active and confident with movement as she used to be. We continued learning from the teacher, John, who was in his eighties. John had moved from the Yang style to Chen after "having direct access to Master Chen" as one of his senior students explained. However, he would sometimes refer to figures in the Yang style such as Zheng Manqing (Cheng Man Ching), who was quoted as advising student to massage their kidneys 49 times in the morning. "Why 49 and not 50?" Asked John with a rhetorical question, "to be in the now." The first class was mentally exhausting for me, as I lay on the sofa before lunch. Relaxation was always a great challenge for me in Wing Chun, and this was even more apparent in Taijiquan. Taking heed from the respected self-help book *The Power of Now* (Tolle, 1999), John again stressed the importance of being "in the now", even making reference to this in cricket, a sport he admired for the concentration needed of the players. Later, I found myself drawn to such books, when perusing book shops in different towns, reading into topics such as *The Miracle of Mindfulness* by the late Vietnamese monk Thich-Nat Han (Han, 1975). Although I am very quick at selecting clothes to buy, I do take a long time making decisions about which book to buy when visiting different towns. Like many martial artists, I am a keen collector of books on different systems, and this has recently extended to antique books on historical martial arts such as archery (Hargrove, 1970), as well as armour and ancient arms (Stone, 1960).

Sadly, John passed away during the beginning of my PhD, as I called his number to check on classes during the university holidays. His adult son answered with the bad news, adding that "some of his students are keeping the classes going." However, as I hadn't formed a bond with them, I felt the class would not be the same. Some of them seemed to look at me with distrust, possibly due to my significantly younger age and background in the external martial arts. This meant I continued with my own Wing Chun training while I reduced my time in the gym, other than the occasional cardio workouts. Then, one evening out with friends, I got talking with Johnny, one of the bouncers in a favourite nightclub. Johnny was an Afro-Caribbean man with a muscular frame and relaxed manner who I found approachable. "I need someone to spar with." He noted. However, when he came to my home all the way from Birmingham for a private lesson, I quickly realised that he would be my teacher rather than my training partner. I told my friend Tim about these lessons, and he was able to join us for several classes.

Although Johnny was surprised to know that I had been learning Wing Chun for eight years at the time (with the techniques not readily transferring to the different punching mechanics and higher kicks), he was impressed by Tim's incredible kicking ability, telling me in private: "He's going to be a legend…he's either going to be in the movies or he'll be a legend in competitions." The latter prediction would prove true for Tim, who has won many gold medals for the last decade in a glittering Taekwondo career. Johnny ensured me that "the high kicks will make your low kicks better." Inviting Johnny to stay for dinner at my home, I was surprised to learn that Johnny was actually 44 years old, which was twice our age of 22. Hearing this, my brother Matt joked that Johnny was, "a 44-year-old trapped in a 20 year old's body." Johnny lived an active lifestyle, although he admitted that although he looked fit, he wasn't. Like me, he regarded himself as being "quite traditional" and has a dislike of competitions that didn't understand some of his more subtle technique. Johnny's background was in a hybrid Kung Fu style combining Praying Mantis with Hung Gar, as taught by a mysterious Chinese teacher who "used to fight for China" and now ran a chain of Chinese restaurants. The determined and hardy Johnny took Tim and I though tough physical workouts involving many push ups, sit ups and isometric exercises, and he sometimes shared stories of his own tough training, noting proudly that "you couldn't wait for it to end" and, "In the winter, I used to walk four miles in the snow."

Johnny and I kept in touch as I returned to university for the autumn term, although he turned his attention to a new self-defence course in a college in Gloucestershire. It was interesting to note his devotion to travelling out of the multicultural city of Birmingham to the rural Cotswolds. While getting some cash out to pay him for the class, Johnny noted the lack of people of colour in the area, and how people would stare at him, a well-built, six foot black man in a white, middle-class village.

Becoming a Fighting Scholar

Following my childhood exposure to Chinese and Malaysian culture, I have been very open to people hailing from other cultures and ethnicities. During my PhD years, I worked alongside Nuno, a charismatic Portuguese researcher who became a close friend and role model for me. A few years older, he read broadly into human development, including the topic of emotional intelligence. I often emulated by reading about these topics which I started to consider in terms of the self-cultivation process in the martial arts.

Nuno was a BJJ practitioner who was training up a friend through informal sessions together, sometimes texting me with the question "fancy some Jiu?". I soon joined these exchanges in some lunchtime exchanges in the university sports hall. When several Spanish PhD students visited Exeter for a research exchange, we managed to gently spar and grapple, learning from each other's fighting style. All of this was managed by Mark, a veteran Judoka and British MMA champion who had joined our School from another university. He sometimes taught us techniques such as anti-takedowns, although much of the training was about free sparring. I often chased opponents with my Wing Chun chain punches, although Mark got used to these, and noting my frequent change of guards, he struck me with a hook, only to split my lip. This was later noted by my Wing Chun teacher, who became slightly annoyed about my MMA training. One senior returned to the class one evening, and eventually pinned me down to the floor, proclaiming that, "there's nothing you can learn outside that you can't learn in your own gym!" After Nuno and I started to work in different halls of residence as university wardens (resident tutors), my lunchtime training diminished as I continue other avenues of exploration through the classes available in Bridge's Academy. The centre was a 45-minute car journey from my flat, but it did offer a nice break from my university identity – with a connection to a different demographic of people who had never entered higher education. On Saturday morning, I was able to learn the basics of the lion dance while taking a more active role in the dragon dance, which involved youngsters from the local town. We sometimes gave demonstrations in local schools and community centres, and with my increasing confidence in public speaking, I was given the responsibility of making the announcements over the microphone, sometimes making impromptu jokes, such as the commentary on a student performing a bench weapons sequence, "you can see from this demonstration that a bench is not just for sitting on!" which drew laughter from my classmates, teachers and the audience. I have tried to use humour in my talks ever since. Humour has come to me naturally in my teaching and presentations, and this application of it (and receival of many a joke) has led me to study it in my research on HEMA and the humorous stigmatisation of left-handed people like me (Jennings, 2022).

During my time as a resident tutor, I lived on the larger, more international campus of the university. Within its library was a collection on world cinema, and my Friday evening tradition consisted of renting a classic Kurosawa film, which included *Seven Samurai*, which one PhD student in film studies regarded as "probably one of the best movies ever made." He also recommended others such as *Throne of Blood*, and I soon devoured the collection available on campus. It was during this period that David Brown and I first collaborated on our first article together (Brown, Jennings, & Leledaki, 2008), which was for a collection on sport in film for the journal *Sport in Society*. Working with another PhD student, Aspasia, as our critical friend, we examined the performing male body in Asian martial arts films, which included Bruce Lee, Jackie Chan, Jet Li and Tony Jaa, which the final figure becoming increasingly popular in my conversations with my Wing Chun class mates, including young Nathaniel, who was an avid parkour practitioner. This article showed a movement away from trained martial artists as actors to actors and dancers trained as martial artists (often with Computer Generated Imagery [CGI] assistance) to the hallowed return of real-life martial artists training for their own students and learning a martial art in depth. The films were important reference points for my fellow martial artists, although many others were interested in the Ultimate Fighting Championship (UFC), especially Nuno, who was proud of Royce Gracie's triumphs in the first two events. One classmate lent me his DVD copies of these events, noting with a smile that "it always goes to the ground with Royce." This circulation of films added to the sharing of copies of Sifu Li's (my teacher's teacher) instructional video tapes from the 1980s, which a junior class mate and friend then used for his own development. "He makes it look so easy" he noted in wonder. We would sometimes meet up to train together, although I often spent more time with our Kung Fu sister Sarah in sessions focusing on *chi sau* in her local park.

Leaving the Academy was something that I dreaded, as I had invested seven years of my time and energy into learning a very specific approach to Wing Chun. Moving to South West London for my first academic post, I was overwhelmed with the choice of clubs in the capital city, of which there were at least 50. However, as this post was a maternity cover, I thought not to learn a new style of Wing Chun, which would require me to unlearn what I had acquired with my Sifu. Instead, I trained hard at home, sometimes returning to my teacher when I could. My next stop was Scotland, where I took up a post in sports development.

There was scope to teach a class in the university gym, so I opened this up to staff, students and members of the public, which was a very rewarding experience. One former practitioner of another style of Wing Chun joined my class, referring me to "Sifu", despite his eagerness to demonstrate the aggressiveness of his other teachers on me, hitting me hard in the sternum. One student persevered with the training, and we kept in touch over email, with him kindly saying, "you're like Grandmaster Ip Man to me." Although I was first introduced to Bruce Lee's teacher as *Yip* Man, the name of *Ip* Man started to be recognised thanks to the series of films starring Donnie Yen.

"There must be a Mexican martial art. There's got to be!"

After an enjoyable year living in Scotland, another exciting opportunity beckoned: Mexico. My partner at the time was from there, and as she had struggled to find a graduate job in the UK, we thought to give Mexico a try. I had enjoyed holidaying there, and loved the culture, food and rich history. But what could I research and write about while over there? Although some people had start to pigeonhole me into a scholar of the Chinese martial arts, one colleague in Abertay remarked on my leaving: "There must be a Mexican martial art. There's got to be!" This comment helped to open my mind to studying other kinds of martial arts, and fortunately, after one month of living and setting up work opportunities teaching English to business people, my partner and I came across an advertisement for a free course in Nahautl, an Indigenous language of central Mexico. Then, when entering the community centre for my first Saturday morning class, I saw a giant banner with a woman in Indigenous dress in a low, deep stance that I immediately recognised of being from the martial arts. "Xilam: Mexican fighting art." Stated the banner, which advertised the class for Saturday afternoons. This was an ideal combination, learning Nahautl in the morning, taking a hearty lunch in the food market followed by a gruelling mental and physical workout in Xilam, which enabled me to practise my Nahuatl in the counting of one to twenty (a special number in the Mesoamerican worldview) during the warm ups and other exercises. My teacher Tonatiuh told me, "George, your Spanish pronunciation isn't very good, but your Nahuatl is very well pronounced." I sometimes joked that I was Mexican in a previous life, and Mexicans were often impressed – eyebrows raised and mouth open – with my rendering of complex words such as Quetzalcoatl, Nezahualcoyotl and Huitzilopochtli. Xilam raised me awareness of different movement patterns missing in the very tight, linear Wing Chun, and I started to blend Xilam with my previous Taijiquan and Wing Chun training during the late afternoons, mixing exercises to balance my plane of movement and physique.

When I first began my martial arts research in 2004, the field of martial arts studies had yet to be coined. Library searches at my university returned with scant references that were on diverse topics, from phenomenology to family, which led me to draw on research from a range of academic disciplines within my literature review. However, since my PhD completed in 2010 (Jennings, 2010), there has been a tremendous acceleration in the volume of research produced by scholars all over the world. Now, after Farrer and Whalen-Bridge (2012) and Bowman's (2015) seminal texts, there is term in English for the field of studying the martial arts, combat sports and related fighting systems from the perspective of humanities and social sciences. I was eager to learn more about this in the first series of Martial Arts Studies conferences in Cardiff, which was also where my old supervisor has moved (at Cardiff Metropolitan University). Asking him if he would like to meet up for a beer, David replied that there was a job opportunity at the university, which I would be perfect for. The only issue was that I was far away in Mexico. However, I spoke to my partner at the time, who said I should apply anyway, as this would change our lives for the better, with the salaries being relatively poor and the working conditions tough.

Mexico has solidified my work ethic and drive to succeed in my career while also considering a balanced lifestyle and multicultural mixture of friends. Through martial arts studies and other conferences in the sociology of sport, I have struck up friendships with people from Italy and Spain who have become close collaborators. I am certainly British, but a cosmopolitan person who is fascinated by other cultures – just like the primary schoolboy who delved into books on far-away countries in the lonely library. To date, I have expanded my analysis to examine French Savate with the renowned scholar Sara Delamont, who has become an incredible mentor and role model for me. She and I live close by, and are able to meet for coffee on a regular basis. With her extensive networks in the scholarly world of Capoeira research, Sara has connected me with David Contreras Islas, with whom I am now planning a book chapter on practitioner-researchers of the martial arts as part of an edited collection on scholar-practitioners in a variety of fields and professions. This will be my first time collaborating with a Mexican martial arts researcher who is studying the teaching of Brazilian Capoeira in his home country, where the instructors (*mestres*) tend to be Mexican rather than Brazilian (see Contreras Islas, 2021). No longer am I a scholar of the Chinese martial arts or the new Mexican styles, but an inquisitive scholar interested in all the world's fighting systems.

Re-connecting with the Kung Fu Family

Upon my return to the UK, I got back in touch with my old Wing Chun teacher, who also reminded me that an old student of his lived in Wales. For the last five and a half years, my namesake George and I have been training together during the weekends when he passes by in Cardiff. We work on familiar drills while preparing for the upcoming quarterly seminars that Sifu announces with several months' notice. This involves a long trek of two and a half hours, chatting about training methods and reminiscing about times gone by. Thanks to today's technology, we have even gained feedback and guidance from Sifu in terms of how we interpret his written list of drills, which are normally a mixture of English and Cantonese terms. This is because Wing Chun, like all martial arts, is open to interpretation. Even the pronunciation and spelling of technical terms differ, and it varies within a given club, with non-native speakers of Cantonese trying to pronounce terms from a language with eight, subtly different tones. In my old Wing Chun school, a senior student who had visited Hong Kong shared a funny story of how the Chinese students found the British counterparts' pronunciation of Gan Sau ("splitting hand" block used to defend the abdomen) very funny, as how we say it sounds like "raping hand." My teacher is now in his fifties, and is no longer the tough, shaven-head man that I initially found to be a daunting figure. He has relaxed his demeanour, allowed some grey hair to grown on his scalp and offers more hugs to his students as he opens up about his issues in life, including unexplained aches and pains.

    I still retained an interest in Taijiquan and the internal arts, which stemmed from my personal investigation into the standing postures of Wing Chun and the potential internal aspects developed from them. In Mexico, I would stand in my office for 45 minutes or more, taking extensive notes on the sensations of heat that built up, along with the knowledge I developed from this training. This was eventually published in conjunction with my colleagues in the Health Advancement Research Team (HART) led by another excellent academic mentor of mine, Professor Jaqui Allen Collinson (Allen Collinson et al., 2016). This four-way collaboration continued as we moved away from our disparate physical cultures of running, Wing Chun, MMA and boxing to a more unifying one: running (Allen Collinson et al., 2018). I returned to running in the first few years of living in Cardiff, especially when visiting scholar Lorenzo Pedrini stay with me for six months while he finished his PhD under the guidance of David Brown. He and I would run around the iconic Victorian Roath Park Lake for several laps, although he continued for a few more, thanks to the endurance he had built up from his ethnographic study of Italian people's boxing or *boxe popolare* (see Pedrini, 2018).

Over time, I have drifted away from my core identity as a Wing Chun practitioner and specialist researcher on the Chinese martial arts. Now I am less of a martial artist who writes about the specific martial arts that he practises and teaches and more of a writer with a specialism in these fighting systems, among other physical cultures. I spend more time on my Taijiquan training and movement training than I do on Wing Chun techniques, although I am grateful for the foundation that my Wing Chun teachers and seniors have provided me with. Each day, I try to stand in a posture from Taijiquan or Qigong (and sometimes Wing Chun), while also maintaining the resting squat and, more recently, hanging off a bar, in order to improve my posture for greater wellbeing. This offsets the excessive anterior movement from Wing Chun but also academic life, as I have my hands in front of me while typing. Much of this book has been written from my standing desk, which I use for around five to six hours per day. Posture and alignment have been an issue for me following my early engagement with weight training, which left me with rounded shoulders and a noticeably hunched back (kyphosis), as well as over development on the right side (scoliosis) – partially due to carrying by backpack on the right shoulder, but also because of the tendency to train techniques on the right side in Wing Chun, most notably in *chi sau* (sticking hands). This chi sau involves the central activity is "rolling", which employs the shoulder muscles while raising the elbow into the *Bong Sau* (wing arm) position. As many people resisted going to the "dark side" of the left, I ended up with an overly developed set of muscles on my right side, leading to the scapula rotating forwards and for the bones to stick up against my back.

With this postural imbalance becoming a concern within my normally sedentary job, I try to take regular breaks to squat (as in when listening to videos and podcasts for this book), walk and take some fresh air and rest my eyes through specialist exercises. My choices of which martial art to study and to what extent I should be involved in them is also dictated by the question of health. When applying for some internal funding for HEMA equipment, I tried to build a compelling message to secure the money and convince the committee. However, the Dean did pass on a message through the director of research, warning me: "There is no point of damaging your health for the pursuit of knowledge." This was during the

COVID-19 lockdown, a period in which I began reading about concussions in HEMA due to my fear of getting brain damage from this ethnographic research project. Once training resumed, I was more cautious in sparring, trying to maintain distance, leading me to be given a new nickname of "running away George." This fear was exacerbated after a strike to the head from a young, rather eccentric university student who had brought a denser sword manufactured by a different supplier. He had sometimes brought protective equipment in the form of a Roman legionnaire, which was permissible due to it all being in black. Our basic, Level One Red Dragon helmets were not designed to withstand such force coming to the head (as the sword was for the stronger Level Two helmets), so I cried out it anguish, and later struggled with a complex drill. Perhaps I was just rusty, but I decided to take the next few weeks off the direct class because of my fear of concussion. Fortunately, as COVID-19 was still a concern and with some local lockdown measures in some of the counties surrounding the gym, Billy allowed me to join the class from my kitchen through a livestream on Zoom. Later on, I went to a rugby supply shop to purchase a scrum cap – not for rugby, but for extra cushioning below the HEMA helmet. I had read about that in a scholarly blog by the respected HEMA instructor Keith Farrell (2014), and my instructor Billy had reinforced this message in the class and through our members' Facebook group. When I was training with a female classmate, she noticed this cap, remarking: "It prevents micro-concussions, doesn't it?" My gradual move away from HEMA coincided with the writing of the book, as both activities demanded a great deal of mental and physical energy.

South Wales seems to be a thriving hub of martial arts activities, and living in Cardiff has opened my mind to other martial possibilities. The Fightingandspirit project that featured in the chapter on Martial Arts as Therapy enabled me to learn some of the basic exercises and principles of Systema. Although this style has been criticised among social media figures for being a potential McDojo due to the stretching of the truth in terms of its history, I did find the training sessions to be beneficial. Putting on a Russian accent, the South African instructor quotes one of the leaders of the Systema movement who believes it is wrong when "people learn to deliver the strikes, but not to learn to take the hits." A similar motto was uttered by Johnny, the Kung Fu instructor and bouncer who taught Tim and I to toughen our abdomens and pummel each other in the stomach. In Systema, the hit is received by blowing out air via short, sharp exhalations – normally in groups of three outbreaths. The instructor, Jeff, admitted feeling a fear of heights while on holiday in France with his children, who wanted to dive of a cliff. As his sons were waiting behind him, and a young French girl had passed them by to splash into the water, Jeff decided to use the breath to steady himself and drop into the sea. He also spoke of more serious situations from the perspective of a survival psychologist from a significantly more violent society. In a break from the physical training, Jeff told the participants about the infamous Tsotsi gangs in South Africa (known to the world through the film of the same name, *Tsotsi*), and how they would work with the people's sense of security by using one member of the gang to approach a victim, whose adrenaline would rise as they readied themselves for a fight. Then two others would come to the scene to chase of the supposed assailant, giving the victim a great feeling of release and comfort. Once their victim's neurological and hormonal system has been auto-suppressed, the entire gang would pounce on the unsuspecting person, who would not be ready for the attack.

Dragon Kung Fu in Wales, The Land of the Dragon

Some months later, in a postgraduate research conference at Cardiff Metropolitan University I was introduced to Brian, one senior colleague who worked on the other campus. I had been told about him in a tour of their facilities after mentioning my research area in the martial arts. Brian was in his early sixties, slightly built, but had the energy of a much younger man. Talking about his experiences of different styles of Kung Fu from the 1970s, he was keen to tell me all about the Southern Dragon style of Kung Fu that he practised under a Chinese teacher. Showing me his fighting stance, which guarded the centreline with dragon-like claws and elbows tucked into the body, he told me of the deficiencies in the Wing Chun, stating frankly that: "your weakness is your bong sau." As Wing Chun was very well established in the UK, it was easy to look at images and photographs of the art to find points to exploit should a martial artist of another style face a Wing Chun practitioner. Brian noted that Wing Chun was no longer particularly tied to the Chinese culture, whereas it was still deeply embedded in the little-known Dragon Kung Fu, which was led by a Chinese community that was also involved in public lion dance displays. His teacher, Thomas Chan, was a man in his early sixties from Hong Kong who ran a Chinese takeaway with his wife, "as they can make so much more money that way", despite them having university degrees. I was also told that another respected Chinese Sifu was submissive to Thomas due to his seniority and skill in his own art.

Thomas, Brian's teacher was a quietly spoken man who I was introduced to in a car park to an outdoor centre where we could exchange some martial arts ideas. The night before I had asked Brian if I should bring a gift for his teacher, and he replied that many people with the Chinese community give Sifus fruit. So I went to the local shop to buy some nectarines, hoping to make a good first impression. Greeting me in the car park, Thomas's first question to me was "who's your teacher?", which reflected some of the kinds of immediate reference points used in other Chinese martial arts communities (Partiková & Jennings, 2018). I used my teacher and his teacher's name to give Thomas an idea of my lineage. Beginning with the typical coffee and chat (accompanied with some Welsh cakes that the two men ate in a ravenous manner), Thomas asked me technical questions such as: "When you punch, what do you think about? The fist, the elbow or the shoulder?" He told me that he had also studied four or five different forms of Taijiquan, and when I performed a technique from that art from my chair, he corrected me: "Taijiquan doesn't just move the arm." However, after demonstrating our punches and defences in one of the open-air bays along a footpath, Thomas concluded: "You don't just move your arm. A lot of Wing Chun people just move their arms." Our discussion also entered the realm of martial arts politics, with a recent feud between the Wing Chun and Pak Mei clans in Hong Kong. However, I didn't recognise the men in the photo. "You don't know who this is? He's your chairman." Thomas replied with shock and slight disappointment in my lack of awareness. The photo was part of a post in Cantonese on Facebook that he translated for me, reading the conclusion to the story: "The Wing Chun and the Pak Mei are now friends again."

Thomas's view of the body was one that was elastic and explosive, which made sense given his prior training in Taijiquan. Like my own teacher's teacher, Master Li, he used Taijiquan as a supplement for his Kung Fu development. Looking through archive photographs, he and Brain spoke of one student who was a bodybuilder whose physique was setting his martial development back. Moving from the café, our open-air training began with some interesting warm ups involving rolling the shoulders and opening and closing the mouth with intensity, which seemed to be working on our tendons and ligaments. I had seen the Mexican pound-for-pound great Saúl "Canelo" Álvarez use such jaw movements before his boxing matches, but I had never learned this movement in the martial arts. Thomas even spoke of some Chin Na joint locks (using pressure point techniques) that Brian didn't recall mentioning, joking, "you must have taught those to your indoor students." We had tested each other's defences by having Brian punch me with his Dragon style punch, which I just managed to defence with a *pak sau* (slapping hand) defensive block against the outside of Brian's forearm. It managed to penetrate my first line of defence, only for my rear defensive Wu Sau to pick up the defence. It was a painful bone-on-bone contact as Brian's punch was one of the most powerful I had ever received.

When I returned the punch to him, he showed how effective the Dragon blocking was, using a movement similar to *pak sau* only to switch to the second hand, twisting it round as in the demonstration in the air that he gave me during the conference. "Good!" Called Thomas, watching us from the side. But Brian had finished with his demonstration, noting my right elbow being exposed to his counterattack. He pressed me elbow with immense force, forcing me to stagger back several metres, only for Sifu Thomas to stop me by pressing behind my back. My poor choice of footwear might have been a contributing factor, as I was wearing relatively smart brown shoes on this working day, but I did feel the power, which my stance couldn't tolerate. How did Brian deliver such power, despite his thin frame and ageing body that had recently been struggling with a long-term illness that left him "crawling through the car park" at work? He was due to take an early retirement, which would enable him to return to training under his teacher.

Walking back to the car park, Thomas reminded me, "if something goes wrong for you [in a fighting scenario], don't blame it on the style. It's because of you, not the system." Although the focus of the discussion was on Southern Chinese Kung Fu styles, we three men also make mention of British heavyweight boxer Anthony Joshua's shock loss to Andy Ruiz Jr., which was only the other weekend. "I hope he managed to get it back, because he comes from a humble background." Commented Brain, as Thomas said, "yes, but it's a sport, it's play." Brian seemed excited by this exchange, hinting to me as we walked to his car, "I think Thomas likes you; I think he is going to take you on [as a new student]." Giving me a lift back to my campus, the training wasn't over, as Brian wished to interact with me by asking questions are we exchanged attack and defensive movements. After showing me some of the movements from his form, which included some closed-fisted blocks akin to those found in Karate and Taekwondo, Brian asked me questions such as: "What would you do next?" after I had trapped his arms with one hand. For some reason, I made a less efficient counter to the lower body, when the upper gate was open. "I would hit me here" he said, indicating to his sternum. We then walked into the campus for Brian to give me some parting advise: "You could do with loosening up; it will improve your speed…I'm saying that as a friend." Later that day, I encountered a colleague in my school who had filmed some of the short exchange on her phone (without our permission!) who asked me in surprise of Brian's ferocity, "did he knock you out?" As an outsider, this colleague was not aware of the playful nature of our inquiring exchange, as we asked questions of each other's style and decision making.

Summary

I began this book with a story, so it was only fitting to end with another. This autoethnography has shared some stories from my journey in the martial arts to date, from the age of 14 to 37. Now moving into the realm of the mid-career researcher, I hope to learn and research about many of the world's fighting systems while developing myself as a human being, so this story is of course in development. It is positioned at the end of the book to enable to reader to understand my positioning within the martial arts, which has shaped my research interests and writing over the years. I aimed to show the reader how the East Asian martial art of Taekwondo and the meditated representation of Ninjas and Bruce Lee opened gateways to for me as a white Westerner with no known Asian heritage or family background in martial arts and combat sports. These gateways offered me different avenues in life, such as physical activity and fitness, sport science, postgraduate study, Chinese culture and philosophy, movement cultures and Western martial arts such as HEMA.

The short tales also touched on topics revealed in the life histories of the instructors and students examined in the previous two chapters, such as fatherhood, role models, the body and embodiment and the importance of cultural texts for motivation and passion in the martial arts. My work has taken me to South West England, London, Scotland and Mexico. Now settled in Wales, I feel my research moving in three different directions: the historical world of HEMA and reenactment; the Chinese cultures and bodywork seen in traditionalist styles such as Dragon Kung Fu, and health, healing and therapy as revealed in my work with Fightingandspirit and the Trauma Informed Martial Arts Network, and more recently, a planned project with Annette (Anna) Drews and Alex Channon called "Finding Strength", using bodymind practices such as the martial arts, Qigong and Yoga to help people with their wellbeing in an age where many people are suffering from isolation, loneliness and mental health issues.

Like me, Alex and Anna are practitioners of such arts, as in Aikido and BJJ. It is important to note that martial arts studies are driven by scholar-practitioners (or practitioner-researchers) who study and often teach one or more martial arts. However, despite an increasing amount of reflexivity and some confessional tales revealing the undertaking of fieldwork (see Van Maanen, 1988; Sparkes, 2002), detailed autoethnographies of martial arts are relatively rare. I hope this story helps pave the way for more narratives of the self (another term for autoethnography) alongside life histories of everyday martial artists, whose stories can enable us to grasp biography and history through the sociological imagination that C. Wright Mills (1959) called for. This is the promise not only of sociology, but also for martial arts scholarship: to study the martial arts, society and people's lives within them.

References

Collinson, J., Jennings, G., Vaittinen, A., & Owton, H. (2018). Weather-wise? Sporting Allen embodiment, weather work and weather learning in running and triathlon. *International Review for the Sociology of Sport* (online early) http://journals.sagepub.com/eprint/Vd8iJVvbCUicA72VR8Xs/full

Allen Collinson, J., Vaittinen, A., Jennings, G., & Owton, H. (2016). Exploring lived heat, "temperature work" and embodiment: Novel auto/ethnographic insights from physical culture. *Journal of Contemporary Ethnography* (online early).

Bowman, P. (2015). *Martial arts studies: Disrupting disciplinary boundaries*. London: Rowman & Littlefield.

Brown, D. H. K., Jennings, G., & Leledaki, A. (2008). The changing charismatic status of the performing male body in Asian Martial Arts Films. *Sport in Society, 11*(2), 174–194.

Contreras Islas, D. (2021). Mexican Capoeira is not diasporic! On glocalization, migration and the North-South divide. *Martial Arts Studies, 11*, 56–70.

Farrell, K. (2014). Dementia pugilistica in HEMA: Brain damage from repeated head hits. Unpublished paper, The Academy of Historical Arts. Available at: https://www.academia.edu/10813311/Dementia_Pugilistica_in_HEMA_Brain_Damage_from_Repeated_Head_Hits. Last accessed 27 May 2022.

Farrer, D. S., & Whalen-Bridge, J. (Eds.). (2012). *Martial arts as embodied knowledge: Asian traditions in a transnational world*. Albany, NY: SUNY Press.

Han, T. N. (1975). *The miracle of mindfulness*. London: Penguin Random House.

Hargrove, E. (1970). *Anecdotes of archery*. London: Thames Valley Press.

Jennings, G. (2022). "Filthy lefties!": The humorous stigmatisation of left-handed fencers in historical European martial arts (HEMA). *STAPS, 136*(2), 17–36.

Jennings, G. (2010). Fighters, thinkers and shared cultivation: Experiencing transformation through the long-term practice of the traditionalist Chinese martial arts. Unpublished doctoral thesis, University of Exeter.

Jennings, G. (2005). Wing Chun wins all: An ethnographic study of Wing Chun Kung Fu focusing on social class, subculture and identity. Unpublished dissertation, University of Exeter.

Law, M. (2007). *The pyjama game*. London: Aurum Press Limited.

Lee, B. (1963). *Chinese Gung Fu: Philosophical art of self-defence*. Oakland, CA: James Lee.

Little, J. (Ed.) (1997). *Bruce Lee: The Tao of Gung Fu: A study in the way of Chinese martial art.* North Clarendon, VT: Tuttle Publishers.

Little, J. (Ed.). (1998). *Bruce Lee: The art of expressing the human body.* North Clarendon, VT: Tuttle Publishers.

Mills, C. W. (1959). *The sociological imagination.* Oxford: Oxford University Press.

Partiková, V., & Jennings, G. (2018). The Kung Fu family: A metaphor of belonging across time and place. *Revista de Artes Marciales Asiáticas, 13*(1), 35–52.

Pedrini, L. (2018). 'Boxing is our business': The embodiment of a leftists identity in boxe popolare. *Societies, 8*(3), 85. https://doi.org/10.3390/soc8030085

Sparkes, A. C. (2002). *Telling tales in sport and physical activity: A qualitative journey.* Champaign, IL: Human Kinetics.

Stone, G. C. (1960). *A glossary on the construction, decoration and use of arms and armor in all countries and in all times together with some closely related subjects.* New York: Jack Brussel.

Tolle, E. (1999). *The power of now: A guide to spiritual enlightenment.* San Francisco: New World Library.

Thomas, B. (1994). *Bruce Lee: Fighting spirit.* London: Pan.

Van Maanen, J. (1988). *Tales from the field: On writing ethnography.* Chicago: Chicago University Press.

Wacquant, L. J. D. (2004). *Body and soul: Notebooks of an apprentice boxer.* Oxford: Oxford University Press.

Zarrilli, P. B. (1998). *When the body becomes all eyes: Paradigms, discourses and practices of power in Kalaripayattu, a South Indian martial art.* New Delhi: Oxford University Press.

11

Conclusions and Future Directions

Summary: Returning to a Working Definition

The martial arts are undoubtedly invented traditions, and it is fair to suggest that many more styles will be created throughout the 21st century in all corners of the world. Existing styles are reimagined, reconstructed, repackaged and redistributed to new generations of students with different needs and interests. Although I could have set on a path of deconstructing the longstanding myths of martial arts as many esteemed colleagues have done to great effect, I wished to consider the contemporary reconstruction of arts for health, movement, performance, human betterment and flourishing, cultural expression and relationships. This analysis required an initial definition and delimitation of what I was going to look at. There are many definitions of the martial arts posed by various authors from distinct academic disciplines, time periods and training backgrounds, with these three factors often merging to form a position on the object of study in question. All of these definitions are to some degree informed by theory or even the start of theory – something very important in any academic field. They are also open to scrutiny and revision over time as new theories emerge, different empirical examples become accessible and when the scholar matures. *A martial art is an imaginative, adaptable system of physical human fighting techniques designed in order to deal with perceived problems in combat and society.* That is a new, working definition that I posed in the Introduction chapter (Chapter 1), setting the scene for this monograph and its examination of various forms of human imagination, adaption and design in various Western societies.

With the time period being 2022, I decided to open up the analysis for contemporary happenings in the 21st century, mainly set in the past two decades, but including ongoing debates and issues as well as future possibilities. I first turned to the imaginative and adaptive elements of martial arts using the case study of the Chinese martial arts in Britain – a context I have been immersed in (both physically and virtually) for over two decades.

The first part of the book, "Reimagining the Martial Arts", was concerned with the imaginative dimension of the martial arts. Following the establishment of the aims and scope of the book, Chapter 2 provided a case study of one cultural expression of the martial arts – the Chinese martial arts – focusing on how they can act as art forms. This reflects the imagination of the leading teachers of organisations that they have founded – in this case, in Britain. The diversity among the Wing Chun and Taijiquan communities in terms of what their focus is on, with this focus reflecting the perception of what is important in the martial arts (for example, self-defence, sporting competition, health and wellbeing, holistic human development, cultural expression or even individual expression). Chapter 3 then moved to tackle the topic of movement in the martial arts. The human physical fighting techniques of the martial arts use many parts of the body in complex and often holistic ways that can be used for more than combat. The chapter highlighted the ongoing work of pioneering movement coaches Ido Portal and Cameron Shayne to show how they have combined specific martial arts movements with wider movement training as in the resting squat and yoga movements to train celebrities, members of the public and elite martial arts fighters.

Chapter 4 delved into the topic of self-help through the martial arts, arguing that the martial arts provided a structure for people's self-help. Three case studies of Shannon Lee, Geoff Thompson and Steve Jones provide contrasting examples of the adaptability of martial arts for the purpose of helping people in wider society – the majority of whom are presumed not to be martial artists. After that, Chapter 5 closed the section to offer an insight into the different relationships between martial arts and therapy. It looked at cases of Fightingandspirit and the Martial Movement Method as interrupted projects that I have been involved in through delivery and design of the material for members of the public, psychotherapists and counsellors.

Part II ("Reconstructing the Martial Arts") then moved onto how specific individuals and groups are trying to regulate the reinvention of martial arts. With the reinvention process being so open and flexible, it can be manipulated by martial arts instructors operating as charlatans or even criminals, teaching people ineffective techniques while also preying on vulnerable people unaware of their ill intentions. In Chapter 6, I examined the McDojo critique, beginning with the humorous exposé that it offers the public on the unregulated martial arts industry before moving onto more serious critiques from martial arts influencers working as entrepreneurs and solopreneurs via social media channels. This ties to efforts to restore the lost martial arts traditions of Europe and Mexico by innovating teachers and researchers, seen in Chapter 7. This revivalist movement connects with the global effort to consider martial arts as forms of (in)tangible cultural heritage through UNESCO and related organisations, which are covered at the end of the section, finishing with an example of Wales, a country steeped in martial heritage.

Following the consideration of these international efforts, Part III ("Living and Breathing the Martial Arts") moves on from the case of Wales and Welsh martial arts heritage by exploring the life stories of committed martial arts instructors (Chapter 8) and long-term practitioners (Chapter 9) living in the country who have become some of my main research informants and gatekeepers to other arts and practices before moving to my autoethnography as a martial arts practitioner who became a scholar of these systems (Chapter 10). This final section of the book gives voice to the people who have been involved in the reinvention process of Taijiquan, HEMA, Wing Chun and Cheng Hsin in terms of both the reinvention of the art and the practitioners. Findings from these chapters are touched upon here, in the final discussion and conclusion.

Contributions to Knowledge

With martial arts studies / research / science expanding at a rapid rate, it is increasingly difficult to remain abreast of all the latest developments, especially given the international nature of this research in different cultures, regions and languages. However, I remain confident that this book offers numerous contributions to our growing knowledge on the martial arts. The definition I offer is original but more importantly, robust in its flexibility across the arts and contexts. For instance, a martial art can be reimagined and repackaged as a form of self-help that can be adapted to a book or an audiobook in order to deal with societal issues such as people's low self-esteem or lack of physical fitness. I hope this definition might be considered by my peers in martial arts research to expand on it and improve it, perhaps building it into theories and other forms of empirical research.

The open nature of the project has allowed me to explore new topics for my research such as self-help, therapy, the "movement movement", the McDojo critique as well as more familiar topics of the Chinese and Mexican martial arts. During the writing of the book, the COVID-19 pandemic struck, and this of course had to feature in the book about the key issues facing martial artists in the 21st century. Identities and personal relationships are also covered alongside the more global themes of cultural heritage and regulating the martial arts industry.

With empirical research in mind, this book has added to the knowledge in several ways. It has combined considerations of the Chinese martial arts in Britain while examining new areas of research in the form of the mixed movement systems and self-help, which have yet to be examined in any detail by martial arts scholars. And while martial arts therapies are now expanding in their delivery and academic reception (with a conference in Germany on this very topic), there have been no writings on the interrupted Fightingandspirit project and the fledgling Trauma Informed Martial Arts Network based off the excellent work in the Fight Back Project in Australia. The chapter on martial arts therapies also provided some theoretical ideas for examining martial arts reinvention more broadly, such as the 8Ps, which could transfer to martial activities of different formats. This is also an unusual book with its breadth of coverage across both Eastern and Western martial arts and those from Latin America (Mexico) along with other hybrid forms of combat and movement. Most martial arts monographs tend to be studies of individual arts or cultural phenomena, but this book, based on the last 18 years of research since my undergraduate dissertation, cuts across these areas.

In terms of the methods used to obtain these findings, this book is also a rare one that combines autoethnography (in my own story), ethnography and online ethnography / netnography (of Wing Chun, HEMA and Taijiquan both online and offline around the time of the pandemic), life histories of instructors and students (Billy, David, Aidan and George) and textual and media analysis of self-help books, TEDX talks, YouTube videos, official institutional websites, open discussion fora and podcast episodes. This is appropriate given the complexity of the task of accounting for a range of martial reinventions in the 21st century, which requires one to consider the lives of individuals being transformed along with their institutions and the external influences such as celebrity martial artists, cultural critics and emerging forms of governance. It is also a pertinent strategy given the fact that people live their lives with their close friends, family, loved ones, training partners, teachers around them while also engaging with books, films, television and streaming series, podcasts and audiobooks. Although the main parts of the book were divided into three sections, the final one reveals how all of them interconnect, with mention of governance of the martial arts, commercialisation, influential figures and writers and Hollywood creations that inspired the participants in my research.

Finally, in terms of theory, I have tried to keep an open mind in terms of the concepts and disciplines I have drawn upon. Some chapters will appeal to different kinds of readers and specialists, but within it, I have considered ideas from the likes of Pierre Bourdieu, Nick Crossley and George Ritzer in sociology along with theorists from interdisciplinary fields such as Marcel Mauss and Ben Spatz with their use of techniques of the body. This is not a pure sociology text, as I consider myself an interdisciplinary social scientist whose home is the cultural sociology of sport and physical culture.

Limitations of the Study

There are many possible forms of martial reinvention that were not covered in this book, a product of one person with a specific academic and martial arts trajectory. As someone with a background in the exercise, sport and health sciences and the social sciences who is also a qualitative researcher, I focused on what interested me and what I understood about the martial arts in contemporary society: health, healing, self-help, human movement and therapy. These are topics I have studied but also fields that I have worked in to a certain degree. Meanwhile, my focus on the Chinese martial arts in the second chapter is indicative of my background in those arts, particularly Wing Chun Kung Fu and Taijiquan. This book is a text about the reinvention of the martial arts in the Western context, and might tell us relatively little about the Eastern societies from which many of those fighting and human development systems originate. The qualitative data helped me focus on my strengths in research, which are about interesting case studies, rich characters and intriguing projects that they are involved in. However, with my limited skills in quantitative research, I did not endeavour to analyse big data such as by comparing statistics across countries.

Language is always a limitation in research, and I have reserved my own analysis to sources in the English and Spanish languages. This means that some regions in the Western context have been missed (such as French-speaking countries and provinces). Also, there were many martial arts left out of my analysis due to my focus on my ongoing ethnographic and life history research as well as my focus on other formats of the martial arts, as in therapy, self-help and movement systems. Other avenues of martial arts might include stunt work (with some of my HEMA research participants being stuntmen), which also leads to 21st century phenomena of martial arts within streaming services such as Netflix, YouTube Originals and Amazon Prime as a form of instant entertainment and edutainment. I hope to contribute to this avenue of research through a collaboration with Craig Owen on the hit YouTube turned Netflix series Cobra Kai, with a focus on the intergenerational ideals of masculinity (for an insight, see Owen, Jennings & Channon, 2018). Gender is also something that skews the sample somewhat, with my interview participants featured in the book being male. However, women's voices are featured in the text, as in Shannon Lee and Marisela Ugalde, and the important role of life partners are considered in different chapters. Nonetheless, more research on women's stories would add to the growing body of literature on females in combat sports and martial arts (e.g., Channon & Matthews, 2015). The Fight Back Project lead by Georgia Verry, and the development of her Trauma Informed Martial Arts Network are further examples of women leading important projects that can benefit people of all genders.

Finally, the scope of the book cast a very broad net that covered numerous topics. With breadth comes the danger of missing various other themes that require investigations of their own. With the richness of each of the four men's lives, the four life histories in Part III could have sat as individual chapters per life story. At the same time, I did have more interview data from other martial arts instructors and practitioners as part of my study of HEMA and Taijiquan, both in and out of the case study schools featured here, which I was not able to feature in this particular book. Some themes that formed part of chapters could actually be the basis for an entire chapter or book in themselves, as in heritage, which is a very important topic for the martial arts in this century. Other themes that scholars might consider researching is activism. With young sport activists highlighting the plight of marginalised and disadvantaged groups, it will be interesting to note the initiatives set up by martial artists. Body image is another important theme in contemporary society, with more young people becoming addicted to social media such as Instagram and TikTok. Could the martial arts reinforce this bodily dissatisfaction, or might the introduce new views on the body concerned with the living movement of the active body over the aesthetics of the passive body?

Future Directions

It has been fascinating examining the broad range of topics, from self-help to McDojos, to movement systems to life histories. Part Three raised some very interesting findings from the four male martial artists I interviewed and studied over the past few years in terms of the relationships they have formed through the martial arts. These relationships, often among men, are often connected in some way to their identities as fathers and sons. Some of the men had distant and estranged relationships with their own fathers, and this contrasts to the return of Shannon Lee with her father's words and legacy (albeit with commercial reasons in mind). Such a study of martial arts and fatherhood would connect well with the established body of literature on martial arts and masculinity, which continued to expand (see, for instance, the special issue edited by Schiller, 2020).

Another feature of martial arts relationships are martial arts couples that were formed in the training halls of various styles. Both Billy and David met their spouses during martial arts action, and I know of several other martial arts couple who train and teach their beloved HEMA together, living an active and inquisitive life that feeds into their selected lifestyle and art. Even martial arts-themed weddings have been related to me in several conversations with colleagues, which raises the possibility of observing more special gatherings such as anniversaries of the founding of schools and the gift bearing and receival that goes with them. This might draw on the pioneering work of Marcel Mauss in terms of *The Gift* (Mauss, 2001[1925]), making use of ethnographic research to capture those moments of planning for, purchasing and preparing a surprise gift for the teacher and their assistants (and, as very often is the case, partners). More research on such couples, gift bearers and receivers could be undertaken using interviews with couples and also focus groups.

Meanwhile, in terms of the power relationships in martial arts, more work is needed in terms of taking the McDojo critique seriously. Although it can be comical and associated with memes and cartoon images, the McDojo can have very powerful messages as in that of Rob Ingram from McDojo Life. This connects to the other topic of hustle culture, a theme that Billy Marshall first introduced to me in one of our regular coffee meetings. In a recent podcast interview with My Jiu Jitsu White Belt, Rob admitted that he wakes up in the morning determined to work 15 hours a day (My White Belt in Jiu Jitsu Podcast, 2022). He left the hosts astounded when he explained that this routine of 15 hours a day was seven days a week, even on supposed holidays. What drives such figures to devote their waking lives to alerting others of dangerous martial arts instructors? How might the martial arts industry be better regulated across the nations? This is likely to be the case for people like Ido Portal and Cameron Shayne, as people who live, eat and breathe the martial arts and movement while always seeking to increase their following. Making a living as a martial arts influencer will undoubtedly require many sacrifices in their lives along with some tales of creativity and adaptability, just as in the martial arts. Access to these people might be difficult in some cases, but an interview-based study would be very original and rewarding. Observational work of their day-to-day activities and research within their custom-made home studios would also be very insightful. This also connects with the role of advanced technologies such as Virtual Reality (VR) for martial arts training, as well as performance analysis used in sport science, which could motion capture techniques and forms that are soon to be lost, with the last generation of teachers passing away.

At a time of increased economic insecurity with a potential shortage of grain due to the conflict in Ukraine, social class and martial arts might need to be revisited in the next few years. There are studies of martial arts and social class, but not in relation to specific economic cycles such as recessions and depressions. Other topics worth noting might be Russophobia and the views of Russian martial arts such as Sambo and Systema among different cultures in the world. More broadly, the pursuit of martial arts as lifestyle activities would follow on from Jaquet, Tuaillon Demésy and Tzouriadis writing on HEMA (2020) in which they identified HEMA as a form of serious leisure. Other concepts from leisure studies and the sociology of sport might help to understand how and why the martial artists invest so much time and energy into their chosen arts, which are rarely used for real-life combat. The martial arts practitioners might make use of new forms of recording their own thoughts via voice memos on their mobile phones and vlogs in a 21st century form of self-observation (see Rodriguez & Ryave, 2002), especially as many of them engage with podcasts as hosts and participants.

In terms of methods, martial arts scholarship has well established strengths in areas such as history, ethnography and now philosophical / conceptual enquiry. However, life histories remain an area to be fully developed. This is perhaps surprising given that many martial arts are long-term pursuits studied over many decades and into old age. Life histories of veteran martial artists and teachers would enable researchers to study various themes from a historical, psychological and sociological perspective. Autoethnographies are also needed in martial arts studies, with the majority of scholars being scholar-practitioners with years, if not decades, of experience behind their writings. However, do date, there is a shortage of such narratives of the self (for exceptions, see Abooali, 2022; Martinez, 2014; Stenius, & Dziwenka, 2015). Finally, there is scope for action research projects involving local communities and martial arts groups who perceive a problem to be overcome. This might be around other, pressing themes such as economic uncertainty, guaranteed spaces to train and more sustainable materials and training venues. This would help martial arts move from an interdisciplinary stage of the coming together of academic disciplines (Bowman, 2015) to a transdisciplinary stage involving stakeholders with a say on the questions posed and the methods utilised in research. I am fortunate to be involved in a planned project of this sort – Finding Strength – with Annette Drews and Alex Channon, with our aim of examining how martial arts and related body-mind practices might help people's wellbeing.

I hope the readers have enjoyed reading the book, perhaps even finding it funny in some places. Humour is located in many places of the book, especially in the McDojo and life history chapters, where the lively characters share their stories and memorable moments from their training and travels. After my forthcoming article on humour in HEMA (Jennings, 2022), I would like to examine humour in Taijiquan, but other scholars could find excellent cases of jokes during warm-ups, demonstrations, partner exercises and during social events, not to forget the online environment where humour can turn aggressive. There are numerous theoretical positions on humour (see Eagleton, 2019), which provide researchers with various frameworks to examine jokes and laughter through ethnographic, survey and video analysis strategies.

The time spent online can remind us of the COVID-19 pandemic, which has prepared societies and martial arts for future outbreaks of other infectious diseases. As I write this conclusion, Monkeypox is beginning to strike communities around the world, and with their close association with touch and intimacy, martial arts schools might be at risk. This links to the other serious theme of loneliness and isolation, and how to maintain an inclusive, positive martial arts community at the most challenging of times.

In summary, the invention of martial arts has and will always occur, but so too will reinvention: of the arts, the institutions that support them and the people who live and breathe them. This is all because *a martial art is an imaginative, adaptable system of physical human fighting techniques designed in order to deal with perceived problems in combat and society.*

References

Abooali, S. (2022). Exploring the somatic dimension for sport-based interventions: A refugee's autoethnography. *Sport in Society, 25*, 506–522.

Bowman, P. (2015). *Martial arts studies: Disrupting disciplinary boundaries.* London: Rowman & Littlefield.

Channon, A., & Matthews, C. (Eds.), (2015). *Global perspectives on women in combat sports: Women warriors around the world.* Basingstoke: Palgrave Macmillan.

Eagleton, T. (2019). *Humour.* New Haven, CT: Yale University Press.

Jaquet, D., Tuaillon Demésy, A., & Tzouriadis, I.-E. (2020). *Historical European martial arts: An international overview.* Chungju-si: ICM UNESCO.

Jennings, G. (2022). "Filthy lefties!": The humorous stigmatisation of left-handed fencers in historical European martial arts. *STAPS*, 136(2), 17–36.

Martinez, A. (2014). No longer a girl: My female experience in the masculine field of martial arts. *International Review of Qualitative Research, 7*(4), 442–452.

Mauss, M. (2001[1925]). *The gift: Forms and functions of exchange in archaic societies.* London: Routledge Classics.

My White Belt in Jiu Jitsu Podcast. (2022). Episode: McDojo Life's Rob Ingram!. Available at: https://www.listennotes.com/podcasts/my-white-belt/mcdojo-lifes-rob-ingram-OT1AzlNuHSf/. Last accessed 31 May 2022.

Owen, C., Channon, A., & Jennings, G. (2018). Cobra Kai: Karate Kid spin-off is a social parable for our times. The Conversation. Available at: https://theconversation.com/cobra-kai-karate-kid-spin-off-is-a-social-parable-for-our-times-101530. Last accessed 31 May 2022.

Rodriguez, N., & Ryave, A. (2002). *Systematic self-observation.* London: SAGE Publications.

Schiller, K. (2020). Masculinities in martial arts and combat sports – An interdisciplinary issue. *Sport in Society, 40*(3), 291–295.

Stenius, M., & Dziwenka, R. (2015). "Just be natural with your body": An autoethnography of violence and pain in mixed martial arts. *International Journal of Martial Arts, 1*, 1–24.

Index

A

Abuse and abusers 115, 118, 123
Aesthetics and beauty standards 53, 106, 212
Age and ageing xv, xvi, xvii, xxiii, 22, 30, 39, 43, 82, 105, 120, 172, 187
Aikido xxii, 110, 173
Art 21, 22, 23, 24, 73
Athletes 47

B

Bartitsu 82
Blogs 108–109
Body cultures 55–56
Books, inspiration from 154
Boxing 116, 175–176, 202
Brazilian Jiujitsu (BJJ) 110–111, 114, 152, 193

Brothers and brotherhood 198
Bruce Lee 61–67, 157, 167, 174, 184, 186
Burnout 69, 73
Bushido 187

C

Capoeira 44–45
Career in martial arts 145
Charisma 52–54
Charity 166, 172
Cheng Hsin 174–175, 176
Children 106–107, 120, 186
Chinese philosophy 22, 70, 158, 159, 191
Chow Gar 170–171
Climate change 25
Concussion 129
Conditioning exercises xvii, 28, 48, 149, 164, 166, 171, 192

Conspiracy theories 169
Couples in martial arts 150, 154, 158, 161, 178, 186, 213
COVID-19 ix, x, xiii, xix, xxi, xxiv, xxvi, 11, 72, 108, 159, 176, 199
Crime 200
Cults 118

D

Definition of martial arts 6–10, 21–22, 24, 115, 207, 209
Disability 48, 65
Dissemination of martial arts 145, 157
Dragon style Kung Fu 200

E

Eastern movement forms 59
Ethnicity xviii, 73, 146, 168, 192
Ex-pats 164

F

Family 21–32, 36, 171, 183–184
Fathers and fatherhood 147, 150, 157, 158, 161, 172, 173
Feldenkrais Method 41–42
Fightingandspirit project 199–200
Films, inspiration from 129, 147, 184, 186, 194
Financial issues 88, 165
Followers 118, 134

G

Gender xviii, 73, 76, 104, 212

Gifts 154–155, 156, 201, 213
Governance 31, 32, 156

H

Health xvii, 40–41, 70, 81, 83, 89–90, 198–199, 215
Heroes 63
Historical European martial arts xvii-xxii, 23, 124–125
Humour xiii-xvii, 105–106, 132–133, 193–4, 215
Hustle culture 213
Hygiene xxi, 68

I

Indigenous heritage 131, 140
Influencers 30, 214
Injury xvi, 41, 43, 113, 153, 158, 170
Internal/external debate 28, 29, 39, 155

J

Jeet Kune Do 64
Judo 84, 188

K

Kalarippayattu 190
Kendo 185
Krav Maga 3

L

Laughter xix, xxiii, 119, 156, 189, 193

Legitimacy 110–111
Lightsabre combat 130
Limitations of study 4–5, 202
Lineage 35, 168
Live action role playing (LARP) 121, 129
Loneliness 72, 215
Longevity 71, 95

M

Martial activities 21, 77
Martial arts studies 10, 196
Martial movement method 55, 80, 88–91
Materials and materialism xx, 125, 126, 152
McDonaldization 103–104
McTaiji xxv
Medicine 82–83
Meditation xxiv, 159
Memes 105, 115–116
Methods 203–204, 210, 214
Mexico 131–135
Mixed martial arts (MMA) 193
Mobilities 33, 156
Mok Gar Kung Fu 166–167
Muay Thai 170
Myths and folklore 22, 26, 207

N

Neoliberalism 69
New martial arts 1
Nicknames xix

P

Physical education 188

Play and playfulness 43–44
Podcasts 108–109
Portal, Ido 42
Positionality 3–4, 15, 198
Posture 178, 180, 198

R

Reenactment 149
Reinvention 1, 2, 10
Relationship in martial arts 175
Religion 172, 177
Resting squat 43, 46, 51, 198

S

Safeguarding 31, 35
Safety measures 127, 129, 157
Sedentary lifestyle 46, 48, 51, 53, 54
Self 59–60, 65, 85
Self-defence videos 116–117
Sexuality 85
Shayne, Cameron 42
Singing 178
Socialising xv, xix
Social media xiv, 214
Spotify 108–109
Systema 49, 86–87, 199

T

Taekwondo 184–185
Taijiquan xxii-xxvi, 28, 29–33, 40, 113, 191
Techniques of the body 40, 42–43, 91
TED Talks 62–63
Television, influence of 173, 184
Theory 6, 7, 8, 25, 56, 211

Theory of Martial Creation 22
Theory of the 8Ps of Martial
    Therapy 92–95
Therapists 86
Tradition 2, 35, 50, 101, 131, 147, 207
Trauma 92
Tribes 45

U

Ultimate Fighting Championship (UFC)
    47, 49, 102, 112, 194
UNESCO 135, 137
Unit combat 151
Ukraine 86, 166

V

Virtual reality (VR) 214

W

Wales and Welshness 34, 138–139, 140

Warrior philosophy 85–86
Willick, Jocko 107–108
Wing Chun x-xvii, 2, 25–29, 189 193,
    194–195, 197
Workouts xx, 143

X

Xilam 89, 132, 136, 195

Y

Yoga 49–50, 51
YouTube 52, 101, 106, 114, 167–168

Z

Zen 48–49
Zoom 159–160

Sport in East and Southeast Asian Societies
Geopolitical, Political, Cultural and Social Perspectives

J.A. Mangun *Series Editor*

Modern sport is emotionally essential to billions worldwide providing ecstasy, escapism and excitement. It is simultaneously witness to a tectonic geopolitical, political, cultural and social shift in performance— West to East! It is experiencing a global transformation in the wake of contemporary East Asian confidence, self-belief and performance symbolised dramatically by Beijing 2008—a harbinger of shifting geopolitical 'plates'!

The editor of this new series from Peter Lang, Professor J.A. Mangan FRHS, FRAI, FRSA, D. LITT., welcomes and invites proposals for the series. Please send details to profmangan@gmail.com

To order other books in this series, please contact our Customer Service Department:

    peterlang@presswarehouse.com (within the U.S.)
    orders@peterlang.com (outside the U.S.)

Or browse online by series at:

    www.peterlang.com

Printed in Great Britain
by Amazon

b6ebf00e-bd54-4e30-b547-1817d0195f49R01